THE DEMISE OF AMERICAN DEMOCRACY
SECOND EDITION • 2017

BY
WILLIAM R. DURLAND, J.D., Ph.D.

UNDERSTANDING the CRISIS and RESISTING THE THREATS

Denver Colorado
Createspace

TABLE OF CONTENTS

DEDICATION

This book is dedicated to all those unsung heroes who lost their human and civil rights and even their lives as a result of the autocratic and malicious actions of rulers elected by a minority of American voters. They, through ignorance, acquiescence or intention, allowed American democracy to be threatened to the extent that it could suffer its demise. A call to action for resistance, a restoration of what has been lost and a resurgence of the movement to a more perfect union has been initiated. The sacrifices of these unsung heroes must not be in vain.

With this call to action, we are inspired by the historical experiences in the evolution of democracy, *Magna Carta*, Roosevelt's Four Freedoms, and in this year, 2017, the 100th anniversary of the birth of one of our most vigilant and dedicated presidents who gave his life to ensure such efforts, John Fitzgerald Kennedy. This year is also the 50th anniversary of the permanent placement, in 1967, of the eternal flame, which watches over the gravesites of the Kennedy brothers. It is an inspiration for the cover of this book, a display of light that energizes our resistance to tyranny.

ACKNOWLEDGEMENTS

I wish to publically acknowledge the work and efforts over hundreds of hours of my wife, partner and companion, Genie Durland, who without her editorial and imaginative persistence, this book and my other ten books and eleven plays would never have happened, and to thanks friends who contributed financially.

OTHER BOOKS by the AUTHOR

No King But Caesar: A Catholic Lawyer Looks at Christian Violence, 1975

Ethical Issues: A Search for the Contemporary Conscience, 1975

No King But Jesus: Matthew 25 and the Biblical Basis of Christian Nonviolent Assistance, 1977

People Pay for Peace, 1978

Conscience and Law, 1980

The Illegality of War, 1982

God or Nations: Radical Theology for the Religious Peace Movement, 1989

William Penn, James Madison and the Historical Crisis in American Federalism, 2000

Immoral Wars and Illegal Laws: History, Religion, Militarism and Peacemaking in the Human Rights Struggle for Palestinian Independence, 2011

The Price of Folly: A Layperson's Guide to American Plutocracy, 2013

The Demise of American Democracy, 1st Ed. 2016

Preface to the Second Edition

RESISTANCE, RESILIENCE, RESURGENCE AND RECONCILIATION

"Each period is dominated by a mood with the result that most men fail to see the tyrant that rules over them" Albert Einstein

The first edition of *The Demise of American Democracy* was completed in September 2015 at the very beginning of the 2016 presidential election campaign and published in February 2016. Since that time the saga of the Trump era has begun to unfold. It became real to a majority of Americans only after Hillary Clinton received almost three million more popular votes and the Electoral College gave Trump a majority of theirs. We then realized that the conservative policies started by Ronald Reagan in 1980 and jump-started again as the Tea Party took over the Republican Party could now be completely implemented.

For twenty years I had been a supporter of the Republican Party. Republicans then were inclusive, with a majority of conservatives, and a minority of moderates and liberals that included Eisenhower, Dewey, Rockefeller, Ives, Javitz, Lindsey, and many others. But for some time, we have known that the modern Republican Party is espousing ultra-conservative issues and policies that are not representative of the American spectrum as a whole. As such, it has been a chief cause for the demise of American democracy, as we have known it from the time of Theodore Roosevelt, Woodrow Wilson, Franklin Roosevelt, Harry

Truman, John Kennedy and Lyndon Baines Johnson. Donald J. Trump is a shallow echo of the heavier substance of the discriminatory and undemocratic principles and practices of a party committed to plutocratic economics and unjust politics. Trump has waffled back and forth so it is hard to know what he stands for or what his words mean to intelligent and logically trained, educated and ethical Americans. But one thing is sure, he has moved in the direction of autocratic rule with the capacity of one who has been called "kleptocratic."

So what this second edition has that the first did not is this introductory note, and an Afterword, bringing up to date the events of the last year that have threatened the collapse of American civilization, and quickened the path to the complete demise of our democratic government. To compare how we saw the scene in 2015 with what is before our eyes today we have left the original text as it was, but with significant re-editing for better clarification, without changing any of the substantive importance of what was written then.

I decided to preserve the original text with my chief editorial associate, my wife Genie Durland, so that those of you who have gone through the process of shock, mourning, anger and resolution to rise up and resist, may have the benefit of a real record composed at the time of its birth.

In March 2017 I was asked to be the keynote speaker at the annual spring gathering of the Colorado Regional Meeting of Quakers, and to reflect upon the first 100 days of the Trump administration. The presentation was entitled "Resistance, Resilience and Restoration: Truth is Power." I urged Quakers and non-Quakers in attendance to an organic resistance with resilience for the long haul, with the aim of restoring what has been lost and to begin again the resurgence of what was eroded years ago, the American experiment to form a more perfect union. Below, I have paraphrased some of what I said at that meeting that is relevant to the revitalization of this book.

I was a slow learner. It took me 27 years to realize that the practice of democracy required more than the brilliant structure given it by James Madison. For it to work, he said that the voters must be educated politically and our representatives be possessed of a virtuous character. Jefferson reminded us "The price of liberty is eternal vigilance." My childhood was spent in the shadow of the Statue of Liberty. I read the words there many times. "Give me your tired, your poor, your huddled masses yearning to breathe free, the wretched refuse of your teeming shore, send these the homeless tempest-tossed to me."[1] My evolution towards understanding all of this began when I was 10. My parents told me that a Jewish friend of theirs could only live in our neighborhood if he kept his ethnicity a secret by changing his name. The neighbors were republicans then and they told me that Franklin Roosevelt was either a crook or a communist.

Twenty-seven years later in 1958, after service in the army as a closet pacifist and a law school graduate, specializing in constitutional and international law, I became an advocate of human rights and liberties. President Eisenhower's Virginia candidate for congress, where I lived twelve miles from the White House, was a segregationist republican, Broyhill of the millionaire furniture family. His

---

[1] Lazarus, Emma, Inscription of the Statue of Liberty.

democratic opponent, Freehill, was against segregation. Historically, Jews, Blacks, Italians, Irish and women were victims of racism and sexism. I was told that we fought World War II to do away with such things. So I became a Democrat.

Through the *resistance* of the Civil Rights movement and the *resilience* of its participants, we were able to *restore* and move ahead on the original hopes and needs of our founding citizens. I began in the law courts, and seven years later was elected a Virginia state legislator and served on national campaign staffs. I finally graduated to direct action on the streets at the March on Washington in 1963. Successes in the legislature between 1966 and 1970 included the end to interracial marriage prohibitions and voter restrictions, such as the poll tax and blank registration, the beginning of healthcare reform and the election of intelligent presidents and vice presidents – Kennedy and Humphrey - whom I worked for.

Earlier, from 1955 to 1957 I was stationed in Germany with the military, giving me an opportunity to examine how an unpopular politician, Hitler, was able to take over a democratic nation with less than a majority vote, empowered by the negative values of a minority over the positive concerns of the majority. He did this by first attacking the media, then the intelligencia, and finally the vulnerable. He did not do it alone but received the support of reluctant powerful factions of the conservative culture primarily business corporations and military veterans. He said he would make Germany great again by providing jobs for White Aryans through a military build-up and confiscation of the savings and public services of the scapegoat population. He became rich on his autobiography, *Mein Kampf,* requiring it to be purchased as mandatory reading. Once he was entrenched by showing that Germany could win again, his conservative government remained in power for twelve years before its end came and democracy was restored after 1945.

Some of us whose lives take us back to that time see a somewhat similar, but not identical process, playing out before our eyes. It calls us to resist and restore our democracy once again, and with the resilience needed for the long haul. Re-education of the majority and election of candidates who are both moral and intelligent is also essential for the realization of these hopes.

In passing, I would call your attention to Philip Roth's novel *The Plot Against America.*[2] Written thirteen years ago, it is about a fictitious conservative president elected in 1940 who supported the Hitlerian dictatorship and railed against Jews and Blacks. I knew Philip Roth when we both attended Bucknell University where I suffered minor prejudice and discrimination because I had friends at the Jewish fraternity house and as a Catholic in my own fraternity. One interesting similarity with the Trump administration in Roth's book was the establishment of "the Office of American Absorption" to benefit White Supremacists so that they could regain control of their country. The stock market rose, profits were up, business

---

[2] Roth, Philip, *The Plot Against America,* New York (Vintage: 2004). See also William Durland, "History as Prologue" for details on the rise of Hitler and similarities to Trump. (See Appendix and Bibliography for further details.)

boomed. Roth's dictator called his policy "America first." His opponents called him unfit. He was finally removed under Article 2 §1 of the U.S. Constitution as unable to perform his duties according to the Constitution after being blackmailed by a foreign power. Interestingly, the FBI first detected evidence of Russian influence in the American election designed to encourage the election of Trump in July 2016. Another similarity is that presidential senior assistant Jared Kushner has been appointed by President Trump to head the newly created "Office of American Innovation." In addition Trump propagandist Steve Bannon has called for the "destruction of the administrative state," referring to the national government and its regulatory protections of the middle class and poor, existing environmental protection, national parks open space, healthcare, immigration and other democratic actions of the Obama administration.

Let's contemplate the choices before us apart from resistance. We can be passive, acquiescent, adjustable, and oblivious to what's happening to our representative government or simply conclude that it's not our kingdom, as dropouts of old did, and it can go its own way. Then there's conflict avoidance stemming from a fear or dislike of conflict and a rationale that if left alone it will resolve itself. But since the inauguration, many of us have decided that we need to consider active resistance as a community. We've had our share of conscientious objectors and the civilly disobedient, so resistance is nothing new to us when human lives are threatened. Even those of us who, for many years, were of the view that we were called to be outward activists and others of us inward spiritualists, have joined the new movement because of the consequences of what this particular threat could mean. And if it is not we, then who will it be? Rather than passivity or conflict avoidance, resistance requires activism, and that is of two sorts – violent revolution or nonviolent direct action.

Resistance through nonviolent direct action is a choice now that seems clear. Many ways to resist nonviolently come to mind. These include 1) direct action of various types including vigils, witnesses, protests, demonstrations, accompaniment, many augmented through conscientious objection and civil disobedience. 2) Education, both of ourselves and for others on how to practice nonviolent direct action through nonviolence training and how to persevere through arrest, trial, jail and other serious consequences. 3) Boycotts, giving up benefits and pleasures of corporate advantage, living under the taxable level as war tax resisters and other actions of simplicity. 4) The use of the media through oral and written statements. 5) Court litigation and legislative work, lobbying through national and international organizations, and 6) Learning and practicing conflict resolution with people of varying political viewpoints, but most importantly, electing representatives under a fair and equitable voting system.

During the past months, there has been a huge renewal of energy, much greater than expected, with the women's march on Washington, climate change and science protests, numerous sanctuary cities established from coast to coast, many large and noisy town hall meetings about immigration and health care, and massive Tax Day demonstrations.

An early article in *The Nation,* called Americans to "Mourn, Resist, Organize."[3] Written a few days after the election, a stunned editorial board stated "a man who campaigned on a platform of hostility to immigrants, contempt for women and disregard for civil and religious liberty has been elected President of the United States." "The same Republican Party," it goes on "that for eight years obstructed President Obama at every turn, now controls the Senate, the House and soon the Supreme Court." Later articles blamed the Democratic Party for not being vigilant enough as the historical party of the vulnerable, the poor, the victimized and the protector of the environment.[4] As the months unfolded, Trump attempted to make true his predatory promises to protect the profit-makers, the privileged and the powerful. *The Nation* wrote about "How to Fight Back."[5] It said: "Resistance must balance the monitoring of his reckless acts through the work of challenging the savage policies put forward."

The Nation listed a guide, available on the Internet, composed by a handful of current and former congressional staffers that outlined the most effective ways for ordinary people to lobby their representatives. The website crashed under the weight of the traffic it was drawing – 1.8 million people, 5,387 different groups in March. Some of the projects were entitled 1) Town hall meetings, 2) The Pussy Hat Project, 3) Knock on every door, 4) Swing Left, 5) Adopt a State, 6) Flipable, 7) Run for something, 8) Grab

---

[3] "Mourn, Resist, Organize," *The Nation,* Nov. 28, 2016.
[4] *Ibid.*
[5] "How to Fight Back," *The Nation,* March 27, 2017.

your wallet, 9) Movement 2017, and 10) Operation 45, consisting of Freedom of Information Act requests.[6]

We no longer have the luxury of a slow but sure movement "to a more perfect union." Our efforts have been sidetracked into stopping the racist, misogynist and kleptocratic practices of dismantling the public services we were able to protect and slowly move forward in the past. George Orwell's *1984*[7] is flying off the shelves of bookstores as "alternative facts and fake news" become commonplace. "Big Brother is watching you," as his Ministry of Truth, announces alternative facts: "war is peace, freedom is slavery, ignorance is strength."

As they join the resistance movement, activists will find that there will be a tension between a more militant resistance and a more spiritual one. We should not be taken up with the need to be effective. Rather we should be truthful about what we pursue. For if our consequences become more important than our principles we will find, as has been the case in many predominately secular movements, we will become more like that which we are trying to resist and less like what we are called to be. The call to nonviolent resistance, on the model of Gandhi, Martin Luther King and Dorothy Day can no longer be selective, as some have said in the past "politics is not my thing," or espoused a false dichotomy between individualism and community. So we must resist together and combine our resistance with the resilience needed in order to make it holistic.

---

[6] *Ibid.*

[7] Orwell, George, *1984*, New York (Signet Classics: 1980).

The long haul includes a resistance with resilience that will restore what has been lost and restart our 250-year movement forward again. What is resilience? It's defined as "the ability to recover from or adjust to misfortune or change; the capability of withstanding shock without permanent deformation or rupture; elastic, flexible." It is a state of being rather than doing. Probably the greatest American experience of resilience was the manner in which Americans, during World War II reacted to the Pearl Harbor attack and the suffering required of them over four years until victory. As a child, I was cheered up by the words of that beautiful song, which told me "there will be blue birds over the white cliffs of Dover, tomorrow just you wait and see." In those days I knew nothing of the detention of Japanese-Americans and their ability to endure until release and vindication many years later by constitutional lawyers protecting the rule of law. My participation in the Civil Rights Movement began with Jews, Blacks and women and moved to include anti-war resisters, undocumented refugees and mistreated prisoners and poor.

Today, as then, the shock comes first, then the sadness, then the outrage, and then the will to gather in community and commit to a unified resistance. Laurence O'Donnell of MSNBC, after the shock and sadness wore off, expressed his concern that the progressives would revert to type and exhibit too much adjustment and acquiescence to what had happened. He said outrage is good. After all what we are facing then and now, as he said early on, was the collapse of American civilization and the destruction of constitutional democracy as we know it. One should be very angry and that anger may then be captured in a will to overcome what had happened. That energy may then be transformed into hope, fortitude and action. Spiritual folks may describe that as faith in the power of truth, hope in the future of democracy, and love for all those involved on both sides of the conflict. Our own experiences, my wife Genie's and mine, have marveled on the need to sustain our resilience with humor as well as faith. I recall, with renewed laughter, such experiences quite often.

Restoration is defined as "to put or bring back into existence or use to a former position or condition; to reestablish, renew, revive." What will we have to restore by such resistance and resilience? Many of us are aware of Trump's campaign promises during and up to the past one hundred days, of what he has successfully or unsuccessfully done in that regard. His failures so far to May 2017 have been his attempts to destroy the Affordable Healthcare Act and his failure to eliminate the American tradition of welcoming immigrants by arbitrary deportation, wall building and threats to "sanctuary cities." His so-called successes can be found in numerous Executive Orders such as ending our movement to challenge global warming by deregulating carbon emissions and pollution prohibitions and many more. He appointed to the U.S. Supreme Court his own candidate in spite of the fact that republicans violated the Constitution's requirement that Obama's nominee receive a hearing by the Congress. (Art.2 §2) The new member of the Supreme Court takes his seat in complicity with that violation, while at the same time he swears to uphold the Constitution. Finally, the President now seems to feel confident from the accolades and approval he has received for rejecting diplomacy in favor of missile attacks, the use of the Mother of All Bombs, and nuclear threats.

What lies ahead? His tax reform aimed at reducing corporate taxes from thirty-five to fifteen percent even though only one out of every five corporations pays a tax at all. And a budget to transfer funds from public services to private profit and military spending are on the agenda as well as further attempts to repeal Obamacare. Some of us may not be familiar with what his proposed budget entails, which he announced in April, but by June Congress had not passed it. A temporary six-month budget was necessary to prevent a government shutdown thereafter. I will paraphrase an early summary in opposition to it from *The Nation* magazine.[8] There is an additional 54 billion dollars to be added to military expenditures and that sum will be subtracted from domestic programs even though the Pentagon accounts for over 40 percent of the world's current military spending. The budget is a blow to science, medical research, renewable energy and education and training. The National Endowments for the Arts and the Humanities are abolished. They constitute only 0.02 percent of the Obama budget and their elimination seriously jeopardizes public radio and television. Education and training programs – preschool and after school, work study and grant support to help low income families pay for college, job training for workers, teacher training and more – are all savaged. Spending on sorely needed infrastructure is cut as well with a thirteen percent reduction in the Department of Transportation and the elimination of the Department of Agriculture's water and waste disposal loan and grant program.

Other programs decimated are infant nutrition, daycare for lower income families, public housing and rent

---

[8] "Trump Budget, GOP Values," *The Nation,* April 18, 2017.

support, meals on wheels, home heating aid for the impoverished and disabled to prevent freezing in winter. Rural economic development programs – the Appalachian Regional Council, the Delta Regional Authority, and the Great Lakes Restoration Initiative – are ended, as well as support for rural airports and radio stations. Job training and legal aid are eliminated. Programs to help middle and high school students prepare for college and after school and summer enrichment programs are cut out. The assault on public education is escalated with money going rather to subsidize charter and private school vouchers. Support for enforcing health and safety regulations in factories and mines, minimum wage and workers' rights programs are eviscerated. Food stamps and Pell grants are cut.

In order to compensate for some of the excessive discretionary spending on trips to Florida and proposed for building the wall, mandatory programs like Social Security, Medicare, Medicaid and interest on the national debt will be cut and privatized. More tax cuts for the wealthy and corporations are featured. The final proposed budget was released in May and is discussed in the Afterword.

Few of us know that the republican administration has recently passed legislation so that the mentally ill may obtain firearms without background checks. This will further escalate the gun violence domestically, as Trump gives enthusiastic support to NRA lobbyists, while at the same time, military action will only increase the violence internationally and diminish our reliance on nonviolent alternatives. Violence begets violence. The Afterword provides a more complete and comprehensive explanation of all the Trump threats, commonly called "Trumpthink."

If that list is not enough to cause wholesale resistance, I don't know what else would do it. It's a huge task to restore and then restart where we left off before Trump. Priorities for resistance must be set. How would you do it? After the tremendous task of restoration, we may again begin a resurgence of what we were pursuing before Trump, even though there has been continued conservative, far-right Christian corporate, confederate, and militaristic opposition to it. Fortunately, there is already in progress the passage of legislation in eleven states, constituting 165 electoral votes, requiring state electors to cast their votes for the candidate who won the popular vote.

Western history has been identified as a slow evolutionary progress toward the elimination of violent discrimination, prejudice and bias and the progression of democratic freedom, security, human rights, equality and neighborliness. This great movement began long before there were American political parties. The terror of tyrants has been with us from the beginning, Trump is only the latest version, but uniquely the first to gain such power in America. Unfortunately, an acceptable pragmatic American culture justifies as ethical whatever "works" as long as you don't get caught breaking the law.

We may make a difference based on a principled morality that proceeds from rightness and not mightiness. "Yes we can." We *can* make a contribution in the effort to resist, empowered by our resilience, restoring human dignity for all and restarting the resurgence of the continuing movement towards a more perfect union.

So read again the Foreword and original text and then finish off with the second edition's new Afterword of our current challenge covering the first one hundred and sixty days of the Trump administration. Compare the republican, conservative positions prior to the Trump election with the Trump/republican efforts, both successes and failures, since the election. The challenge before us becomes self-evident. Do we want to lose the progress made by American civilization because we elected an aspiring autocrat to govern us, leading the present administration in the worst way possible?

A movement towards democracy began over 800 years ago in earnest and progressed in a way, heavily powered by the American and French revolutions, to disintegrate the power of the one percent then represented by kings, lords, nobles and bishops, and inspired the emergence of the ninety-nine percent gaining a more equitable place in the world – the peasants, serfs, vassals and slaves. Today the titles have changed but the percentages, that a generation ago were finally moving to that more equitable relationship, have once again seen the top one percent now composed of CEOs, employers, plutocrats, corporations and autocrats rising to dominance over the workers, employees, middle class and poor, disabled and vulnerable. Let us employ all our efforts to resist, restore and move forward with a resurgence that will pick up the efforts where we left off during "Trump time" and begin again to form a more perfect union for Americans with liberty and justice for all.

FORWORD: It Takes a Renaissance Man to Spot a Tipping Point

By Loring Wirbel

For every dozen climatologists who warn us it is almost too late to do anything about a warming planet, you will find a Bjorn Lomborg ready to feed us the positive news that the Earth's environment has actually improved a bit since the late 1980s. And along some dimensions, Lomborg is not entirely wrong.

Similarly, for every student of democratic institutions who warns us that these institutions are being hollowed out, one will find the new Extropians or Objectivists who insist that a 24/7 Internet-connected world populated by citizens staring at smartphones with more computing power than 1970s supercomputers, gives birth to a new form of democracy only dimly appreciated by traditionalists. In a very limited sense, the Extropians may have a point.

But if we are willing to shift our focal point to wide angle and apply all the institutional memory we can muster, from the classical Greek and Roman eras to the decades immediately preceding our own, we can conclude that something has been lost in American democracy in the past 50 years. The problem is, there are few surviving individuals with a broad enough eye on society any longer to spot the true flaws in the body politic that may well be fatal wounds.

William Durland is such a renaissance man. The books and plays he has published in the last two decades remind us that it is still possible to synthesize Greek and

Roman dialogues on democracy, High Middle Ages texts on the role of feudalism after the *Magna Carta*, and philosophers' observations on the proper governing of humans, from Hobbes to Sartre.

Durland uses examples from his eight decades in academia, the military, politics and activist organizations to weave his observations taken from the classic critical texts most have either forgotten or have never read. Certainly there are plenty of tunnel-vision activists who have warned of narrow elements of *Citizens United,* Christian influence in politics, and the superficiality that has displaced rationalism. But not may activists in the 21st century even attempt to weave together so many elements to create one unified quilt.

Durland's research and on-site activism into the Occupied Territories during the 1990s and 2000s did more than fuel the passion for his written studies on the Middle East. He applied a careful and critical eye to the relationship between Israeli expansionists and Christian Zionists, recognizing the way in which devout groups put faith before reason. The conclusions regarding the armor used by the devout to deflect rational discussion fit many other topics in American discourse outside the Middle East.

In the course of developing his readers-theatre plays, Durland assumed an enlightenment-empowered audience that could take is distillation of ideas at face value. While the plays have met local praise in Colorado, it is evident that the mere existence of enlightenment baseline values and ideals can no longer be assumed, even outside the legions of the devout. Recent generations have grown up pursuing degrees in business management, marketing, programming or highly specialized science and engineering domains, and simply have no background in the ideas that shaped Western humanities disciplines.

This is why the concrete examples used in this book are so important. Young activists may stumble upon a holistic view of justice and righteousness through specific callings in gender identification, anti-racism actions, environmentalism and the like. But it is only by bringing up the founding ideas of democracy in the context of specific struggles that Durland can make his case.

It is often said by leading environmentalists like Bill McKibben that the planet is already past its "tipping point." Certainly, it makes sense to fight climate change and reduce our carbon footprint, but we must recognize the contextual reality that at this point, we can only alleviate in part the damage already done.

In considering the revitalization of democracy in the 21st century, Durland may be playing the role of the canary in the coalmine, within the confines of a coal mine where all the workers have died. There are many signs that we have already passed the tipping point.

In more centralized societies outside our own, Egypt reversed the Arab Spring simply by getting citizens to call for army intervention. Viktor Orban of Hungary turned racism and hatred of the other into a point of pride. Russia under Putin, long accustomed to living under ethical fantasies where Putin calls upon the Russian Orthodox Church to bring the people to sacrifice, while making up stories out of whole cloth to justify a climate where surreality reigns supreme

And what of the United States? Karl Rove was quoted as saying, during the buildup to the Iraq War, that facts and lies did not matter any more, as the Bush administration was building its own reality, and by the time critics would have called them on inaccurate points of that reality, the White House would have moved on to create another new reality.

This certainly characterizes most of the political and corporate surrealities defining the United States today. The crowded GOP dance card already included candidates with strange personal surrealities, from Mike Huckabee to Ted Cruz to Rick Santorum. When a brash, bullying, lying-as-strategy candidate like Donald Trump came along, it was only natural for him to explode in the polls among citizens who fully accept lies as truth, and have no means for distinguishing their emotion-based beliefs generated in their pontine brains, from the rational search for truth that takes place in the cortex. They cannot favor rational logic or the scientific method because they do not understand the value of this type of thinking. Many, for evangelical independents to Trump supporters, even tend to dismiss scientific method as Satanic.

So do we stop attempting to bring back democracy to citizens in a post-tipping-point world that seem to have little appreciation for it to begin with? Like McKibben with climate change, Durland would utter an emphatic "No!" I would join him in such a conclusion. The struggle to identify right ways of living, and to serve as an example to others, is worthy even it if is a Quixotic effort against impossible odds. While we live, we fight. While we live, we try to follow the scriptural call to "Go then, and do likewise." Durland has done this kind of thing all his life, because it is his calling. We can listen and try to understand, we can listen and refuse to understand, but we cannot afford to clap our hands over our ears and refuse to hear the canary in the coalmine.

Loring Wirbel is an author and activist living in Monument, Colorado. He is author of the book *Star Wars: US Tools of Space Supremacy,* and is a two-time winner of the Project Censored awards of Sonoma State University, for articles in *The Progressive* and *Covert Action Quarterly.* He is a state board member of the Colorado ACLU, and has served on the boards of Pikes Peak Justice and Peace Commission, Mobilization for Survival, and Poetry West, among other organizations. Wirbel has written lengthy critiques of a variety of modern computer and bioengineering technologies, at daily papers in Tucson and Albuquerque, and at technical journals such as *Electronic Engineering Times.* He currently works as a technology analyst for The Linley Group in Mountain View, California.

PART I - THE THESIS: EVOLUTION, PROGRESS AND CURRENT DECLINE OF AMERICAN DEMOCRACY

CHAPTER ONE – INTRODUCTION

"IF MEN WERE ANGELS, NO GOVERNMENT WOULD BE NECESSARY" JAMES MADISON, THE FEDERALIST PAPERS, BOOK 51, 1788

The Question Raised

James Madison called it "an American Experiment." We have been at it for over 200 years, making progress through adversity. How valuable is that experiment to Americans today? The premise of this book is that American democracy and specifically its representative form, is in a state of demise. The progress of our past has been reversed over the past 35 years. Unless we restore it and move forward again with vigilant oversight and action, its fate is sealed – "the American dream" is dead.

My conclusion that a demise in American democracy is underway started to form in 1989, when in my second book, God or Nations, I expressed the opinion that in nation states, "violence exists … and generally to a greater degree than in former times.… It is the violence that convinces the United States and other super powers that they must manipulate and exploit their weaker neighbors for their own aggrandizement."[1] These comments were made in reflection

---

[1] Durland, William, *God or Nations*, Baltimore, (Fortkamp Publishing Company: 1989), p.142.

on Ronald Reagan's eight-year presidency. I went on to quote Robert Nisbet who concluded that "it is sometimes said that political nationalism is the contemporary man's substitute for religion in the ordinary sense.... The political state has taken on many of the attributes medieval man found in the church alone."[2] But it also seems that part of what I then called "the demise of the modern state" in America was not only a political institution substituting religion for politics but American conservative Christian religious institutions substituting the political state in place of their rejected nonviolent early Christian characteristics. Centuries have proved that modern Christians rely much more on Moses and Joshua than Jesus and the violence found in the Hebrew Scriptures attached to the Christian New Testament has legitimized current American political practices.

In 1995, while a professor at Trinidad State Junior College, I wrote an essay for the college literary magazine on the theme of the de-evolution of American democracy. Once again, I saw this de-evolution beginning in 1980 and described its purpose as follows. "It is designed to regulate our federal laws, provide more tax cuts for the rich, persuade us that our enemy is the national government and that each of us has little responsibility in regard to a national political authority, which it assumes interferes with our personal freedoms, and it promotes greater attachment to a state

---

[2] *Ibid*, p. 143. A quote from Robert Nisbet's *The Social Philosophers*, New York (Washington Square Press: 1982) at p. vii.

government, which it says will serve us better."[3] Once again the reference is to the Reagan administration's successful attempts to replace FDR's New Deal with a conservative, southern, confederate Christian corporate "deal."

Nevertheless, there were many who in the midst of the 2016 presidential election year asked the question "where is the crisis?" After all the economy is on the rise, and America is the dominant world power. There are more jobs and the party of business is again in power in Congress and that's good for our economic system – capitalism. More Americans than ever have the right to vote and that means both our economic and political democracy, demonstrated by our representative government, our Republic is flourishing. What's all the fuss about? The fuss would turn out to be Donald Trump.

The fuss became a crisis, the result of the demise of just those precious characteristics. There is a greater degree of irresponsibility and at the same time of inequality than ever before, where less than 40 percent of those eligible to vote in the last two national elections did so and charges of voting interference were made. Numerous roadblocks have been placed in the way of minorities who wish to vote, but can no longer do so. That plays a big part in the perpetuation of what we have known as representative democracy. In international affairs, a conservative President and Congress hawk war in the Middle East and support the secular theocracy of its closest ally – the State of Israel. I call Israel a secular theocracy because it declares itself both a

---

[3] Durland, William, "The De-evolution of American Government," *Purgatoire Magazine of Literary Arts*, Philip Tate, ed., (1995) p. 58.

democracy and a privileged Jewish state, while dominating indigenous peoples and occupying their lands. One reason for this is that many Americans are oblivious to what is happening, while another group of powerful Americans are making sure that it happens.

My own evolution of these thoughts reached articulation in my first Mellen publication, *Penn, Madison and the Historical Crisis in American Federalism.*[2] My experience and research in the year 2000 indicated that out of this crisis four alternative powers would emerge and combine in complement to seek constitutional power from the national government. These were a coalition of conservative, confederate corporations, Christians and militias. Just before the presidential election of that year, I pointed out that a de-evolution and dismantling of the federalist structure of the national government of our republic was taking place with the transference of national powers to these entities. The first part of that process was the states' rights southern third confederacy. Their aim was to do away with the national government they so long resented. But their modern reason would be that it was too "big." To say that the national government is too big and leave the impression that its power will simply be diminished and not reside elsewhere is a faulty notion. Power knows no vacuum.

That transfer of national governmental power predicted then is taking place politically and economically through corporate structures - internationally through

---

[2] DURLAND, OP. CIT, *Penn, Madison and the Historical Crisis in American Federalism,* Lewiston, NY, (The Edwin Mellen Press: 2000), pp. 210-213.

globalization and domestically either by transfer of power to state governments or to private corporations. A third powerful group, the American Christian right has become an instrumental mover in these political and economic changes that have religious characteristics as well. The fourth element I mentioned then was the militias, which were very powerful before they were assimilated into the NRA-supported Bush administration's gun-friendly policies.

The first American confederacy in 1776 was well-meaning wherein an attempt was made, successfully, to establish an American national government that did not have a monarch at the top of political, economic or religious power, such as was the case in England where the King was supreme head of the Christian church. That first confederacy, however, was unbalanced in another way, where an over-reactive extreme structure placed most power in the hands of the legislatures and little with the executive or judiciary. A constitutional form of government was later designed to rectify that and put an end to the first confederacy. The second confederacy in 1861 was an attempt, based on economic, political, as well as religious propositions, to perpetuate the dominance of White southern Christian slaveholders over their "property" stolen from the shores of Africa. Beginning in the 1980s, the Reagan administration began setting up what looked like a return to confederacy with the shift of powers to the states with the privatization of services by corporations. Christian church influence, and for a time, private militias, rounded out the power base. Since the accession of the Bush administration and republican power, the National Rifle Association lobby has adequately represented private militias. The NRA has convinced

Congress that guns in the hands of "good people" can solve all our problems with "bad people" who oppose us. The only problem with that reasoning is that in many cases, bad people were good people to begin with.

What provides the basis for this insidious transfer of power is the acquiescence and/or obliviousness of the major part of our representative democratic constituency, which is allowing this to happen. Twitter, Facebook, U-Tube, blogs, texting and other instruments of individual entertainment and absorption keep a large part of our population technocratically active, but essentially ill-informed publicly in this so-called information age. Too many citizens are unaware of the significant loss of their own freedoms as they become preoccupied with their new technological freedom of entertainment and superficial information. Others are aware of what is going on but are comfortable enough to acquiesce to such changes or just don't care. Some say: "politics is not my thing" as if it were another entertainment choice. And still there are those who feel that things are bad and have been convinced by the media that it all resides in Washington and that nothing can be done about it unless we take away or reduce the power of the national government. A majority of Americans recently polled are agreeable to the loss of freedoms to the extent that they will provide us with a greater security from the threats they fear, which are extreme Islamists or neo Cold War Russians.[5]

---

[5] A Gallup Poll in 2014 noted that 79 percent of Americans were satisfied with their freedoms being restricted, a drop from 91 percent in 2006. A previous 2013 poll noted a stark shift from prior percentages in favorable responses to surveillance of telephones and Internet. Revelations leaked on NSA surveillance and violations of privacy were claimed to be the cause.

Will Big Brother protect us? Will we be the new "good Germans?" If the past is prologue and history not only repeats itself but also informs us of the future, why would it happen now? This book is about not only that it can happen here but that it is happening here right now, in a similar and more subtle way than how it took place in 1933 in Germany.

Some say the Republican Congress has reduced itself to nothing more than a quasi-judicial Star Chamber-like inquisitorial body. It investigates the opposing party through allegations and assumptions about supposed wrongdoings instead of performing its primary function of passing legislation that represents the will of its citizenry.

In this introduction I will only attempt to gather together an overview summary of the arguments and supporting evidence and claims that are presented in succeeding chapters. The numerous and particular areas affected that give credence to the basic thesis of demise have been the result of 75 years of continual thought and experience on my part in the area. I intend to conduct a concise conversation with the reader on the truth of such assertions and no more. My hope is to create a wake up call to consider the possibility that what the likes of such giants as Socrates, Plato, Aristotle, Cicero, Augustine, Aquinas, More, Coke, Locke, Montesquieu, Madison, Jefferson, Marshall, Lincoln, Wilson, and the two Roosevelts worked to establish philosophically, politically, and economically is worth keeping and protecting and will not pass away. Rather, a new birth of freedom can be ours. This book is for students of public life to reflect upon. But the message is for the public citizen to act upon. For me it all begins at the age of nine.

A Personal View

My father's family was of Dutch origin, quite suitable for a New York homestead, first in Brooklyn and then in Queens, Long Island. My mother's family, from Ireland, lived in Spuyten Duyvil, adjacent to Kingbridge, in New York City. Her mother's name was Kilcullen and her father, Henry James Seymour, a distant relative perhaps of the English Seymours. The Dutch Dorlands made money, the "shanty Irish" didn't. So it was that my father's father, president of the Canadian General Electric Company, bought my parents a $35,000 home during the Depression in Scarsdale, New York, when I was five years old.

I may not have been the first Scarsdale Galahad, but the place where we lived in Berkeley Park was a Camelot to me. The new houses were built around a beautiful park with two lakes. A few yards behind our property to the east was the White Plains Post Road, where close by George Washington was said to have spent a night in what was a town library in my school days.

Down our road lived a Mr. Herbert and his southern Protestant wife. He was a photographer for Life magazine, well off and with a farm to boot. There was only one problem, he had a secret. I overheard my parents one evening talking about him. Not all grown-ups were of interest to youngsters like me, but Mr. Herbert was different. With the other fathers of our neighborhood households, he worked in New York and most of them came home by commuter train and a few of them walked home from the train station. During the summer, when we children played football or baseball in the park before dinner, Mr. Herbert and other parents would walk by. But Mr. Herbert always gave us a big Hello and sometimes would throw the ball with us. We came to appreciate his attentiveness and singled him out as one of our favorites.

That's why, when I heard my parents talking about him, I paid attention to what they were saying. It turned out that Mr. Herbert's secret was that he had to change his name to live in Berkeley Park. So my reaction was a natural one if you take into consideration I would some day become a logic professor. I asked my parents, since Mr. Herbert had to change his name, what was our name before we changed it? Their answer was we didn't. Mr. Herbert was Jewish and had dropped the foreign ending of his name to conceal that. Jews, Blacks, and Italians were prohibited from buying a house in this wonderful place. Most Blacks and Italians generally couldn't afford it so in those days they lived to the north or south of us. But Jews could and lived in other parts of Scarsdale. My nine-year old sense of fairness was offended.

Shortly thereafter war came to America. I was told that Jews were persecuted in Europe and we were in the war to save the Jews. I was angry. Mr. Herbert was my friend and I couldn't understand why everyone in Berkeley Park or elsewhere could not be treated like everyone else. It seemed so unfair. That was my first lesson in cultural relations. It was disturbing, and that disturbance has never left me. I am sure that this isolated experience at a very young age was a motivating factor for my involvement in international and constitutional civil rights as a lawyer, legislator, teacher, author and activist. Certainly it remains a reason why I would undertake to write a book of this sort that I feel is necessary.

All of this has never gone away. Even though progress has been made on the issues of race and others like it, that progress is now in a state of demise. By the time I bought our own home in 1959 in Fairfax County, Virginia, I was again to experience the same prohibitions in my own deed, wherein it stated that I could not sell my house to Negroes. And I was shortly to find out that in the case of Jews, there continued a de facto discrimination in such places as country clubs. Fortunately, I was aware, having just graduated from Georgetown Law School, that in the Supreme Court case of *Shelley v Kraemer*[6] the U.S. Supreme Court ruled such provisions null and void constitutionally. And yet segregation persisted in the south right up to the borders of the nation's capital.

It would be a long battle to end it, as those of us who were elected to the Virginia State Legislature in 1965 were

---

[6] *Shelley v. Kraemer*, 334 US 1 (1948). The Court held that state judicial enforcement of agreements banning persons from ownership or occupancy of real property on racial grounds violates the Equal Protection Clause of the Fourteenth Amendment of the U.S. Constitution. A Black person purchased a home the deed for which contained a racially restrictive covenant prohibiting the sale property to "people of the Negro or Mongolian races." The restriction had been in force since 1911. The Supreme Court decision did not specifically require the deed to remove the language. (It was obvious that it was intended, however in the South, the restriction was still included even though knowledgeable home-buyers might know, as I did, that the provision was unenforceable.) That is the reason why the deed I was given in 1959 still contained the restriction and why most buyers understood it to be enforceable upon them. I joined the NAACP in 1950.

able to accomplish by authoring bills to abolish such restrictions as the poll tax, voting registration restrictions and the privatizing of schools so that Blacks could not attend. Even sterilization laws had been introduced prior to my election. Anti-miscegenation laws prohibited people of color from inter-marrying with Whites. We overcame that in 1967, when, after I announced my intention to provide legislation to abolish such laws, the Supreme Court did so in their decision in *Loving v. Virginia.* The evolution of American representative democracy took a step forward. It is from my experiences as a young adult and my years in the Virginia Legislature that I developed my life-long drive to work for justice. Today, and for some years in the past, that drive has been tested as progress has been reversed.

An Overview of the Book

In order to put into writing a cogent argument for the thesis that American representative democracy is in a state of demise, or disintegration, or at worst destruction, I would like to provide an outline of my method of doing so drawn from the structure of this book. In the not-too-distant past America was the most respected country in the world. That reputation had emerged from its revolution, followed by the evolution of an American republic, a representative democracy with a compassionate concern for its neighbors around the world. If this were not true it certainly was the belief of many here and abroad during and after World Wars I and II. It was anchored in such events as the Declaration of the Four Freedoms, the creation of the United Nations, the formation of the Nuremburg Principles and the restoration and reconciliation of world relationships among the victors and vanquished designed to end destruction and discrimination against minorities and indigenous people everywhere.

Madison's great accomplishment was to study the current understandings of his time of two political philosophical and practical extremes - one on the right of autocracy or monarchy, and the other on the left of libertarianism or anarchy. These isms were played out in real life in small city-states or huge empires. Madison invented a new federalist structure, of neither extreme - confederal nor unitary - but instead a representative democratic republic, and for the first time workable in a sizeable nation-state. He saw the great threat of factions, whether a majority or minority, usually represented by political parties, but envisioned that in a large state neither the extremes of right or left could destroy the design. Two prongs of this structure were its separation of powers horizontally among balanced executive, legislative and judicial powers, and vertically by a national, state, and local separation. He had one fear, nevertheless, that structure alone would not do it but that the people's representatives would have to be virtuous and, as Jefferson said, the people would have to be vigilant to make sure that it succeeded. Jefferson added that an educated rather than an illiterate electorate was necessary and that a great wall of separation would protect both church and state from each other. If these things were established, this new form of government would be insulated from anarchy or autocracy, as had not been the case in Europe and elsewhere.

The new nation would be considered a vast public community where its citizens would not feel separated or isolated from the government over which they would become sovereign. Nevertheless, Madison realistically acknowledged that men were not angels. A divergent but reasonable economic interpretation of the Constitution has been around for years. The Democratic Socialists of America argue that the founders' main motive was to enhance the power of educational elites and make rapid democratic change difficult to achieve.[7] Any deviation could allow political, religious or economic factions to ruin the design. And so the evolution and progress flowing from this plan became the history of the United States of America, with its great birth of potential democracy, held back only by its continuing system of human inequality in slavery, then segregation, and finally deprivation. But after the 20th century unfolded and world wars exposing dictatorships of the left and right, the anchor of a post world war world was variations on a theme of Madisonian democracy.

The so-called "American dream" continued to envision that the sociological stratification of old would wither away and kings, bishops and nobles - the lords - could no longer dominate over their servants, vassals, serfs and slaves. The reality is many of them remained under more modern and comfortable names with some of the same

---

[7] *The Federalist,* No. 51; See Hutchinson, William and Rachal, William, eds. *The Papers of James Madison,* Chicago (University of Chicago Press, 1969); Smith, James M., ed. *The Republic of Letters,* New York (William Norton & Co: 1995) this is a compilation of correspondence between Jefferson and Madison; Peterson, Merrill, ed. *Jefferson: Writings,* New York (Library of America, 1984); Bailyn, Bernard, ed. *The Debate on the Constitution,* New York (Library of America: 1990). See Schwartz, Joseph, "Socialists and the U.S. Political System," *Democratic Left,* Summer 2015, pp. 3-5; Beard, Charles, *An Economic Interpretation of the Constitution of the United States,* New York (Macmillan: 1913).

stratification. The hope was that the people, as sovereign, would make sure that their own representatives would perpetuate a truly equitable system of human opportunity. After World War II and for a generation this would not only be the hope but an emerging reality. But this was not the case both here and abroad. It is the thesis of this book and its chapter-by-chapter argument and evidence, that the de-evolution presently taking place as a result must be halted and reversed.

My outline of parts, chapters and sections is an attempt to offer the reader a glimpse on these pages of how that American dream has stalled, been allowed to reverse itself and is in need of recovery. The Table of Contents details the numerous subjects and issues covered. The chapters are not uniform in length. I decided that substance should prevail over form, which might have dictated that the various chapters should be equivalent in size. The book begins with a Foreword and has three parts and nine chapters. Part One is entitled "The Thesis: Evolution, Progress and Current Decline of American Democracy." Chapter One is entitled Introduction and divided into three sections setting the stage for the heart of the crisis, which is unfolded in Chapter Two, a chronology of historical events demonstrating the etiology of this present demise. Part Two begins with Chapter Three, perhaps the most detailed of my presentation – the dismantling of representative government – the crux of my argument. Chapter Four covers the dissolution of democracy abroad with its present disuse of international law, the United Nations and treaties on universal human rights.

Part Two, "Domestic and International Examples of Demise" builds on the arguments of Part One and presents the evidence for the disintegration of democratic norms, providing specific details, more than generalizations found in Part One. Chapter Five is entitled "The Right to Live." It makes the point that our nation's promiscuous and indiscriminate weapons development, war making, punishment system, and personal gun-worship legally, logically and morally make no sense. Harsh imprisonments, spying and surveillance round out examples. The examples given are intended to serve as illustrative vignettes. A book of this limited size, treating so many diverse issues cannot provide a comprehensive analysis of each of them. The purpose, rather, is to bring these issues together in one place and to provide an opportunity for the inquiring mind to examine the arguments and evidence offered to support my thesis of deteriorating democracy. It is noted that others, mentioned as we proceed, are of similar mind.

Part Three entitled "The General Welfare Under Attack" brings together in five chapters nine examples of specific areas of demise. Chapter Six shows how economics plays a central part in public life and is related to the problems facing the preservation of our environment. The two should not be in conflict with one another, but they are. The rise of corporate power has increased inequality by obstructing people of color, and the poor from access to public benefits designed for those in need. It also fails as well to keep safe our infrastructure. The problems facing our environment, such as global warming, grow without significant action. Our environment faces eventual if not irreversible destruction. The Earth is not ours, we did not create it, and we must limit the extent of our dominion over it.[8] National borders treat humanity as criminal invaders when such boundaries make human beings illegal, primarily to protect a select few from a disenfranchised many.

Chapter Seven is entitled "Religion, Science, Sex and Sanity." It considers the extremes of civil religion and secular theocracy as they attempt to dismantle the great wall of separation between church and state originally built to protect church and state from each other. The experience of the Church of England and the monarchy of England, as one, was enough to warn us of this evil. But today, often with the aid of political power at the Supreme Court level and through state legislatures, a faction of Christian religion attempts to legislate, at the national level, their own Christian form of Mosaic laws and Islamic sharia in the form of the religiously validated violence that has ruled the three Religions of the Book – Judaism, Christianity and Islam.[9]

Under science, sex and sanity, we talk about the evolution of humanity. Most people in America don't believe it but many do - that we were, in fact, created just as we see ourselves today only some 5,000 years ago. When creationism fell into disrepute, "intelligent design" was substituted and that wording became popular, particularly in

---

[8] Genesis 1:26; Exodus 19:5, *New Revised Standard Version* of the Bible, London (Harper Collins: 1993).

[9] See Durland, William, *Tribal Tales: A Parody on Paternal Gods and Predator Peoples,* a play, (2015) highlighting Old Testament violence and laws adopted not only by Jews but Christians and Muslims as well. These writings and stories have justified religious and political violence in the name of religious faith.

the southern, conservative Christian states. Most Americans believe in dinosaurs but all creation is stuffed into that 5,000-year period. One of the results is that since the design is now called intelligent we can't mess with what God created. Interesting, when we look back on religious violence at the beginning of this chapter, and at the end contemplate our immigration and boundary limitations, we are certainly messing around with the Judeo-Christian God who pronounced that "the earth is mine."

Then there are gender rights, homosexuality, and same-sex marriages. This seems to be one area where depending on how ne defines progress, progress is being made. For example, women's right rights are improving. Science often affords a factual, objective basis for deciding issues like these. Certainly the tension between right to life and the right to choose must be informed by compassion. Lastly, the human incentive to discover who we are and to explore our universe of intelligent design also gets stalled when it is seen as an intrusion upon religion. And along with that, stem cell research for health and saving human life has experienced a bumpy road with some of the same people, preferring the unborn to the born.

That brings us to Chapter Eight, "Health, Education and Welfare," where we see that health care as a human right has been pursued by presidents and others for half a century without success until recently. When a modest step was taken to provide affordable health care through the conduit of profit-maximizing insurance companies, we have found almost everybody having a gripe about it. Liberals sought a more egalitarian single payer plan, while conservatives viewed it as an interference with free enterprise and example of big government trying to control people's health care. No wonder polls indicated disapproval and then presidential candidates and confederate-leaning states did all they could to destroy it and return to what some people saw as snake-oil pill pushers, doctors reduced to technicians and insurance companies practicing medicine. A pleasant surprise was the conservative Supreme Court's constitutional approval of this congressional legislation.

Reflecting upon Jefferson's emphasis on education, we have taken a look at some of the present drawbacks of what the national government has been able to provide in alleviating the costs of college education and the violence that threatens public education. Without a well-educated electorate we have people with degrees yet lacking the intellectual acuity necessary to understand the complexities of religion, politics and economics. Affordable higher education is generally non-existent and those who get it may find it's impersonal, rather than relational, approach to learning not worth doing in the information age, which holds out that the Internet and it's progeny such as Twitter, Facebook, etc. can provide all the information necessary for us to be technocrats. Madison's emphasis on virtue, which he derived from Montesquieu, might help us restore a modern understanding of an out-of-date word. Virtue is still available to us through the serious study of such disciplines as religion and science. Critical thinking and logic help us form the ability to analyze the words and actions of some political candidates and parties that we need to make intelligent and balanced political and civic decisions. All of this is just more evidence that representative government and democracy today is in need of immediate attention of a thoughtful populace as the general welfare is threatened.

We close on a call to action asking the question: will we let the American experiment die? Chapter Nine sums up the evolutionary rule of law, ever persistent in the pursuit of justice and always dependent on the vigilant. The replacement of evidence and fact by simple allegations and opinions has created a fast-track justice undermining the legacy of our legal democracy.[10] Conspiracies and cover-ups and violent war making and massacres have called for removal of First Amendment rights. A call to action for a restorative democracy goes up, not only in the pages of this writing but among many in America. I have presented the argument and theme and will follow with evidence and a methodology to thwart the threat and ensure that the American experiment will not perish from this earth. A new birth of action can restore what we are losing and continue the progress called for in the Preamble to the United States Constitution to form a more perfect union. So let us begin to

---

[10] "Fast track" justice is a device practiced by judges to move cases along more quickly without, some people say, sufficient evidentiary proof. Such inequities exist in domestic relations courts, at least in Denver, Colorado, where attempts have been made to rebalance the disadvantages of women in past domestic relations cases. The tables have been turned so that discrimination against men has allowed allegations rather than evidence to be sufficient in winning cases against them. In one case a man was put in jail overnight for domestic violence on what proved later to be spurious allegations. In another case a judge called for an evidentiary hearing after the woman's attorney alleged wrongdoing by the man without proof, the judge decided that that was good enough and refused the man the right to present evidence in rebuttal and ruled in favor of the woman.

bring some clarity to what is the case before us and what needs to be done about it. Are we in demise? If so why is that so? What are the examples and how may we begin to reverse the trend and restore progress?

CHAPTER TWO

THE HEART OF THE CRISIS

"THE PRICE OF LIBERTY IS ETERNAL VIGILANCE" THOMAS JEFFERSON, 1888

Introduction

The heart of the crisis, I propose, is the disintegration of representative government, as it existed in its progressive, evolutionary movement up until some time between 1963 and 1980. Both domestic and foreign relations have been affected. This part of my book, Parts One and Two, is "the forest" while Part Three is "the trees" – generalities followed by particulars. First I will present a broad view of the problems facing us today, while afterward I will provide the details in our syllogism, which will help us to eventually decide whether the argument and evidence justify the conclusion.

As we piece together our picture, there is an unusual amount of gossip in the news in recent years in the form of *ad hominem* attacks from the legislative and more subtly the judicial branches, and even more obviously among the presidential candidates on the conservative side of the election of 2016. Donald Trump is a prime example. A President of the United States elected twice to that office has been subjected to personal attacks upon his integrity as well as upon the bills he initiated and which became law such as the Affordable Healthcare Act. His color and ethnicity, some say, is the reason behind all for that, but I would add that this

21

attack is also made as a device to help in deconstructing the American national and federal structure. A still somewhat representative democratic majority has vindicated the President and the laws he sponsored so far until January 2016.

Two examples suffice to illustrate this point but many more will follow. The traditional international proposition that war, boycotts and sanctions should be last resorts is less and less a reality. The Obama administration put negotiation first into practice with Iran and gained an agreement that includes other nations as well (but not the Republican Party, of course). The nuclear agreement with Iran finalized by his administration is a stellar example and one, which Republicans (and Israel) reject out of hand, favoring instead a bombing campaign without a declaration of war. Steadfast negation is a far harder course than attack first and ask questions later as we did in 2003 in Iraq. On the domestic side, the only major western nation without a universal healthcare system for its people is the U.S.A. Decades after Truman, Johnson and John Kennedy began such a drive, a crippled and compromised but better-then-nothing healthcare bill passed both houses of Congress in 2010. It has been maligned ever since by a conservative legislature, but finally upheld by the Supreme Court in June 2015. Congress provided, all along, for itself with superior healthcare coverage while fighting to demolish "Obamacare," upon which it was based until compromised.

What should be expected of Congress in the case of Iran is simply to treat Iran and Israel similarly. Yet Israel's illegal nuclear weapons are ignored while they are one of the loudest voices demanding no nukes for Iran. Israel, as will be discussed later, obtained nuclear weapons by illegality and stealth and to this day will not acknowledge its possession of them and so does not abide by the same rules all other nuclear nations do by treaty. Moreover, the same parameters Israel achieved in its own independence are denied to Palestinians with singularly aggressive military occupation of those people in their own land.

The impetus behind the kind of stands the conservative Congress adopts is ultimately the intention to relocate public governmental power to wealthy, private corporations and religious organizations. With such a shift, nothing like free voting and representation would continue to exist. In its place will be elite and greatly overpaid CEOs and a Boards of Directors. In order to be included in decision-making, common folk would be required to buy stock (if they can afford it). The wealthy may do so, of course, so all the cards will be in the hands of the corporate few instead of a representative majority that votes for free. No separation or balance of powers or federal system will continue. In fact they will be intentionally eliminated. Volatile and adventurous forms of capitalism will dominate its political counterpart with domestic corporations expanding through international globalization. This is what I expect in the future and have been seeing on the rise for the past 25 years.

But one may say at this point that I am still dealing with assumptions and allegations and not hard evidence. So let us take a look at what specifically constitutes evidence of this transfer of power from where it once made American democracy the envy of nations.

Before proceeding, it may also be said that there is nothing wrong with believing what one cannot prove as true without sufficient evidence. What is wrong is claiming that certain beliefs, allegations and opinions should be enforced without evidence, simply on the basis that a faction, either political or religious, holds them, on faith, to be objectively true. The practices of today's republican-controlled Congress are a prime example. Their conservative committees are constantly investigating or interrogating what they believe is an abuse of the democratic process instead of legislating. Harm to others is often the consequence. Doing so can constitute an immoral act. To require of oneself the necessity to prove by evidentiary fact that which one asserts, alleges or applies in accusing others of wrongdoing is a moral act. So it is that which we will follow here and in succeeding chapters will be the facts and expert opinions and studies upon which my own allegations and hypotheses are based.

Another distinction should be expressed at the outset. There are always improvements and points at which progress is lagging that can be made in a democracy. But when progress generally recedes and the progressive movement retrogrades, it is those forces causing it to do so that are the ones to be identified, proved and brought to the attention of the citizenry so that damage is minimized and a dedication to renewed progress declared and activated.

The Evolution of Democracy

What are those historical foundational points upon which to build our more detailed study? The underpinnings of the evolution of American democracy predated the colonial period, and take us back to the period of the emergence of common law in the England of Henry II and his disputes with Thomas Becket and his son King John in the 13th century. The *Magna Carta* began the transfer of power from the elite to the common folk. In the 16th century Henry VIII's disputes with Thomas More highlight church and state conflict. Sir Edward Coke and the laws of the House of Commons in the 17th century set the stage for the adaptation of common law and a written constitution in America. The U.S. Constitution and its Bill of Rights take us away from the failed first Confederacy, an overreaching response to British monarchial dominance, to an attempted second Confederacy by the southern states against the union and Lincoln. A young nation flexed its muscles and took on grandiose views of manifest destiny as it ran roughshod over indigenous peoples and imported slaves, eventually to be freed but segregated. America emerged as a world power through two world wars and a resurgent economy. Progress in post-war representative democracy accelerated with a growing movement towards real equality for all citizens, in the war on poverty and civil rights movements. A strong development in international organization accompanied these domestic improvements, but would be short-lived.

That brings us face-to-face with the "Great Communicator," the Hollywood actor, Ronald Reagan, whose administration in 1980 began the end of the great New Deal and aborted the New Frontier of JFK, as well as, the "Great Society" of Johnson/Humphrey, all parts of the progressive climb of American democracy. (Richard Nixon offered mixed signals.) As the efforts of Ronald Reagan continued to influence us, a political Supreme Court, in 2001, saw itself strong enough to intervene in a national election divided by a few hundred votes and still counting. The Court ordered the count terminated and declared George Bush the junior the winner over Al Gore ensuring more backward movement. That leaves us in a thwarted democratic attempt to elect a president and a congress that would continue the progressive adventure. Not until 2006 would a congressional majority again arise and a democratic president be elected in 2008. With a small majority obtained, would it be enough to renew the evolutionary progressive trip forward?

Current Impediments and Media Influence

In a true representative democracy a majority should be enough to pass progressive legislation. But was this to be? Two impediments in the permanent rules of the Senate constituted an obstruction to the majority will from 2008 on. Although in the first two years of Obama's presidency there were enough votes to pass compromised legislation on a universal health care bill that had been in the works but obstructed since Harry Truman's time. But when in 2010 a republican majority was elected in the House of Representatives and Supreme Court appointments by Bush had already given the republicans control of the judiciary, Obama offered progressive democratic proposals in the U.S. Senate. But there was the problem of 60 votes now needed, instead of a simple majority to end debate or filibuster. The democrats had a majority in the Senate from 2008 to 2010 but not 60 votes. So the minority ruled simply because of this Senate rule imposed on the will of the majority by both democrats and republicans as their security blanket when threatened as the minority.

This was a key factor in the polarization of actions in the congress and the stagnation of legislative progress as a result of it. There was yet another impediment in the Senate because legislation could be amended by words that were not germane to the body of the original legislation proposed. What havoc did this wreak? It meant that the minority conservative party could amend the majority party's more progressive legislation with irrelevant conservative changes or additions requiring the democrats to choose whether to vote for their own proposal with hostile or irrelevant additions or kill their own proposals because of them.

These are but a few examples but not all of the devices available to create a crisis in the democratic process. With the advent of a militant faction of ultra-conservatives called the Tea Party an attempt was launched in the next several years to stalemate the democrats and re-gain a conservative majority knowing full well that the electorate in off-year elections, such as would be the case in 2014, would be acquiescent, oblivious or just non-voters. The republicans gained control of the Senate in the off-year election of 2014, perhaps as a result. Some have concluded that voters spend only a few hours determining how to vote if they vote at all, yet it has been said that the average person uses a cell phone 150 times a day.

So what has the media been doing to uncover truths behind what is going on? The media just reflects whatever is going on and not what should be going on because primarily giant private corporations that have their own special interests, supporting the diminution of the democratic process, own American media. They are the private corporations that are absorbing powers rightfully belonging to government with the help of conservative politicians. But that certainly is not stereotypical of the whole industry. For example, Jackson Lears writes for *The Nation* that he believes the situation is serious.[1] He reviewed David Runciman's book *The Confidence Trap*, which claims that democracy has been in a state of crisis since World War I. He notes that the usual state of affairs in democratic institutions, such as the United States, is that they "lurch from one crisis to another ... without collapsing altogether."[2] This doesn't seem to be an historical problem for that old favorite Alexis de Tocqueville. He contended that he had "faith in the survival and ultimate triumph of democracy" as part of "the providential plan of the universe," which sustains it as "the conventional wisdom."[3] It therefore will withstand all challenges. That may be, but I and others like me are anxious that this may not always be so if we act vigilantly. Jackson Lears compares Walter Lippman's approach to this phenomenon with Runciman's a century later, the former wanting to master "the currents of change" whereas Runciman, after decades of "degeneration of government" according to Lears, is simply dealing with the one issue of executive overreach as the only problem. Lears points out that currently the power relationship between the governors and the governed is dysfunctional.[4]

Runciman takes a first necessary step in approaching this controversy by defining what he means by democracy –

---

[1] Lears, Jackson, "Mistakes Get Made," *The Nation*, Feb. 9, 2015. Lears' article includes a book review of David Runciman's *The Confidence Trap: A History of Democracy in Crisis from World War I.,* published by Princeton University Press.

[2] *Ibid.* p. 32.

[3] *Id.*

[4] Lears, *Op. Cit.* p. 33

"any society with popular elections" or a "relatively free press and open competition for power." He contrasts it with autocracy and concludes that it will one way or another "muddle through." But Lears comes to his own conclusion that Runciman "pays little attention to the role of concentrated wealth and power in greedy structural constraints as the exercise of democracy." He assumes majority rule to be a continuing *fiat accompli* because the influence of public opinion on policy will be direct and unproblematic.[5]

In foreign policy and practices the United States has been convinced of its "divinely ordained destiny to promote democracy" around the world, and that becomes its excuse for foreign intervention. I would agree. Lears notes later "people not abstracts, make policy."[6] But I would add that there is a semblance of the abstract when, if I'm correct, multi-national corporations, known from birth to be legal fictions, are replacing the national government, and making policy and instituting practices as "persons" that attempt to control governmental power and its representatives. *The Confidence Trap* highlights and confirms some of the major threats to democracy that we deal with here, but does not rise to the level of crisis that I am proposing and Lears seems to infer.

The federal government, popularly called, is more properly described as the national government (because it

---

[5] *Id.* p. 34.

[6] Lears, *Op. Cit.,* p. 35

forms a major part but only part of the federal government structure that includes state and local governments). My thesis is that if the national government is in a state of dismemberment and being reduced by corporate power domestically and globally, we have a crisis. And that crisis is taking place in so many particulars that their combination may spell destruction rather than simply disintegration or demise. *The Confidence Trap* is valuable because it exposes the proposition that no matter what happens Americans are used to sitting back and letting democracy correct itself as they acquiesce to these ups and downs or are oblivious to them. You might say it is something analogous to the economic capitalist theory of Adam Smith's "invisible hand." Somehow or other everything outside our own doing will rectify everything. In Marxism it was the withering away of the state. But this is our time and there is a withering away, not as Marx described but one, nevertheless, taking place before our sightless eyes.

Bruce Katz, Vice-President of the Brookings Institution, and co-author of "The Metropolitan Revolution" writes about how this is already happening.[7] His article in 2014 was entitled "How the Federal Government Became Irrelevant" and called the national government "feeble." He claims this is because it has been limited by the powers that be in such areas as education, infrastructure, research and development. It therefore has a shrunken pool of resources at its disposal. This has happened because its discretionary

---

[7] Katz, Bruce, "How the Federal Government Became Irrelevant" Perspective Section, *Denver Post,* Dec. 7, 2014, p. 10.

money to spend is limited by Social Security, Medicare and Medicaid expenses on the rise. But that's not the only cause. The defense budget is about 47 percent and the social programs just named are "absolutely crucial" but only represent 17 percent of the national budget. These two media analyses are typical of a rising critique as they question the soundness of American democratic representative government and who is causing the turn downward to make it become a permanent reality.

The Crisis of Collapse

I intend to show, in this analysis, the national governmental structure is in disintegration and why that *ipso facto* is making it feeble and irrelevant as claimed. Suffice to say for, whatever reasons, others agree. We began this democracy trek, piggy-backing English common law and its own evolution of democracy with a Declaration of Independence by the our original forbearers. Our own evolution of the rule of law and the pursuit of justice slowly established a more democratic identification, not easily recognized due to the inclusion of slavery and segregation. It became obvious to many, after an economic collapse in 1929, that the political structure necessitated a great leap forward in order to deal with the economic slide occurring ever since the Gilded Age.

In the next chapter we will concentrate on one of my several arguments proving my thesis, that of the demise of representative government. We will show that this is taking place by such obstructions as voting restrictions and gerrymandering and de-regulation of campaign expenditures in *Citizens United*. Threats from the controlling faction of the present Republican Party, hell-bent on making feeble the national government, took place with greater force since the Obama administration took power. Sequestration, shutdowns, and threatened defaults became the characteristics of what was once a moderate party. In fact the Republican Party, not long after its birth, and its successful ending of the Civil War was described as radical. The Democratic Party was the confederate, conservative breakaway. When the national government is able to pass compromised legislation, southern state nullification acts, reminiscent of those passed by the same states prior to the Civil War, have popped up. In the name of free speech religious and health issues are challenged. Rather than pursuing its own legislative agenda, to counter of the Obama administration, the then minority republicans, once capturing the House of Representatives, began to function as an investigatory committee in regard to such past democratic legislative achievements as the Affordable Care Act and the workings of the State Department. These accusatorial groups brought notoriety to the Congress as one of the least active in many years. In some ways it did more to divest the national government of its identity and power than did the Soviets in the long Cold War. American representative democracy has come up lacking as well in recent years, as we have mimicked the State of Israel and it's American-born Prime Minister Benjamin Netanyahu, of whom we will have more to say later, by taking on Mossad-like international tactics. Obama, the CIA and national security organizations called for means of protection, such as torture, rendition and assassination, since 2001 that were, in the past, considered inappropriate in a representative democracy.

The effect of all of this internationally is to perpetuate a war-like atmosphere, pumping up corporate investments and military sales in which the U.S. leads the world, while at the same time. At the same time we developed mechanisms such as drone warfare and targeted assassinations, which violate national sovereignty and human rights abroad. Counter terrorism, indefinite detention, and extreme rendition and kidnapping as public policy, persist. Guns, the main instrument of international warfare, become so honored and prolific that domestically they increase in unregulated amounts so that American culture itself has been militarized. Public police organizations are being replaced by private civilian action backed up by "make my day" laws, and privatizing residential security aimed mainly against unpopular minority groups. Police budgets have dropped, but as the crime rate dropped, isolated massacres, police brutality, murders and suicides by veterans are on the rise. While treaties and international law are ignored, public projects and services at home are reduced. Chapter Three will summarize effected domestic issues and Chapter Four international ones.

For those who might conclude at this point that my thesis is outlandish, we will take a look at some of the proposals calling for a reorientation of American politics that are being made daily by conservative presidential candidates. It seems that anyone with money and some kind of national media presence is eligible for participation resulting in a greater numbers of candidates. By money, I mean millions or billions and by national presence I mean people who have gained notoriety such as Donald Trump, or even Ben Carson as examples.

Most of you might say at this writing that you still don't know Ben Carson. But apparently he has the money and is seeking the acclaim. When you are one who has the former and not the later it takes some kind of exciting campaign proposal to get yourself known. In Ben Carson's case, he wishes to undo Chief Justice John Marshall's seminal decision in 1803 in *Marbury v. Madison*. The U.S. Supreme Court confirmed that it is a separate part of the government, equal with the legislative and the executive branches. Its independence is identified by its authority of judicial review of the constitutionality of acts by the executive and legislature.[8] Marshall laid down the principle, which means that the Supreme Court, limited only by other legal parameters has the power to review allegedly unconstitutional acts.[8] That was the effect of *Marbury*. But Ben Carson would change all of that and substitute his own personal view for 200 years of Supreme Court precedent establishing the separation of powers and an independent judiciary. A monarchial type executive power would allow the president to enforce laws the Supreme Court declared unconstitutional. Carson also attacked the Constitution's freedom of religion clauses stating that Muslims should not be President.

One might remember that probably the only instance of a president getting away with ignoring Supreme Court judicial review was Andrew Jackson. The Supreme Court

---

[8] Carson, Ben, "U.S. Should Rethink Court Review of Laws," *Denver Post*, May 11, 2015.

ruled that the removal of the Cherokee Indians from their ancestral territories in the east to a distant Oklahoma reservation was not within the president's constitutional powers since the Cherokee, themselves, were a nation. He did it anyway, creating the notorious Trail of Tears blot on American history. He justified his actions by saying: "does the Supreme Court have an army? No, I do. They can't enforce what they do but I can." This is but one example of the outlandish propositions that are offered in this presidential year to replace the stable and slowly but well evolved democracy in America by citizen representation and oversight. The heart of this crisis to which we have devoted our attention in this chapter is whether the American form of representative democracy has been put in a state of serious deterioration by the intentional actions of conservative politicians who have limited the access of minorities to the vote in several ways, including gerrymandering, and increased the ability to control elections where money counts more than people by Supreme Court conservative politicized decisions such as *Citizens United*. To this we will now direct our attention.

PART II: DOMESTIC AND INTERNATIONAL EXAMPLES OF DEMISE

CHAPTER THREE

THE DISMANTLING OF REPRESENTATIVE GOVERNMENT

"ALL MEN ARE ENDOWED BY THEIR CREATOR WITH CERTAIN UNALIENABLE RIGHTS…. THAT TO SECURE THESE RIGHTS, GOVERNMENTS ARE INSTITUTED AMONG MEN." THOMAS JEFFERSON, *THE DECLARATION OF INDEPENDENCE*, 1776

Introduction

In this and subsequent chapters, I will back up my general arguments, allegations and assumptions with evidentiary proof. This take place in two ways – logically deduced and inductively accumulated examples of causative reality. Although this work is a scholarly abstract one, it is offered as an academic tool to induce a reversal to the decline of democracy currently taking place. In this chapter we will concentrate on the intentional dismantling of representative government at home, that being the very heart of our democratic institution. It will be followed by the disregard for international obligations in Chapter Four.

It was in 1788 that a constitutional democratic republic emerged from a failing confederacy and began its evolution to our own times. Representative governments require, as Madison and Jefferson have told us, virtuous and educated candidates. It was said of America that pure or direct democracy would not work here. The democracy being referred to was practiced in city-states there such as Athens and much later Venice. This form of democracy, that we Americans know only at town hall meetings or in the form of referenda, recall or ballot initiatives of the people at election time, was considered possible only in small republics. The reason is that it required voting citizens to be vigilant and knowledgeable of every major issue and to vote on it themselves frequently. Madison's plan overcame this by choosing, rather than a pure democracy, a representative one in which every so many thousands of American citizens would have one representative. This would work in a large republic, he said, without the necessity of political parties that in Europe were simply special factions. But over the years very general political positions of what we might call today conservative or liberal government, became identified with the emergence of two major parties. Nevertheless, because of the size of the Republic, and the cultural limitation to only two major parties rather than many minor ones of numerous factions, the system proved adequate.

However, where the system of federal states became associated with one major issue that identified one of the two parties, the manipulation of voting and boundaries of election districts became a problem. This abuse emerged early on as the two parties competed for election and upset the nature and purpose of true representation. The citizen, as voter, was now the holder of sovereignty in a democratic state, replacing the monarch, as was the case before the American Revolution in the colonies. But along the way and still obvious in our own times, attempts were made successfully to obstruct a large voting electorate. First it was slavery, then it was money and property, then it was segregation, and finally gender. We have taken care of those variations that were so overt, but several more haunt us as subtle abuses. These are: 1) voting restrictions, 2) gerrymandering, 3) inequality of campaign financing abilities, 4) privatization of power moving from national government to private corporations, and 5) replacement of legislative function with investigatory activity. These influences are all negative, are generated by self-interested motives, denigrate the representative system, and have been expanding at a greater rate in the last generation.

Jared Diamond, Professor of Geography and Environmental Health Sciences at U.C.L.A. is well known for his bestselling books, *The Third Chimpanzee* and *Guns, Germs and Steel*, which received the Pulitzer Prize for nonfiction in 1998. As an expert, from these works on the hominid species, he recently wrote an essay on how our kind interacts politically in community, and exposed current threats to American democracy. He believes the recent crisis over the federal budget and debt ceiling, caused by government shutdowns and sequestration, was the result of extremist attitudes obstructing positive legislative and executive actions over the last five years, e.g. the Obama period. Examples he gives are Senate Republican rejections of presidential nominees whose approval heretofore by democrats and republicans alike were usually routine, and the increasing number of filibusters made possible by the Senate 60-vote cloture rule causing the decline in the passage of legislation, the main function of Congress.[1]

Second, he notes the increasing restrictions on the right to vote. This, he says, has weighed disproportionately

---

[1] Diamond, Jared, "Four Threats to American Democracy," *Opinion/Voices*, UCLA Mewsroom, Feb. 8, 2014.

on voters for the Democratic Party and has been intentionally created to restrict minority citizens' right to participate in choosing their democratic representative, both at the national and state levels. He singles out state Republican parties in the south and west. The end result has made representation and voting more difficult for minority and poor voters who primarily are shown to vote democratic. This creates an unfair advantage in the party system of one party over the other and creates an abuse of our democratic system. Recent state legislation in these regions requires registered voters to show documentation, such as passports, which many voters usually don't have updated and available. This device has been successful in unbalancing the vote for the reasons stated. He supports the thesis here argued that there has been progress over fifty years and that only recently has it been abridged by the "proliferation of restrictions" reversing a long positive trend. In the last major national election of 2014 only 37 percent of Americans voted. It's hard to tell whether that is from obstruction or simply disinterest of voters. In any case the number of American voters in national elections has dropped at least 15 percent over the period of his study.

The third issue he treats is the tremendously increasing inequality of rich and poor in our country, once called a land of opportunity. It seems opportunity no longer exists, except for the rich. We lead all other first world democracies in the disparity between rich and poor.[2]

---

[2] *Ibid.* The Gini Index of Equality Inequality measures income and wealth disparity. See Chapter 6 for a more detailed discussion on inequality.

The public expenditures now made are less for education, infrastructure, non-military research and development. This is an intentional practice of conservatives and a contributor to the destruction of democracy I am positing. As I have said, there is also an attempt through legislation to privatize education, health, welfare and other public services to enhance private corporate profit and eliminate government as a competitor and a provider of services that are more needed by the poor and middle class than the rich. This coalition I've mentioned, of conservative fundamentalist Christians and capitalists, is creating a plutocracy where these minority groups become plutocrats controlling the reins of politics, religion and economics.

Diamond makes a very good point that since the beginnings of governments 5400 years ago, they have served two primary purposes: 1) "to maintain internal peace by monopolizing force, settling disputes, and forbidding citizens to resort to violence in order to settle disputes themselves," and 2) "to redistribute individual wealth ... promoting the good of society as a whole."[3] These purposes are no longer being fulfilled. Specific areas of degeneration that Diamond mentions in detail are 1) education, 2) prisons, and 3) health. We will treat each of these areas with our own specific detail in separate subsequent chapters.

Voting Rights and Restrictions, Gerrymandering and Campaign Contributions

The threats to voting rights have emerged not only from a republican congress but the judiciary as well. Three

---

[3] *Id.*

40

have been pursued recently. First, an effort is in progress to terminate the Voting Rights Act of 1965. A Supreme Court ruling in *Shelby County v. Holder* does just that. Second, the Citizens United case has allowed for control of elections by money rather than people. And last, the U.S. Supreme Court more recently considered the Arizona voters' approved system for redrawing U.S. House districts by an independent commission. That action by Arizona voters is designed to put a stop to gerrymandering by political parties. In March 2015, the Supreme Court heard arguments. The Court's conservative Justices indicated, by their comments, at that time, that they might join the liberal majority, and that's what they did in June 2015.

The conservative stance is that the voters can't take away from their representatives the power given to them by the U.S. Constitution as elected state legislators, to be the only ones who can design or redesign voting districts. This, of course, is a throwback to past times in early America under the first confederacy when the people did not have popular rights and their state representatives controlled the vote, under the Articles of Confederation, before the Constitution was enacted.[4]

---

[4] "Ruling Could Nix Redistricting Commission," *Denver Post*, March 3, 2015. In June 2015 the Supreme Court issued its 5-4 decision, Justice Kennedy joining "the liberal wing" to allow an independent commission to redistrict. *Arizona State Legislature v. Arizona Redistricting Commission* (June 2015); some cases decided in June 2015 were not yet assigned a volume and page number at this writing. Section 2 of the 14th Amendment states that any state that denies or abridges the right to vote shall have its congressional representation reduced in proportion to the number of citizens it disenfranchises. This section has never been used but certainly, from what we have discussed above, it should be.

One bright light in the dim horizon was the Supreme Court decision, announced in its June 2015 releases, on this topic. Ruling five to four, the Court agreed that Arizona voters may utilize an independent commission to draw up voting districts to prevent political gerrymandering. Justice Kennedy was the swing vote.

Because minorities and young people tend to vote democratic and the Democratic Party supports the obligation of the national and state governments to provide public services for the general welfare, the Republican Party has intentionally tried to use ways such as gerrymandering to increase its power in the national government and to lessen the voting rights of minorities and young people in the states.

Let's pause for a moment and consider the end game of these efforts. According to Jim Hightower that game is to replace the American national government with private multi-national corporate government.[5] He writes that the Supreme Court, after declaring corporations to be persons much earlier in its history, is now trying to transform multi-national private corporations into a type of governing organ replacing our own national government. The recently passed trade agreement for the Trans-Pacific Partnership – an effort sponsored by a coalition of President Obama, House Speaker Boehner, and Senate Majority Leader McConnell, proved initially successful in Congress in spite of Democratic Party opposition. It ran into further opposition when presented to the international members of the TPP subsequent to

---

[5] Hightower, Jim, "TPP creates Corporate Nations," *Colorado Springs Independent,* May 1, 2015

Hightower's article, but was approved. It is now before Congress again, but its future is uncertain. Republicans, however, supported it because it gives private for-profit corporations sovereign rights equal to traditional nation-states, as well as taking away the rights of voting citizens and working Americans. Under this agreement a corporate nation, unlike individual citizens of nations, may directly compel the United States or other countries to change their laws for the purpose of increasing corporate profits. Regardless, this kind of dramatic change in American representative democracy is only happening because American citizens are acquiescing to business take-over of the Republican Party.

Many states that regularly vote republican are in the process of trying to prevent minorities and young people from voting. Black, Hispanic and young voters are the targets.[6] Since 2010, twenty-two states have passed strict new voting restriction laws according to the Brennan Center for Justice. The reason given is that significant fraud exists where adequate voter identification does not take place. However, there has been no evidentiary proof of such allegations in any of these states. The real reason is as given above. Fewer such people voted in 2012 than in 2004, even though eight million more voters became eligible by that date. It has been shown that the poor and young have less access to governmental documentation such as picture IDs and passports.

---

[6] Mencimer, Stephanie, "Republicans are Trying to Make Sure Minorities and Young People Don't Vote this November," *Mother Jones,* April 22, 2015.

A contributing factor was the Supreme Court's ruling in *Shelby County v. Holder*.[7] In that decision the Court declared racism to be non-existent and obliterated a key provision in the Voting Rights Act of 1965. That Act became law in the wake of many lives sacrificed in the civil rights Marches preceding it. The provision that some states, particularly former segregationist and confederate slavery states, must receive Justice Department permission for changes in their election laws was voided. Conservative, anti-federal GOP legislatures then passed restrictive laws that the Voting Rights Act had disallowed due to their past and present actions against minorities.

Six states acted very quickly. What they did was to shorten voting hours available to American citizens, placed restrictions on voter registration drives and more stringent rules on government identification or proof of citizenship to vote. Americans have always considered the primary purpose of their passports was to travel abroad and not be possessed, updated or regularly available as proof of their right to vote. None of these laws, alleged to have been passed because of fraud, required any proof or evidence of fraudulent activities. Several of these laws have been challenged but currently remain on the books.

By limiting the votes of Americans, another piece is accomplished towards the general goal of transforming public national and state government into a privatized corporate nation of the United States. Some of the states involved in this movement are Texas, Arkansas, and North

---

[7] *Shelby County v. Holder,* 557 US 193 (2013)

Carolina, but as well Ohio and Wisconsin. The state of Wisconsin, formerly a populist one of Robert La Follette fame, is presently controlled by the Tea Party, a rogue political privy council of the Republican Party. Governor Walker of Wisconsin is a prime candidate for the presidency. Stephanie Mencimer's article included specific information on North Carolina, Wisconsin and Ohio a month before the 2014 elections. The November 2014 election results then correlated, in these and other states, with the premise of an increased conservative control of election results with the reduction of minorities and young people able to participate. Thirteen more conservative U.S. senators were elected and dozens more House members, giving control of the U.S. Congress to the conservatives as a result of the obstruction in voting participation in these states.

The best way to manipulate the vote is first to restrict it, then control it and finally make it irrelevant by transferring power from the sovereign people to the profit-making corporations, now also persons with personal rights, such as free speech. The *Citizens United* case[8] is known to most everyone of the top one percent income earners in America, but much less to the bottom 99 percent. But its impact affects 100 percent of Americans. It is one of many legal cases over the past ten years that have taken negative steps to dislodge positive movements favoring representative government. In a column I write for a local magazine/newspaper I gave my own analysis on the impact of several recent decisions by the U.S. Supreme Court

---

[8] *Citizens United v. Federal Elections Commission*, 558 US 310 (2010).

affecting representative government.[9] In that article, I said that further weakening of our representative government came in *Citizens United v. Federal Elections Commission*, in 2010, which struck down the McCain-Feingold Finance Reform Act, that limited the rich corporate takeover of elections through unbalanced financial influence. The Court, having declared corporations "persons" only as a technical legal fiction many years earlier, extended that concept to a virtual personal, human one. It empowered corporations with a free-speech conscience identical to that of human beings, failing to consider the impact on the general welfare and majority, and equitable voting dignity of real live persons.

Jane Ruskin writes in "Citizens United and the Corporate Court"[10] that the idea of the corporation as a person was limited in *Dartmouth v. Woodward* (1819) to this definition: "An artificial being, invisible, intangible and existing only as a mere creation of the law." But by 1978 in *First National Bank of Boston v. Belotti* the forerunner of *Citizens*, Justice Lewis Powell, whom I knew personally, created a "fivesome" as the Court gave "corporations and banks the right to spend without limit to influence public opinion on ballot issues. "The inherent worth of speech ... does not demand its source." By that he meant speech is not limited to human speech so an artificial legal fiction may speak words that then can be legitimized. In other words,

---

[9] Durland, William, "The Human Rights Report," *Active for Justice,* December 2, 2014.

[10] Ruskin, Jane, "Citizens United and the Corporate Court," *The Nation,* October 8, 2012.

whatever makes the speech is irrelevant, real or fictional, and may not be suppressed. But that doesn't make much sense. It does definitely imply that money can be speech.

Citizens United only amplified these earlier substantive cases allowing hundreds and millions of paper dollars to now be above regulation and infused into political campaigns through non-profit 301(1)(4) advocacy groups and 501(c)(6) trade associations and super PACs. *SpeechNow.Org v. Federal Elections Commission* (2010) then struck down what amounts of money mere human beings can give to "independent" expenditure organizations. The end result is that today thousands of super PAC non-profit organizations with billions of dollars of untraceable money is being donated to candidates in big chunks by big wealth. None of this was unforeseen. Thomas Jefferson feared the rise of a "single and splendid government of an aristocracy of banking institutions and monied corporations … riding and reeling over the plundered plowman and beggared yeoman."[11]

In 2004, the U.S. Supreme began a process of re-legitimizing gerrymandering as a means for political parties to manipulate voting outcomes. In 1962 in *Baker v. Carr*, a more liberal Court ruled in favor the concept of "one man, one vote." What began with Governor Gerry's circumventions in Massachusetts in 1812 was restored in

---

[11] In a letter of March 17, 1814 to Horatio Spafford, Jefferson wrote: "Merchants have no country. The mere spot they stand on does not constitute so strong an attachment as that from which they draw their gains."

2004 as Justice Antonin Scalia embraced the right of political parties to once again gerrymander. This has allowed the House of Representatives to be taken over by a conservative political party that has won it with a minority vote. The end result of that has been the polarized gridlock going on today.

Gerrymandering complements this corporate take-over and has been around much longer. But, in my own time, I thought we saw its demise in 1962 by the cases previously mentioned. The re-designing of districts in strange ways that enhance an advantage to the party in power, has regained usage and popularity. The result is often that those who are not wealthy and powerful believe that their votes will be effective because they are lumped all into one or two disadvantaged districts, creating a majority in wealthier or whiter districts, or, when more feasible, diluting the vote by making sure that it's a minority in many districts. The word comes from its first use on March 26, 1812 in the Boston Gazette in reference to Governor Eldridge Gerry of Massachusetts. He signed into law a re-districted state to benefit his party. These districts, to reach their goal, by necessity must take on convoluted, impossible shapes, hardly oblong or square as one would think they should be. His first attempt looked like a salamander and thus a combination of that and the Governor's name gave birth to the word Gerrymander. It proved to be a success and henceforth unrestrained incumbents are providing recent examples in North Carolina, Texas and Utah among others. It is not limited to southern states, where it has been used most frequently, but also exists in northern states, where the vote has been increasingly close. In the 2012 election in

Pennsylvania, democratic candidates received 83,000 more votes than republican candidates. Nevertheless the republican-controlled re-districting process resulted in the Democratic Party losing in thirteen of eighteen of those districts.

In seven states, where republicans had complete control over the re-districting process, they received 16.7 million votes to the democratic House candidates' 16.4 million; the re-districting resulted in seventy-three of one hundred and seven affected seats. Republicans received only 50.4 percent of the vote but won 68 percent of the congressional districts.

In another closely contested northern state – Michigan – the republican-controlled legislature re-districted just before the 2014 mid-term elections. Cities such as Battle Creek, Grand Rapids, Jackson, Kalamazoo, Lansing and East Lansing were separated into districts with large conservative-leaning hinterlands that essentially diluted democratic votes there. Since 2010, not one of these cities is within a district in which a democratic nominee has a reasonable chance of winning. Another example is in Texas where the Supreme Court ruled in 2006 that the 2003 re-districting based on gerrymandering was perfectly legal.[12]

Allen Rosenthal is one of the leading scholars on the subject of state legislation and voting. A Professor of Public Policy and Political Science at Rutgers University, he supports the attempts of republicans to "waste opponents'

---

[12] Ting, Jan, "Boehner and House Republicans Lack Mandate to Oppose Obama," *News Works,* December 14, 2013; Wang, Sam, "The Great Gerrymander of 2012," *New York Times,* February, 2, 2013.

votes. It is not unusual to see a party with fifty-five percent statewide vote winning sixty percent legislative seats."[13] *Davis v. Bandemere* (1986) opened the federal door to challenging this, but when Rosenthal's book was written in 1998, the Supreme Court had done nothing to correct it. So a June 15, 2015 five to four Supreme Court vote became the first step in a long time to halt the decline in fair voting through gerrymandering. That case allowed an independent commission, as we have said, to set up voting districts rather than the legislators themselves because of their obstructive history, but doesn't guarantee, constitutionally, that an independent commission will operate any more objectively than the state legislators. It is a step forward but more needs to be done.

In addition to gerrymandering and voter registration restrictions, the de-regulation of campaign financing is perhaps the most insidious method of attack on representative democracy in America. As we have seen, *Citizens United* expressly prohibited the national government, under the First Amendment, from restricting so-called "independent political expenditures" by corporations and citizens as their First Amendment right. I discussed the case in detail in a book I wrote on American economics a few years ago.[14] Following is a summary of that discussion.

---

[13] Rosenthal, Alan, "The Decline of Representative Democracy," *Congressional Quarterly*, Washington, D.C. 2007, p. 27.

[14] Durland, William, *The Price of Folly,* Colorado Springs, (Createspace: 2013) p. 132

The matter came before the Court in a much narrower issue involving a solitary film criticizing Hillary Clinton. During oral argument, and after briefs had been filed on the original issue, questions emanating from Roberts and particularly Kennedy, required the attorneys to respond to a larger scope of questions than they were prepared for, involving the consideration of other cases and fact patterns. Roberts asked the attorneys, after their presentations, to prepare themselves for further in-depth discussions on the new question that had arisen and to come back at a later time with arguments prepared. Some felt that by so doing the Chief Justice had manipulated the issue politically to allow an already obvious five-four decision in favor of the corporations to have a wider political and economic scope. The case was withdrawn from the schedule and rescheduled so that the more expansive questions were the subject of the next resumption of argument. As a result, Roberts violated a fundamental rule of the Supreme Court process and which may have motivated him to be so steadfast about a later rule of process that determined, for him, the Healthcare case. Supreme Courts usually considered only the narrowest issue raised by questions presented in cases before them. Any commentary on relevant but broader issues, not specifically to the point of what is called the *ratio decidendi* of the principle on which the case is to be decided, is called dictum. What he did, some commentators consider to be pure politics. It is interesting to note that Roberts was an attorney in the Florida Supreme Court decision that successfully intervened in the presidential process in 2000. Kennedy, Scalia and Thomas were on the Court and successfully determined the election in favor of Bush over Gore.

On June 25, 2012, a case arising in Montana would give the Court a reason to overturn its sweeping five to four decision that unleashed a flood of cash into the 2012 national and state elections. Montana's highest court set up a direct conflict with *Citizens United* by ruling that it was entitled to keep the laws it had for more than a century to eliminate corruption and influence peddling. Montana's position was supported by twenty-two states, including New York. The summary dismissal of the argument about whether *Citizens United* applied to state and local elections came in a one-page answer, "There can be no serious doubt that it does."

Margaret Margaronis in a survey of the Roberts Court from *The Nation*'s London bureau[15] evaluated the Court after ten years. Her conclusion was that it ranks as the most business oriented court in generations, "in which racial and religious minorities, women, workers and consumers have struck out regularly, while the economically and politically powerful have walked around the bases." Treating several different areas, most of which we will discuss in later chapters, she says this of *Citizens United*: "Rather than serve its traditional role as an institution of government where those shut out of the political process can find a voice, the Court has used its rulings to strengthen the already deafening voices of the wealthy and powerful." She goes on to say that the Court has "insulated itself and the lower federal courts from the pleas of the politically disfavored by slamming shut the courtroom doors." She lists ten areas as evidentiary

---

[15] Margaronis, Margaret, "The Roberts Court at 10," *The Nation,* Feb. 16, 2015, pp. 45, 48.

proof, including voting rights, campaign finances, and worker rights.

The Conservative Agenda

As the fabric of American representative democracy is torn apart, what is actively sought in its place by the conservatives? The processes being sought and/or presently used include: 1) Reforming immigration laws so that children already in this country innocently brought here by undocumented refugee parents may not remain in the only country they have ever known; limiting further legal immigration of individuals from south of the border; militarizing the border and finally attempting to do away with Obama's Executive Order of protection enunciated because of the failure of Congress to pass any legislation at all. 2) Ending universal health care. 3) Perpetuating environmental pollution by the passage of one of the few conservative pieces of legislation in 2015 legalizing the Canadian pipeline extensions. 4) Continuing Guantanamo Bay prison. 5) Prohibiting same-sex marriages. 6) Increasing the use of concealed weapons in schools, parks and public buildings while ending background checks for juveniles, felons and the mentally ill. 7) Enhancing confederate nullification acts of federal laws. 8) Ending homeland security financing unless Obama's Immigration Executive Order is revoked. 9) Curbing all federal spending other than foreign relations, military and prison expenditures and increasing tax breaks for the wealthy and corporations. 10) Abolishing various U.S. executive departments such as Health and Human Services, Education, Housing, and Energy. 11) Fast tracking trade treaties transferring governmental power to globalized corporations. 12) Ending diplomatic negotiations with Iran and replace them with increased sanctions and threatened war making. 13) Blocking all Obama federal appointments. 14) De-regulating carbon emissions from efforts by the Environmental Protection Agency to limit them. 14) Obstructing all efforts to reverse Global Warming as not profitable. 15) Abolishing the Consumer Financial Protection Bureau. 16) Reinstating the Glass-Steagell Act by ending the modified Voelker rule on corporate predator activities included in the Obama Financial Reform Act. 17) Continuing the 60-vote Senate cloture rule obstructing the passage of legislation by a minority vote and continuing the practice of amending legislation with non-germane minority issues to obstruct or defeat majority bills. 18) Privatizing Social Security, Medicare, and Medicaid. 19) Minimizing minimum wage levels, unemployment insurance coverage and overtime pay. 20) Ending all trade unions. 21) Continuing the primary use of legislative committees as Star Chamber inquisitorial groups. And, 22) obstructing when necessary, government progress by sequestration, government shut-downs and defaults.

When all these particular attempts are put together in one list, which is not necessarily complete, it is easy to see how those of us who are supposed to be represented by Congress are essentially without representation. Republicans have stymied votes that help improve the economy, fostered tax cuts for the rich, cut spending on scientific research, environmental protection, aging infrastructure and equal pay for women. They filibustered the Obama infrastructure bill, blocked highway repair bills, frustrated decent Amtrak budgets and other transportation and housing necessities.

They have perpetuated sending American jobs overseas and off-shore banking accounts where untaxed monies of the wealthy can be safe. They stymied a bill which would re-hire 400,000 teachers, firefighters, medics and police officers and obstructed Obama's efforts to lessen the impact on college debt for graduates. They proposed bills to limit overtime pay, increase off-shore oil drilling, promote private and religious schools supported by public funds, blocked regulation on coal ash, regulation of oil companies and much more.[16]

These are the domestic tactics, at least some of them, that are being used intentionally for the most part and by some unintentionally, to tear down our democratic representative process. Two-thirds of our sovereign electorate is allowing this to happen by their acquiescence or because they have made themselves oblivious to what's going on. But this is only the domestic part of it except for a few examples. The next chapter will discuss, in a general overview, similar international and foreign tactics and problems. After that we will proceed in succeeding chapters with further details, specific facts and evidence on many of these topics.

---

[16] Johnson, Dave, "The Cost to Our Economy for Republican Obstruction and Sabotage," Campaign for American Future, OurFuture. Org, September 23, 2014. President Obama will use his executive power to provide overtime pay, he announced.

CHAPTER FOUR

DISREGARD OF INTERNATIONAL LAWS AND ORGANIZATIONS

"... THE INHERENT DIGNITY AND EQUAL AND INALIENABLE RIGHTS OF ALL MEMBERS OF THE HUMAN FAMILY IS THE FOUNDATION OF FREEDOM, JUSTICE AND PEACE IN THE WORLD."
ELEANOR ROOSEVELT, 1948

Introduction

As a young child of ten, I experienced my first war when, on December 7, 1941 Pearl Harbor was bombed without a prior declaration of war. My 5th grade class heard Roosevelt's speech on the radio in place of our schoolwork the morning after the attack. Roosevelt described it as "dastardly" (I thought he said "bastardly" and I was shocked) and a "sneak attack." Much later we learned that two Japanese emissaries had been waiting for days in the outer office of the American Secretary of State, Cordell Hull, to present to him a declaration of war just prior to the scheduled attack.

From that point I switched from simply reading the comics or funny papers to the front-page news of a war that would go on until I was 14. Influenced by that experience, I was early on committed to international law and organizations and universal human rights, best expressed in Roosevelt's "four freedoms" speech and the formation of a United Nations that would replace a weak League of Nations created after World War I without Wilson. After victory was achieved in 1945 this came about including a strengthened International Court of Justice. After her husband's death, Eleanor Roosevelt became the moving force in creating the Universal Declaration of Human Rights.

In college I specialized in international relations as a political science and history major at Bucknell University. I worked for the National Security Agency out of college from 1953 to 1954, as an intelligence analyst. While stationed overseas with the U.S. Army in Germany from 1955 to 1957 as a troop information and education instructor, I gained some insight and experience in the area of international affairs. I graduated from Georgetown Law School with legal courses in constitutional and international law. After a failed attempt to land a job in the Legal Counsel's office of the U.S. State Department, I was able to secure employment as Legal Assistant to the Director of the U.S. Commission on International Rules of Judicial Procedure in 1960 and was vice-chair of the International Judicial Cooperation Committee of the American Bar Association.

So looking back, it's clear my interest in American democracy from the perspective of foreign relations arose from those formative experiences. I became a senior partner in my own law firm in 1962. My first international legal client was Mario Montessori, in Italy, the son of the founder of the Montessori method. My last international legal client was in South Africa in 2013, just a year before my retirement. It is my contention, which I hope to illustrate, that there is a corresponding interruption in the evolution of the rule of law in the pursuit of justice in the area of international relations just as there has been on the domestic scene. I propose to highlight some of these events that demonstrate this demise generally here and further illustrate with particulars in succeeding chapters.

A list would include: 1) Intentional violations of national sovereignty in war making. A specific example is the use of drones flying into sovereign nations without their permission, dropping bombs on alleged terrorists and killing civilians as justifiable collateral damage. 2) Indefinite detention, extreme rendition, torture, assassinations and the like. 3) The replacement of the U.N. with NATO and the domination of seven or eight major nations by the United States. 4) The militarization of civilian life. 5) The use of covert terrorist activity in CIA and NSA operation. 6) The disregard for international law and treaties. 7) Various human rights violations. 8) Empire building in the Middle East with ally Israel, and 9) Fast track trade agreements replacing nation-state regulations.

Most of these changes have been on going since the Reagan administration. The Democratic Party has been closer to the Republican Party on international issues than in domestic ones. It continually tries to convince voters that it is tough on our enemies. But the greater emphasis has come from "Christian" organizations moving to extreme conservatism through Tea Party off-shoots.

After World War II the first major international conflict in Korea was an attempt to use the facilities of the United Nations Charter to put down war making anywhere in the world. By the time of Vietnam such attempts were fading as the United States attempted alone to put down what it said were other attempts of international communism to take over the world. Following that unsuccessful venture, the United States waged war against Grenada and Nicaragua and finally an Iraqi dictatorship, to mention only a few such incidents. CIA coups in Iran and Guatemala were so successful that such adventures became common U.S. policy.

Most recently we have been plagued with this permanent go-it-alone policy of non-use of the U.N. and Nuremberg and Geneva Convention principles. The U.S. and its chief ally in the Middle East – Israel – use other methods to control the area, quite often unsuccessfully. Israel, early on, set the example with its covert organization, the Mossad, by kidnapping Eichmann in violation of the sovereignty of Argentina, the nation where he resided in 1960. World leaders raised no objection and acquiesced as they have in many Israeli covert and overt activities.

The most extreme Israeli violation of international law, as far as Americans are concerned, was their attack on the USS Liberty in the six-day war in 1967, unmercifully killing over 30 American sailors and wounding 130 of them with intentional, separate air and sea attacks over a period of many hours as the ship flew its U.S. flag. We have learned a lot from Israel on how to kill people. A U.S. policy of first-strike as a plausible principle of international warfare, which we had so drastically rejected when the Japanese used it against us, and China against South Korea, was made a legitimate foreign policy in the Jimmy Carter administration. These issues provide an introduction on the events, internationally, that have persuaded me that our ethical and moral attitudes and practices, in observing and applying the Nuremberg Principles, Geneva Conventions and other advancements in the international rule of law in pursuit of justice, have fallen into disregard.

Drone Warfare

Drone warfare by the United States began in Pakistan and has spread to Somalia, Yemen and elsewhere. It is the norm for the assassination of specified Al Qaeda or ISIL leaders. When killed, along with collateral damage civilians, they are only replaced by new leaders. Pakistani leaders have failed to register a strong objection to the violation of its sovereign territory. At one count the U.S. had launched more than 100 drone strikes in Yemen since 2002, killing about 900 militants, including an American citizen Anwar-Al-Awlaki, called "the most dangerous man in the world" by us. Collateral damage of civilians fits nicely, for its justification, into philosopher Jeremy Bentham's theory of utilitarian greatest good for the greatest number, although most who engage in that activity never heard of him or his theories. It is impossible, in any case to discern with certainty that civilians will not be killed. Not all countries are against such casualties. Friends and allies of the U.S in Yemen have given us the names of people they want eliminated who may not necessarily be our enemies, but only theirs.

The end result is that motivation is created for subjects of the nations attacked by drones to join Al Qaeda and now ISIL. So even the principle of the greater good may not hold true in this case since the impact of the drone assassinations creates a greater evil, a retaliatory Islam in the form of its extreme militants. It's no wonder that its moral or ethical effects are not considered because the primary policy deciders, such as Obama and democratic and republican leaders, have declared themselves pragmatists. The main principle of that philosophy is that good or right is defined only by effectiveness or what works. So the final justification for pragmatists is that if sidestepping international morals is successful in the sense that it terminates the effectiveness of Al Qaeda and ISIL, then it is seen as moral because it "works." In Jeremy Bentham's utilitarian language it would be morel because the consequences are good.[1]

Kathy Kelly, long time peace and justice activist in the Middle East, wrote recently that killing by long distance is still killing. President Obama has sought to sell drones to other countries to increase their arsenal of weapons. Kelly wound up in prison for protesting the use of military drones.[2] (My wife and I demonstrated recently against drones at the Willow Grove Naval Air Station near Horsham, Pennsylvania with the Brandywine Peace Community. We first joined Brandywine in 1978. We have known Kathy Kelly since we worked with her organization in Iraq in 2002-03.)

In December 2012, the U.S. Air Force revealed that U.S. drones hit 477 targets in Afghanistan during 2011 only.

---

[1] Johnson, Dave, "The Cost to Our Economy for Republican Obstruction and Sabotage," Campaign for American Future, OurFuture. Org, September 23, 2014. President Obama will use his executive power to provide overtime pay, he announced.

[2] Kelly, Kathy, "End Drone Warfare Now," *Houston Catholic Worker,* March-May, 2015, pp. 3-5. In late 2015, the Pentagon announced it wanted to increase drone attacks by 50 percent to include Ukraine, Iraq, Syria, North Africa and the South China Sea. Before drones, there was Ronald Reagan's "Star Wars" enterprise claiming earth's space as ours with first strike potentialities. Loring Wirbel wrote a definitive book entitled *Star Wars: U.S. Tools of Space Supremacy,* London (Pluto Press: 2004). He is an acclaimed technology journalist and the author of this book's "Foreword." Reagan's "peace through strength" policies only resulted in prolonging the Cold War for several years in the 1980s.

Although peace activists have gone to jail simply for nonviolent free expression, a U.S. Air Force officer received an order of protection from U.S. courts, i.e. a restraining order, because he alleged that nonviolent demonstrators posed a threat to his safety. The peace group expressed the opinion that "laws should be made to protect human beings. Laws shouldn't protect ways to kill other people. In Afghanistan, U.S. drones are used to kill many ordinary people."[3] So it may easily be seen that indiscriminate killings by drones are pragmatically counterproductive and morally wrong and are harming people here and abroad in violation of international law and treaty prohibitions. Moreover the reputation of the U.S. is becoming increasingly tarnished.

The Mossad Precedent

The best example of how a nation's intelligence service can be used as an instrument of illegal international intrigue, by virtual killings for hire, is Israel's Mossad. Other examples could be used to illustrate this transformation of intelligence organizations from what they were when I was part of them in the 1950s, but this one has set a new precedent for international illegalities. Mossad is treated specifically in Gordon Thomas's *Gideon's Spies* and best serves to illustrate the point of this discussion.[4]

---

[3] Ibid. "Boos, Allen, Hamilton, BAE Systems have been named as part of a secretive industry worth hundreds of millions of dollars," Fielding-Smith, Abigail, Black, Crofton, Ross, Alice, Ball, James, "Private Firms at heart of U.S. Drones War," *Guardian Weekly,* August 7, 2015, p. 10.

[4] Thomas, Gordon, *Gideon's Spies: The Secret History of the Mossad,* New York (Thomas Dunn Books: 1999), pp. 93-105

In June 2015, at the time of the speech of Netanyahu to a joint session of Congress, I was finishing the reading of *Gideon's Spies: The Secret History of the Mossad.* Netanyahu was invited to speak only by the Republican Party in the House of Representatives and not the elected democrats, the Senate, nor by the President representing the Executive Branch for which international affairs are constitutionally its primary concern. He was brought here because conservatives supports Israel's foreign policy demands for an attack on Iran. That Iran has accumulated, legally, nuclear materials that could in the future develop a nuclear bomb is their rationale. The republicans and Israel want a military solution while the democrats seek a diplomatic one through a ten year treaty during which time Iran would be limited to the use of nuclear energy only for peaceful purposes, would refrain from any development of nuclear weaponry, and would be subject to international inspections. For abiding by those restrictions it would receive an end to the present sanctions.

After reading this book, and particularly that part on how Israel moved illegally to acquire its own nuclear bomb, its demand for another nation to stop the same process, seems hypocritical to me. Israel now possesses several hundred nuclear bombs while refusing to admit it has them and further refusing to submit itself to the Nuclear Weapons Treaty. Nations that have nuclear bombs subscribe to it.

This is how Israel got its bombs. It began in 1956, when France gave Israel a 24 megawatt reactor as an ally plotting with Britain to invade Egypt and re-take the Suez Canal. An aggressive President Eisenhower, who had not been informed of their clandestine intentions, stopped them.

Prime Minister Ben Gurion claimed the reactor that they continued to possess would be used only as a pumping station in the Negev Desert to desalinate seawater. Six out of seven members of Israel's own Atomic Energy Commission protested, saying its actual use was for political adventurism and would turn the world against Israel. Yegal Allon, Yitsak Rabin and Ariel Sharon opposed a nuclear arsenal on the basis that "we have the best conventional forces in the region."

The reactor was located in the Negev Desert at Dimona. The reactor alone was not enough to produce the fissionable material, uranium or plutonium that was required. So three months later, a nuclear processing company was opened in Apollo, Pennsylvania called Nuclear Materials and Equipment Corporation, NUMEC, led by Dr. Salmon Shapiro. In 1962 the U.S. Atomic Energy Commission warned Shapiro's corporation that it had failed to comply with U.S. nuclear security regulations and espionage laws. Israelis, in noticing this, found out that Shapiro was the son of an orthodox rabbi and was placed in an important position with Westinghouse, developing nuclear reactors. Some of Shapiro's relatives and been Holocaust victims. Shapiro had left Westinghouse and with 25 Israeli sympathizers as stockholders, set up NUMEC. It then won contracts to recover enriched uranium.

Ben Gurion was told by the U.S. State Department that if Israel contemplated making a nuclear bomb, it would upset the balance of power in the Middle East. President Kennedy asked Ben Gurion to allow the International Atomic Energy Agency to inspect Dimona. When Ben Gurion objected, Kennedy persisted and demanded a U.S.

inspection. Ben Gurion's attitude towards that was that a Catholic in the White House is bad news for Israel. Ben Gurion's front man in the U.S. was Abraham Feinberg, Zionist supporter of Israel's nuclear bomb ambitions. He also happened to be the most important Jewish fundraiser for the Democratic Party. JFK was threatened to end his persistence or his party would suffer. Even JFK's Secretary of State, Robert McNamara, supported Israel's position just as he did in supporting the Vietnam War. Kennedy then offered, for inspection rights, additional surface to air missiles. So the U.S. was given permission to inspect and found nothing. And Israel joked about how easily the U.S. was "duped" by a bogus, fake control center setup. Heavy water, stolen from France and Norway by Israeli smugglers was placed off-limits to any U.S. inspection.

Next Israel came to Apollo with Shapiro underwriting expenses to make a bomb and ship containers to Israel. The FBI refrained from inspecting them despite discovering the obvious lead sheathing needed to cover the enriched uranium. The FBI was told by the State Department not to "create a diplomatic incident" by investigating what was going on. Nevertheless, the FBI determined that 100 pounds of material were missing. Neither Shapiro, nor Apollo was charged with any crime.

Israel also looked for other places from which to smuggle plutonium – Columbia, Bosnia, etc. - in addition to what they smuggled through NUMEC out of the U.S. The FBI believed that the reason for the lack of action against Israel was due to the power of the Jewish lobby and the reluctance of the U.S. to confront Israel, even though NSA had intercepted Mossad messages revealing Israel's covert action. Meanwhile, according to Thomas, Mossad had broken into sophisticated systems of U.S. encryption codes and spied on us. In 1997, Mossad obtained private messages between Clinton and Lewinski revealing more Clinton illegality than had been made public as a result of the sex expose, and would use this, they threatened, if the U.S in any way resisted Israel. If they made this information public, Clinton most probably would have been removed from office. One result was that the FBI terminated its hunt for an Israeli mole within U.S. intelligence. Later in the 1980s, Jonathan Pollard was arrested for spying outside the Israeli Embassy. But his handler, the mole nicknamed "Mega" remained in place. With other allies available, Israel worked out an agreement with the apartheid government of South Africa for plutonium and uranium to produce its nuclear bombs. Pollard was released in November 2015 from a U.S. prison, some say, in order to placate Israel in its hostility toward the Iran sanctions negotiation.

The Israeli nuclear scientist, Mordechai Vanunu, exposed the existence of Israel's nuclear program in 1986. He was illegally abducted, tried in secret, spent 18 years in prison, 11 of them in solitary confinement, and then released to house arrest in 2004, where he remains to this day. The end result is that Israel is the only Middle Eastern nation having hundreds of illegal nuclear bombs, tacitly approved by the U.S. and with no obligation, pressed by any western nation, to admit its illegal possession, or to adhere to the international treaty regulating nuclear weapons. As Secretary Kerry has said, an agreement with Iran would reduce the threat to Israel. Kerry makes sure he doesn't mention Israel's nuclear stockpile. Israel stands on its power and perceived moral obligation to prevent other nations from doing what it has done. In spite of all the infringements on American sovereignty, including the violent attack on the USS Liberty, in 1967, killing or wounding 160 American citizens in international waters, the U.S. continues to claim that Israel is our closest ally. All this can be reduced to the lust of American politicians for AIPAC money and American votes from its Jewish population. Is this a sufficient justification to perpetuate this relationship between Israel and the United States, which tarnishes U.S. standing internationally?[5]

Regardless of Mossad's acts, the U.S. saw Mossad as effective and helpful from the beginning of its relationship with it in the early 1950s. A successful release of hostages by a clandestine Israeli raid in Uganda established Mossad as the supreme worldwide entity for such activities. Mossad's record spoke for itself. "It has spies in place in every Arab capital," Gordon Thomas writes, "providing a steady stream of priceless information." As early as 1954 its chief, Isser Harel, met with Allen Dulles, U.S. chief of the CIA and brother of the Secretary of State. A partnership was created with the young U.S. intelligence outfit, soon to become heavily covert and espionage-driven by that relationship. Each agency shared intelligence and equipment with the other, as well as establishing a "back channel" link bypassing normal diplomatic channels. Such communication afforded cooperation in emergencies, assassinations, coups,

---

[5] *Ibid*, pp. 43-44, 78-83, 149-150; on Vanunu and Pollard, see *Washington Report on Middle East Affairs,* September 2015, pp. 7, 23-24

and invasions, without serious consideration of international law or treaty obligations.[6]

Russian Relations

Republicans, who were hell-bent on taking away domestic public services, were anxiously replacing them with private globalization and NATO as tools to enhance what looked to other nations like empire building in the Middle East and Asia. Policies in Iran and more recently concerning Russia and the Ukraine are examples.

The Obama administration's attempt to resolve tensions with Iran were strongly diplomatic rather than militaristic. Within the Republican Party, however, it was the reverse. While republicans moved in their preferences from sanctions to war, democrats moved from sanctions to negotiations. It takes a bit of history to understand, more objectively, where these conflicts, both in Iran and Russia that are presently taking up so much of our attention, originated. In the case of Iran, it was born out of the CIA overthrow of Iran's democratic government led by its elected leader Mossadegh, in 1953, to be replaced by an autocratic Shah. The seminal event took place in the Eisenhower-Dulles era and set the scene that remains heavily coloring all relations between the two countries. Today, Iran is a close ally of Russia.

An emerging second cold war between the United States and Russia, originated in Russian eyes, with the deployment of U.S. missiles fixed on the Russian nation from Poland, while the U.S. encouraged the movement of

---

[6] *Ibid.*

NATO membership to the borders of that country from the three Baltic States to the west central Asian country of Georgia. As presented by the media, Putin appeared to the American public, to simply, out of a vacuum, start threatening the west. He was apparently responding to previous western encroachments. Both major parties in the U.S. are in close agreement on the meaning of these suspicious movements along Russian borders. Apparently the same policies we see in Russia through Putin, other countries in Asia and the Middle East see in us - that being the same old cold war attempts to enhance our influence beyond our borders. The most recent event of that kind, and yet to be thoroughly analyzed is the announcement from the Obama administration to expand our diplomatic relations in the South China Sea where islands there are being hotly contested by the indigenous peoples around them, who feel threatened by the Republic of China. America, apparently, is not pleased.

The Russian attitude towards missiles pointed at them and the U.S. response that they are really there because of Iran, is reminiscent of similar events in 1963 when the Soviet Union installed missiles in one of their satellite allies, Cuba, causing U.S. generals and politicians to advise President Kennedy to attack Cuba immediately. He refused to do so and the matter was settled somewhat diplomatically, as Khrushchev came to terms with the consequences. Another reason for the event to have taken place at all was that the U.S. had for some time had its own missiles placed in Turkey pointing at the Soviet Union, as well as flying U-2 spy planes across Soviet boundaries.

If this were not enough for history to repeat itself by the same two powers, the Russians found themselves involved with the Ukraine on its immediate borders. The issue there seemed at the outset to be a regional one with the eastern half of the Ukraine populated by a majority of ethnic Russians. This unusual situation came about because Belarus, Moldavia, Ukraine, Georgia, Azerbaijan, Armenia, Latvia, Lithuania and Estonia were all part of the Soviet Union up until its nonviolent transformation into separate countries, loosely joined together in a confederation. Prior to the Ukrainian conflict, the U.S. had moved to get Georgia to become part of NATO, as Latvia, Lithuania and Estonia had already done. The Russian reaction was hostile to this move, which disintegrated when its own people charged the Georgian president with corruption.

Then came the Ukrainian issue where ethnic Russians, who had become part of the Ukraine by a technical change of boundaries within two parts of the Soviet Union, were moved from the Russian federation to the Ukrainian federation. No one envisioned that this would become a problem later on, but so it has. The Ukrainians want to hold on to their traditional territorial boundaries while the Russians took part of it, the Crimea, back illegally. Next the ethnic Russians east of the Dnieper River wanted to rejoin Russia themselves. U.S. diplomacy, if you could call it that, was to back the Ukraine and not Russia and not to propose a nonviolent conflict resolution strategy. As NATO offered to take them in with U.S. support, the Ukrainians felt secure enough to stand up to what was described as Russian aggression. Since the Russians considered both Syria and Iran as their allies, the U.S. threatened Russia with sanctions and implemented them, as did members of the European Union reluctantly. Russian oil and gas sales play a part in both U.S. and Ukrainian interests. Some western and Arab countries, allied to the U.S., would like to see their own oil markets increase, Russian competition decrease and Iranian production not resumed. Russia will not allow that to happen. Lest we forget it was the western powers that introduced the successor of the Soviet Union to capitalistic ways of economic manipulation. A report of the European Leadership Network in June 2015 calls for both sides to communicate in order to avoid confrontation as each side carries on large war games. Each gives the other the impression that they are preparing for a possible confrontation.[7] Russia's Syrian moves are uncalled for.

The Militarization of American Life

As terrorism abroad increased, it overflowed domestically as protectionism here through our new Homeland Security Department. Concealed weapons permits increased and the legality of weapons personally deployed in parks, schools, and libraries became prevalent. Police departments dress and act like the military and use military equipment, and become more and more visible on U.S, streets. As general crime dropped, massacres – a form of local domestic terrorism by individuals loaded up with

---

[7] "Russia: Are Ukrainians Aggressors or Victims?" *This Week.* March 6, 2013; MacAskill, Ewen, "NATO's Baltic Manoevres Ramp Up Military Stakes in Cold War With Russia," *Guardian Weekly,* June 16, 2015, p. 9; Traynor, Ian, "U.S.-Poland Talks on Placing Weapons in Eastern Europe," *Guardian Weekly,* June 19, 2015, p. 15; Borger, Julian, "Russia and NATO Spar on Borders," *Guardian Weekly,* August 21, 2015, p. 5.

military equipment increased – murdering children in schools, people in theaters, and passersby. At the same time, republicans with libertarian instincts, privatize domestic security in ways that recall historical militias, while reducing police budgets. All this, of course, was a response to increased overt operations worldwide by our security forces and the threat of outside terrorists coming in to upset our historically comfortable and safe lifestyle.

More recent Middle Eastern terrorist and covert operations have coupled domestically with a rise of killings of police. This also comes in response to more indiscriminate police killings of suspects and has created the justification for the militarization of policing at home. So it works both ways. An attack upon us in 2001, now apparently isolated and essentially unrepeated, killed a thousand or more Americans. Such tragedies take place on a regular basis in other parts of the world that live much less comfortably. Our response, as many of our politicians explained, was to keep such attacks away by international attempts to take it to where the terrorists live. And this we have done from Afghanistan to Iraq to Somalia to Pakistan to Yemen and Iran. But nothing seems to change. Perhaps this illustrates that there might be a better response to terrorism than an eye-for-an-eye. Neither side has evolved to the significant level of human maturity called diplomacy.

We would think that no one would never be attracted to beheadings and mass killings without trial or imprisonment, or would be moved to join a movement in the Middle East passed off as some kind of dutiful response to the call of Allah. But it goes on and on.

Terrorism and Counter Terrorism

Covert operations can corrupt the culture of a nation, because lying, deceit, and murder are critical tools of the trade and reflect our enemies' tactics as well. We adopt a philosophy of utilitarianism to justify unethical means in order to reach an ethical end, as long as it becomes a greater good for the "better" people, as we have seen.

Louis Menard asks us to consider the following dilemma: "You are a super power that hopes to convert other nations to principles you hold vital," such as support for liberty, property, and free markets, but not for social equality, state ownership and planning, or another brand of religion. These might be the differing ends but the means used by us and our adversaries, are much the same, an eye-for-an-eye, retribution, retaliation and revenge. Menard writes in "A Friend of the Devil" that the U.S. State Department deals with nations with which the U.S. has diplomatic relations. International comity prohibits a nation "from negotiating with or acknowledging the legitimacy of groups committed to a nation's overthrow."[8] So it is necessary to have a covert agency that operates clandestinely. We have, as all nations do, such groups secretly working "both sides of the street." Legitimized nation-state covert groups are more like than unlike overt terrorist groups described as our enemies, such as Al Qaeda and ISIL. Recent events such as the attack by wanna-be ISIL operatives on a French magazine, which made fun of the founder of Islam, Mohammad, in cartoons, or the Boston

---

[8] Menard, Louis, "A Friend of the Devil," *The New Yorker*, March 23, 2015, pp. 85-88.

Marathon massacre in retaliation for the U.S. intervention in the Middle East are good examples.

Graeme Wood writes in *The Atlantic*, that the Islamic State is no mere collection of psychopaths; it is a religious group with carefully considered beliefs. Among them is that they are the key agent in the coming Apocalypse.[9] Judaism and Christianity, before Islam, acted out their own biblical versions of similar end-times in aggressive violence. Sunni Islamic theocratic writings require the violent re-establishment of a Caliphate, which legitimizes violence called for by Allah. There can be no Islamic State without a legitimized Caliph justifying the violent means we are seeing to establish ISIL. But we are familiar, in Christian end-times theology, that prior to the final judgment several things must happen before there is a new heaven and new earth, two of which are the coming of an Anti-Christ and the return of Christ to terminate the Anti-Christ in an apocalyptic war, bringing on perpetual peace. Some far right Christians see an Islamic caliphate as the expected Anti-Christ.

ISIL is not the first religious or political power to publicize its beheadings. Our ally, Saudi Arabia, cuts off peoples' heads and hands for such crimes as drunkenness and fornication. Stoning to death is another variation on the theme. We might remember that the Jews of Jesus' time did that as a commonplace lethal punishment. In one case, Jesus suggested that he who is without sin should throw the first stone. In that particular case no one did. But Jesus became a

---

[9] Wood, Graeme, "What ISIS Really Wants," *The Atlantic,* March 2015, pp. 79-84.

martyr by crucifixion as a blasphemer against religious authority and a seditionist against the state.

And now we have ISIL, creating itself as an Islamic State, and with a Caliphate formed to justify its right to wage holy war, mutilate people and subject them to mass killings. Most westerners are not aware that the establishment of a Caliphate allows Muslims to move from a defensive to an offensive mode. The justification is the further expansion into countries ruled by non-Muslims. Waging war and terrorism is an essential duty of the Caliph. The Sharia is its preferred order of state, but in its application it is not unlike Moses' laws or medieval Christian inquisitions. The word Sharia means legislation in Arabic. It is considered the infallible word of God as was the Qur'an and the Hebrew and Christian scriptures before it. Its two sources are the Qur'an and the Sunnah, both writings attributed to Mohammad and understood as Islamic law.[10]

Iranian Relations

Writings and activities that we identify as terrorism and modern holy war can be found in our own Judeo-Christian traditions. Perhaps we are paying the price for the dominance in power we, in the west, have employed in African and Middle Eastern cultures. Nevertheless, it makes the preservation of what is best in our culture - representative and relatively free democracy – that much harder to sustain. We cannot do away with our international enemies now, but we don't need to be co-opted by them into imitating their

---

[10] "Sharia," Wikipedia definition

vendettas so similar to what we foisted on them through our religious institutions and our colonial adventures in a violent past. However, the obvious result is more available arguments that are formulated to justify militarizing democratic America. The factions calling for less democracy and more militarism are the libertarian and Tea Party wing of the Republican Party. Steve Coll calls it "republican fear-mongering" and claims it is overblown in respect to Iran and republican refusal to support negotiations and settlement over sanctions and possible invasion.[11] However, Iranians know that in 1974 our policies toward it were the opposite, as we asserted Shah Pahlavi's right to build nuclear power plants. The Shah's coup-appointed regime fell in 1979 to the Ayatollah, who believed that nuclear weaponry was un-Islamic. But after Khomeini's death in 1989, his successors thought otherwise. And by 2009 they were within a few years of an atomic bomb.[12]

Iran's enemies have been from time to time, our own. Al Qaeda and ISIL as Sunni oriented, concentrate on murdering Shi'ites unless Sunnis they run across do not support a Caliphate Islamic state. In that case they are treated as enemies and unbelievers. We have lost an opportunity to find common ground with Iran and just as with Vietnam, we could wind up with an enemy who years later becomes an ally. Our failure to recognize that the Vietnamese had a historical animosity for the Chinese and our insistence that

---

[11] Coll, Steve, "A Calculated Risk," *The New Yorker,* April 6, 2015, pp. 17-18.

[12] *Ibid.* Steve Coll is an American journalist, author and business executive, presently Dean of Columbia University's Journalism School. He has received two Pulitzer Prizes for journalism.

they were being orchestrated by China, led to vast and needless bloodshed.

Most recently, at the beginning of Jeb Bush's presidential campaign, democratic opponents accused him of complicity with his father and brother in fomenting this rise of animosity in the Middle East by the Iraqi and Afghan invasions, while overlooking the Obama administration's drone assassinations. On the republican side, forty-seven House republicans sent off a letter to Iran, obviously attempting to obstruct one decent piece of diplomacy, pursued relentlessly by Secretary of State Kerry, to lessen hostilities in that area. The republican letter, warning Iran of opposition to a successful conclusion to the negotiations, usurped the rights of presidential prerogative in international relations. Soon after, the republicans, without consulting the administration, invited the Prime Minister of Israel to speak to a joint session of Congress in direct opposition of the American Executive's role in nonviolent diplomacy. Benjamin Netanyahu is known to hold a hostile view of most of the nations in the area. The Obama-Kerry Iranian agreement survived in Congress in September 2015. The republicans claimed they would find other ways to kill its implementation. Its effect will be, the administration claims, the significant lessening of Iran's ability to possess nuclear weapons, as Israel now does illegally. For that limitation sanctions will be lifted and normal relations restored, as Obama has done in Cuba. The above series of events has put in jeopardy our understanding of the separation of powers between the executive and legislative branches.[13]

This presidential international prerogative has been accepted at least since 1936 when the Supreme Court decided that "in this vast external realm, with its important, complicated, delicate, and manifold problems, only the President has the power to speak or listen as a representative of the nation. ... He alone negotiates. The Congress is powerless."[14]

According to Steve Coll, the republicans are now "meddling in unprecedented fashion to undermine President Obama's nuclear policy with war. Congress has explicit power to review treaties." But the Iran agreement is not a treaty but an executive agreement, an executive agreement, which may be terminated at the end of Obama's presidency in 2016 with a republican victory. The same could happen to Obama's renewal of diplomatic relations with Cuba and the lifting of travel restrictions after half a century.[15] The Republican Party wants to review the agreement as if it were a treaty. Senator John McCain called America's Secretary of State, John Kerry "less trustworthy than Iran's leaders."

---

[13] Klapper, Bradley, and Riechman, Deb, "GOP Letter Warns Iran," *Denver Post,* March 10, 2015, p. 8.

[14] *United States v. Curtiss-Wright Export Corp*, 299 U.S. 304 (1936).

[15] Coll, Steve, "Dangerous Gamesmanship," *The New Yorker,* April 27, 2015, pp. 19-20. A Rabbi and former Israeli Navel Chaplain, Admiral Harold Robinson who has been "a lifelong Zionist, devoted to Israel, a retired general officer and Rabbi for over 40 years," joined 3 dozen retired American generals and admirals supporting the Iran Agreement. He called it: "The most effective means currently available to prevent Iran from obtaining nuclear weapons." *Peace Now*, August 14, 2015.

Such inflammatory fiction illustrates what this book is all about. Obama has sworn to veto any rogue republican actions motivated by such talk. Coll goes on to say that "the collapse of comity and common sense in Congress is not just a fountainhead of divisive politics, it is also a threat to the Constitution. ...Members of Congress continue to degrade and paralyze the institution."[16] One consequence of this currently failed Middle East policy is the expansion of ISIL and Al Qaeda. If we are sacrificing our liberties at home to bring us national security, the evidence seems to establish that we are losing both.

Free Trade Treaties

Once again in the spring of 2014 "free trade" raised its formidable head. Free trade got a big push forward in the Clinton and Bush administrations, with NAFTA and CAFTA. Barack Obama campaigned for the presidency separating himself from free trade sponsorship because by his time free trade was good for the lords and nobles but not the vassals and serfs. By that I mean the capitalist one percent benefited while the majority middle class did not. Jobs went overseas and domestic decision-making authority was transferred to globalized authority through world trade organizations. So it was that by the spring of 2015, Obama was separating himself from democrats who had had enough of this, as he sponsored the fast track Trans-Pacific Trade Bill. But his party had scruples about workers' rights and environmental protection, seeing free trade as harmful to both. Obama's support comes from the republicans, or shall I say from the very same people, who are presently controlling

---

[16] *Ibid.*

the party of Lincoln, who don't mind harming the environment and the workers by sending jobs overseas, outsourcing, and devaluing regulatory U.S. laws. Minority democrats in Congress put up a fuss when Obama not only supported these harmful practices but also wanted them passed on a fast track. His argument in favor was calling the bill a national security package bringing America into Asia to counter Chinese expansion with the pay-off being the claim of increased aggregate wealth. The 12-nation trade deal, eventually passed into law with some democratic support. It claimed that open markets promoted better labor conditions abroad, actually protected endangered species and promoted national security in the Pacific. Protection for American workers' rights was also claimed.

Many Americans, who have a vote and expect their views to be represented, do not believe that so-called free trade is better than what they call fair trade because fair trade propositions are sensitive to environmental and worker conditions more than they are to maximizing profits or engaging in empire competition in the far off Pacific. Its current location is not far from where we floundered for so long in a place called Vietnam. Some republicans joined with democrats, more motivated by their overall hate of Obama than their love of TPP. It initially cleared Congress and was approved by TPP members and is before Congress again in 2016.

This event further demonstrates how both parties do not benefit from the past but are perpetuating it for the reasons given in spite of the harm that it continually creates. Just another example of how some see the CEOs today as our lords and nobles and the vassals as underling, white-collar merchants, the serfs as blue-collar underling workers and the "slaves" relegated to domestic and international prisons. Of course, that is an over statement and yet it's interesting to note that when the monarchs and bishops and their knights were at the top, they comprised about one percent of the population, very similar to our modern ratio, daily expressed by the media as the one percent and the 99 percent.[17] Inequality dominates many domestic and foreign policy issues, as we shall see.

The Key to Peace in the Middle East

As our national representatives ponder what to do in the Pacific, we can't sweep under the rug what is done and not being done to being peace in the Middle East. It has been known for some time that the west needs to show a new face for troublesome issues like Iran and Palestine to go away. The U.S., to indigenous people, looks like it is playing copycat to British and French imperial aggressions in prior centuries in that area. After World War II with the international power of those nations regressing, the U.S. with the loss of Iran as its satellite ally, anointed Israel to take its place. Israel, at its birth, claimed to be a non-discriminatory secular, but Jewish democratic state. But facts on the ground have not born that out. No nation can be all those things at one time. What Israel does to Palestine and what America does in the rest of the Middle East, spreading as Far East as

---

[17] Younge, Gary, "Free Trade's True Cost?" and Grider, William, "The TPP Tipping Point," *The Nation,* July 6/13. 2015; Obama was having a problem getting his Arian allies to sign on to TPP as late as August 2015, Mufson, Steven, "Pacific Trans Pact in Balance," *Guardian Weekly,* August 7, 2015, p. 17.

Iran and Afghanistan, is taken as just another western attempt to dominate over their rights and freedoms. Much of Israel's leadership has come from western Europe, America or Russian immigration and their present Prime Minister is American born. So it was not surprising to hear him say, after his unexpected re-election in April 2015: "As Prime Minister of the one and only Jewish state, I plan to use that voice for Israel to stand up for itself."[18] That translates into Jewish marginalization of indigenous Arab and Muslim people. The U.S. and Israel are looked upon by the homegrown as attached at the hip, both foreign interlopers.

When Obama makes a reasonable attempt to settle things by negotiation and diplomacy, Israel abuses that effort and uses negotiations only to perpetuate the status quo - occupation and control - and then couples that with calls for sanctions and war against its own enemies, primarily Iran. Domestically, Israel discriminates against Arabs, Muslims, Christians and North African Jews as second-class citizens. It is noted for its hostility and aggression in protecting its ethnic Jewishness against states it perceives as hostile to its way of governing itself.

---

[18] The Netanyahu administration will not negotiate with the Palestinian Authority unless it recognizes Israel as a Jewish State. It recognized Israel as a state in 1988 when that's all it was asked to do by Israel. Having done that Israel maintained that there is no such thing as a Palestinian, first publicly announced by their Prime Minister, Golda Meir. Israel has never recognized Palestine as a State. Netanyahu now wants the Palestinian Authority to recognize Israel as Jewish State. They refuse to do so because that would legitimize Israel's second-class treatment of Palestinian Israelis and Ethiopian Jews while calling themselves a democratic society.

America finds itself in a difficult situation with allies and enemies that don't necessarily equate with Israel's and, as such, in the Obama administration it has been said that American-Israeli relations have suffered. On these issues Congress sides sometimes more strongly with Israel than it does with our own American interests because of lobbying money and American Jewish votes, rather than representing their own country for which they were elected.[19]

Resolution of these issues that would truly consider the democratic rights of all people might go farther than drone air strikes have done. Such an approach might take away the energy created by hostile attitudes that empower groups like Al Qaeda and ISIL on one hand and Israel on the other to frustrate and impugn American Middle Eastern foreign policy.

There are many more aspects to the disregard and disrespect of international law and organizations and support for universal human rights that could be discussed. Numerous treaties have been violated and others unenforced. The premier justification of American international intervention is that it offers something more democratic than others in the region or around the world can bring to the people it intrudes upon. Democratic principles and practices recede from scrutiny inside a country's boundaries, but they are noticed perhaps more quickly and deeply by others

---

[19] For a comprehensive study of the history, theology, politics, law, militarism and peacemaking of the Israeli-Palestinian conflict, see Durland, William, *Immoral Wars and Illegal Laws,* Colorado Springs (CreateSpace: 2011).

around the world. So the dismantling of representative government in the United States certainly gives pause to our allies and others we associate with internationally. At the same time, it is just what our enemies intended to happen after 9/11. That enhances their influence and has become a fact, and *ipso facto* has diluted our own. In our own self interest, if not the moral principles, which we have enunciated on paper and from time to time practice, we should re-evaluate what we are doing as domestic and international factors interact.

If we truly want to continue to profess and practice democracy here and abroad, it is time to make a quick turn-about and stand up to the organizations that are impeding that purpose. For our failure to not do just that, since the time of the Reagan administration, has not only hurt our nation's reputation abroad but threatened our quality of life as Americans to continue to live in an atmosphere of justice and peace. What I call The Right to Live is the title of our next chapter and subject of our study.[20]

---

[20] The Colorado Springs Pikes Peak Justice and Peace Commission's Middle East Peace Project has worked for Israel-Palestine justice since 2001.

CHAPTER FIVE

THE RIGHT TO LIVE

"TO TAME THE SAVAGENESS OF MAN, AND MAKE GENTLE THE LIFE OF THE WORLD." SEN. ROBERT F. KENNEDY, APRIL 14, 1968.

Introduction

The diminution of American democracy not only affects us as citizens in community, but also as individuals. Our personal "right to live" is under threat. An expression most often heard is "the right to life" in tension with "the right to choose" or "free choice." It is a tension that involves abortion and as such the phrase "right to life" has been restricted to the right to life of unborn fetuses.

I developed a personal issue with that tension when I joined what I was told was the first Right to Life group in America. I soon found out how limited its focus was. I was all for it at first but when I suggested that we expand its coverage to include capital punishment and war making I encountered resistance. I was told by the founders that those issues were not their concern and with the Pentagon only eleven miles away not feasible. Most of the people on the original committee were Catholics and military personnel. After many years, it dawned on me that the much broader issue was the one we should have entertained from the beginning. Human beings are said to have, politically and religiously, certain human rights and that we should always be vigilant when those rights are threatened. Most basic is life itself – the right to live. Politically, the right to live, unintentionally or maliciously has been attacked by conservatives from time immemorial. Slavery is only one example. Jefferson held the opinion that people were basically good and should have their life, liberty and the pursuit of happiness protected under the Constitution in order to create a more perfect national community. (He did not include slaves in this opinion, apparently.) This chapter is about how, in our own current times, our own individual lives have been made somewhat comfortable, yet progressive American democracy is more imperiled than ever. Succeeding chapters will speak to the specific issues that threaten our lives and well-being. This chapter is unique in that it concentrates on how each of our personal lives is now at risk more than ever by life threatening power mechanisms. The threats that affect us personally, whoever we are or wherever we go, are the ones to consider. A list includes guns, wars, the death penalty, assassinations, torture, indefinite detention, imprisonment, punishment, racial discrimination and police brutality and most recently terrorism here and abroad.

Gun Violence and Police Power

The subject of guns and the logic of their control began for me at about the same time that I joined the Right to Life committee in Virginia, specifically, the day after John Kennedy's assassination. I helped found the first gun control citizens' committee in Northern Virginia some 50 years ago. Progress has been slow while the massacres have increased, and more assassinations and random shootings have taken place. Research and studies made by many, myself included, have not confirmed that there is an originalist constitutional justification under the 2nd Amendment permitting individuals an absolute right to possess guns, free from significant regulation. But some of the 50 states, particularly those in the southern former Confederacy, cling to this individualist, nihilist view of gun ownerhsip.[1]

A recent Supreme Court case, *District of Columbia v. Heller*[2] prohibited the District of Columbia from enforcing handgun laws that required citizens, who may legally possess them, to keep them unloaded, disassembled or trigger-locked when not in proper use. Handguns have never been included under the aegis of a right to bear arms. None of the Bill of Rights guarantees an absolute right, in this case, ownership of property. This case was followed in 2014 by *Peruta v. San Diego* where the Supreme Court, in its 5-4 permissive republican majority, allowed any gun to be carried, cowboy style, into schools, tents and parks without universal background checks. These rulings created a culture of libertarian, anarchistic defiance of otherwise adequate national and state regulations protecting us from the random violence created by the use of guns.

---

[1] I have written and spoken extensively on gun control and the meaning of the 2nd Amendment to the U.S. Constitution beginning in 1968. These include Keynote Address, Conference on Firearms, A Memorial to Senator Robert F. Kennedy, Fairfax, VA, June 1968; Main speaker, Citizens for Effective Firearms Legislation Forum, Reston, VA, June 1969; The 2nd Amendment to the U.S. Constitution: A Critical Thinking Approach, Class Guide, Pikes Peak Community, College Ethics Course, Colorado Springs, CO, Fall 2009; Keynote Speaker, The 2nd Amendment: Guns and Legal Rights, ACLU Conference, Colorado Springs, CO, June 28, 2010; Main Speaker "Guns and Spies" ACLU Summer Forum, Colorado Springs, CO, July 13, 2013.

[2] *District of Columbia v. Heller*, 554 U.S. 570 (2008); *Peruta v. San Diego*, 742 Fed.3d 1144 (2014).

These and other rulings, such as "Make My Day," (from a Clint Eastwood movie) and "Stand Your Ground" (associated with the Zimmerman case) laws have enhanced the permissiveness of the so-called "good guys." The "bad guys," with NRA support, discourage gun regulation, which would enhance the safety and right to live of we human beings. In my own state, when legislators sponsored successful gun regulation a few years ago, they later faced recall elections, and were removed. It has always made sense to regulate guns so that minors, the mentally ill and, violent felons, are prohibited from possessing guns. The idea that guns might be registered was long ago rejected here on the same grounds as many other pieces of legislation, i.e. that they make for big government. Background checks and limits on ammunition were defeated over and over and only recently passed into law in a few states. In 2015, Colorado congresswoman, Diane DeGette, introduced another piece of national legislation that went down in defeat.

Whatever it is that attracts certain individuals to guns, there are others, who are also citizens, who have been of the long standing opinion that the increased availability of guns without regulation eventually means they will be available and used for which they are designed - to shoot at somebody or something. We hear of so many cases of even small infants dying as a result of the accessibility of guns to them or in their households. There used to be a belief that the police would join the movement for legislation comparable to that which we have for automobiles and drugs. This has not been the case. What is the case is that private ownership of weapons is now commonplace, and that the courts have said it's okay to bring them into parks, libraries, schools, and the like but not, of course, courtrooms or Congress. The police react much faster than before, in pulling the trigger. We can't blame them entirely, but they are approaching this issue in the wrong way and the end result has been more and more "suspicious" unarmed people killed. Police budgets have been cut and "shoot first, worry later" seems to be the rule to make up for it. The latest series of excessive police actions began at Ferguson, Missouri two years ago. Several innocent people were killed in that event and its aftermath, and now in hindsight we see an over-reaction where police are being killed unjustly. Semi-automatic military weapons and countless handguns are as available as smart phones in this country. The tendency towards militias and vigilantes has been somewhat legitimized, it seems, as civilians replace police enforcing the law on the street, such as in the Zimmerman case.

In Hayden, Idaho a two-year-old baby accidentally shot and killed his mother after he reached into her purse at a Wal-Mart Store and fired her concealed weapon, a small caliber handgun. Her permit was next to it. In bordering state, Washington, a three-year-old boy was seriously injured in November 2014 when he was accidentally shot in the face by a four-year-old neighbor. In April 2014 a two-year-old boy shot and killed his 10-year-old sister while he was playing with the family gun in Philadelphia, three examples out of countless such tragic and avoidable events.

How is it possible that some writing or better yet some interpretation of what was meant by a writing several hundred years ago can give private citizens today a constitutional right to possess military-style weaponry? No matter how many deaths arise from this interpretation, it is declared untouchable. I have written extensively on the subject of the 2nd Amendment. That Amendment, like all others, was never intended to be enforced in an abstract, absolute way, but rather in context with all other human rights and duties expressed in the Constitution and interpreted by the Supreme Court. The right to live is at least as important as the right to property. But the NRA argues that the use of the gun, itself, will ensure this very right to live that I am advocating for here. If that's what does it, then all the rest, called freedoms and liberties, and duties and responsibilities, under the same Constitution, dissolve in the presence of the this interpretation of the 2nd Amendment to the United States Constitution.

Constitutional scholars know that constitutional prerogatives are fundamental and more powerful than mere statutes. But they also know that if there are ten amendments in the Bill of Rights, and each qualifies the other, as the Supreme Court interprets them, no one can be absolute over all the others. It is that principle that we have lost in the last five years or so in regard to the 2nd Amendment and must regain in order to prevent further decay in this area from taking place. Or will we continue to acquiesce and remain oblivious to these urgent problems? One's right to live is severely threatened by another's right to possess property – a gun.

The Supreme Court shot down a gun safety law benefiting those who live in D.C. communities constantly under threat by gun violence. We are told that guns should not be in the hands of "bad guys" and should be permitted in the hands of the "good guys." But more frequently than not, the bad guy was a good guy first, before he turned bad.

Currently, the 2nd Amendment is afforded an almost absolute protection to those with guns over against those who have a right to live and to be safe. A close literal interpretation of the context of the language in which the 2nd Amendment was written reveals that it was not an absolute individual right. The current Supreme Court determination that the 2nd Amendment would guarantee an individual right to a handgun does not take into consideration the history of the time in which it was written. The colonial defense of America began and remained essentially in the hands of volunteer militias, men who signed up for a set period. Most of colonial America was farmland and these volunteer farmers were told to bring their guns with them, primarily muskets, when they were called up. They had used their muskets when they joined the British Army in defeating the French and Indians in a recent war. The concern then was not an absolute individual right to own a gun, but a qualified right to bear arms in defense of one's new country, which had only militias and no standing army.

The facts of the *Heller* case are nothing like this. Justice John Paul Stevens, a long serving and well experienced republican appointee who has since retired, offered his view that this modern permissive interpretation in the D.C. case was a "law-changing decision" eradicating decades old Supreme Court precedent, which he wished could be maintained as constitutionally accurate.[3] What is

---

[3] Nan, Yeomans, William, Schwartz, Michelle, "The Roberts Court at X" *The Nation*, February 10, 2015, p. 8. For international observation, see Freedland, Jonathan, "On Guns and Race, the U.S. is Shackled to Its Past," *Guardian Weekly*, June 26, 2015, p. 18. The new Supreme Court permissiveness supports such life-threatening gatherings as the "Machine Gun Shoot" in Colorado Springs, CO where over 200 machine guns were

disappearing in our culture, politics and legal decision-making is balance. What we see here in this example lacks balance. That's why it's called "extremist." We have, not too far in the distant past, prime examples of democracies gone dictatorial when individuals and militia-like groups waged violence against national governments and eventually took them over and enforced the opposite extreme that no one, but the totalitarian regime would henceforth possess a gun. It is an NRA contention that if guns are not given an absolute protection they will be absolutely taken away by the so-called "big government." That belief is counter to the factual evidence of over 50 years. Gun-control advocates do not want to take away the right to own guns but only to regulate them. There is no constitutional right to massacre citizens as in Oregon in October 2015. Hillary Clinton calls for stricter background checks while conservatives call for more guns. The right to live safely is a constitutional guarantee, free from such massacres, always just around the corner.

The Increase in War Making and Treaty Breaking

The problem of war making and treaty breaking is touched upon in several chapters of this book. Here we will comment only on how these events threaten our right to live as individuals and create fear as a cultural norm.

The movement to a more devastating form of war making and international law and treaty violations was set

---

available at "a family event." Its publicity said, "Rent a machine gun and feel the fire power. Kids included." *Colorado Springs Gazette,* August 24, 2015. Recently, in Arizona, a nine-year-old child accidentally killed her father in a "family" machine gun party at a firing range.

off by the events of World War II from the beginning of the attack on Pearl Harbor to the devastation of intentional civilian targets in Great Britain and Germany to the culmination of the war by the use of the weapon of mass destruction – the nuclear bomb – twice, on primarily civilian populations of Japan in August 1945. Foreign policy more than military necessity inspired that rash decision. An Island blockade would have accomplished the end of Japan's ability to continue in very little more time. The Japanese on the mainland were out of oil for fueling their war and out of food to survive. But waiting would have meant that the Soviets, who already had been urged to come into the Pacific war many times, and now were on the verge of doing so, were no longer desired or needed by the allies once they had the bomb. To let them come in at the end and sit at the peace table as an equal partner to Britain, France and America, was seen as foolhardy. More intelligent minds could have figured how to get around that without having to resort to the bomb as a means to keep the Soviets out of the Japanese occupation.

Most of our leading generals, including Macarthur, Eisenhower and Hap Arnold rejected the idea but Truman did it anyway. The week the bombs were dropped, I was, at age 14 finishing a beautiful eight weeks of summer camp in Maine. I was performing an assigned duty of sweeping up a guest cabin, and as I picked up trash on the floor I saw the headlines of a newspaper a few days old. It said something like "atomic bombs dropped – Japanese surrender." My immediate reaction was to smile. Four years of my young life had been spent living through war and now I was secure. All that mattered to me was the surrender. Who knew what these atomic bombs would cause beyond ending a war, as far as human beings were concerned? Of course there were those who knew, but it didn't matter. Some scientists thought the world would blow up and others seemed to have immediate regrets.

A month earlier, the primary scientist involved in the creation of the bomb, Robert Oppenheimer, the director of the Los Alamos laboratory where the bombs were made and tested nearby, had this to say: "If atomic bombs are ... added as new weapons to the arsenals of a warring world ... then the time will come when mankind will curse the names of Los Alamos and Hiroshima.... Atomic weapons are a peril which effects everyone in the world, and in that sense a completely common problem.... In order to handle this common problem there must be a complete sense of community responsibility."[4]

And so there was, for a while, a movement to codify a practice of community responsibility by the formation of a United Nations organization. But it was to be short-lived and the dream of a community of nations became diluted. Further violations of international law and treaties became more commonplace, not only by the Soviets but by the Zionists and the U.S.

Traditional war has again become an extension of foreign policy. The one-time use of atomic weapons fades, but is replaced by possession and deployment by the major powers, whether legally or illegally, of weapons of mass

---

[4] Farewell Speech at Los Alamos Laboratory, New Mexico, 1945.

destruction, as a deterrent. Smaller wars, therefore, have become the norm. We see the threat to our own culture enlarging as western and Asian powers continue efforts to colonize the Middle East. Resistance by indigenous people becomes justified in their own eyes, leading to the current threat of a theocratic Islamic state throughout the area.

The Israelis are the only ones whose leaders are secular but who use their religious documents to justify, with U.S. support, their colonization of the ancient lands of Palestine. The Soviets vanished as a super power, just as Rome and Britain had before them. The U.S. filled the vacuum with the same justification the British used, that is to democratize the region. But a price is paid when the violence comes so close to us now that young people within the United States and other western nations, are attracted to ISIL. As yet there is no sufficient plan to protect our right to live from these international threats partially created by our own shortsighted conservative foreign policy. This is not the American dream and we must awake and put a stop not only to the violence within our own country but the violence worldwide that is threatening us. The Iranian sanctions negotiations are a first step.

Killing People Who Kill People

Returning again to our domestic life, the issues of the death penalty and capital punishment have been plaguing us for the last half century of my life, and now more intensely than ever. The phrase "killing people who kill people" came to my attention from an activist button originating with the Fellowship of Reconciliation. It asks in full: "Why do we kill people who kill people to prove that killing people is wrong?" On its face the question is a logical one and also has ethical connotations. But it also questions our motives grounded in retaliation and revenge more than in retribution, the practice of an-eye-for-an-eye. Alternatives, such as rehabilitation, restitution and diversion have been virtually set aside and are superior to all the motivations named above.

Conservatives have never put the implementation of the death penalty in this country as a way of dealing with crime to the same test as they put liberals to the test when they charge that gun regulations don't stop crime. "Guns don't kill people, people do." Conservatives argue that because people are still killing people, gun control regulations don't work and they have been successful in obstructing them. It would seem to follow that if people are still killing people, the death penalty hasn't worked and should also be abolished. One of the most serious problems in conservative thinking is that it is so often hypocritical in its inconsistency and incoherence. Nevertheless, over two-thirds of Americans, in polls conducted over many decades, have favored the death penalty even though there is much scientific evidence that it has not proved to be a deterrent simply by the fact that we are still threatened by capital crimes. We also know that deterrence only works among a thinking population. Those who are emotionally charged to commit a crime without weighing the consequences or are not mentally able to do so cannot consider the consequences.

I would say that even earlier than when I took my first stand against discrimination, I had decided that I did not favor the death penalty. My reason at that time, probably at age seven or eight, was that I was scared out of my pants that somehow, mistakenly of course by the authorities, I could be walking to the electric chair as an adult. The reason for this, I remember, was an experience I had at an early age. My relatives were great moviegoers and I was taken to the movies often, regardless of the film's suitability for children. So it became a habit that I saw a lot of movies in the 30s. The movies in those days were morally clear – the good guys won and the bad guys lost. In the movie in this case James Cagney, played a hardened criminal. There was no doubt he committed the murders and all that was left was for him to be electrocuted for his bad deeds.

I was certainly given the impression by my parents and relatives, priests, school and country, that capital punishment was part of the moral culture, a just desert fitting the criminal. The movie also included the character of a Catholic priest who confirmed this. The priest's only advice to Cagney was that he should take his just punishment like a man so that the priest could tell everybody that at the end he exhibited at least one characteristic of the good guys - courage. The film terrified me. Of course you can't talk to your parents about such things. Could this possibly happen to me? I wasn't worrying about the world, I was worrying about myself. I gained the understanding that it should not happen to anyone else since I was so sure that it shouldn't happen to me. Mistakes could be made and innocent people killed, unlike in the film. The way for it not to happen was what the Catholic priests were teaching me, which was that we should forgive bad people and help them to be better, not kill them if we were to follow Jesus' teaching. I didn't see Cagney electrocuted. The movie portrayed his walk with the priest to the electric chair with scary music and black shadows. So you can see the early roots of my opposition to capital punishment from this story. I also remember, in growing up, that my very wise grandmother told me that two wrongs can never make a right. In more scholarly language it is intrinsically wrong to do to another what he did to you as a form of punishment. Perhaps there is an upside to taking children to inappropriate movies.

The Supreme Court, in 1972, decided to end the death penalty in America in a Georgia case that I came very close to being part of as an attorney, *Furman v. Georgia*. Four Justices were of the view that the death penalty was just fine. They were the most conservative ones. Three Justices believed that the death penalty should be lifted until such time as it would no longer discriminate against minorities, particularly in the south. Two Justices, Thurgood Marshall and William Brennan, were of the view that the death penalty now, if not always, violated the 8th Amendment to the U.S. Constitution, as cruel and unusual punishment.[5]

In 1976 all that was undone as capital punishment was restored after several southern states claimed they had ended discrimination against Blacks in their areas. Outflanking the two, the three who had been against the death penalty, as discriminatory, joined with the four, who had always been for it and back it came. Today there are

---

[5] *Furman v. Georgia* 408 U.S. 238 (1972), five to four vote; *Gregg v. Georgia* 428 U.S. 153 (1976), seven to two vote. Justices Marshall and Brennan remained steadfast that the death penalty is cruel and unusual punishment. In August 2015 the Connecticut Supreme Court declared that the death penalty "no longer computes with contemporary standards of decency" and violates the 8th Amendment as cruel and unusual. The U.S. Supreme Court may take up the issue in fall 2015.

numerous polls and studies indicating that a disproportionate number of Blacks are on death row. One study claimed 42 percent, even though the Black population is only 13 percent. We are the only major industrial nation that has the death penalty. The others (which are not "major industrial") are Syria, Egypt, North Korea, Saudi Arabia, and Iran.[6] The death penalty is clearly both discriminatory and cruel and unusual, and threatens the right to live in society in safety when innocent people are put to death. Experts claim that number has been about ten percent.

One's position on capital punishment is not necessarily dependent upon whether one is conservative or liberal. The reasons may be different but the conclusions are the same. I lived in northern Virginia for 20 years and each morning I would drive into the District of Columbia, when my office was there in the 60s, and listen to the local classical music station. The host of the program one morning identified himself as a convinced conservative republican, living under the Kennedy-Johnson democratic administration. This host regularly added social commentaries to his musical program, one of which had been the dangers, then, of Halloween for children. This particular morning it was the death penalty. He favored the end of capital punishment and expressed his view quite clearly. He was not concerned about the rights of the perpetrator or even the victims. He said his concern was for

---

[6] Nine states have abolished capital punishment since 1980. In the 2016 presidential election primaries, three democratic candidates oppose the death penalty, Sanders, O'Malley, and Chafee. Shapiro, Bruce, "An unsettling Sentence," *The Nation*, June 8, 2015, pp. 6, 8.

the human race, if it is to remain civilized. The more we legitimize and make a habit of killing people, even those who "deserve" it, whether for retribution, retaliation or revenge, the more we degrade ourselves. Our community psyche is injured. We should stop doing this.

Eventually I would realize that my deeper objection to capital punishment was not simply fear, but its intrinsic immorality. There are those who simply on principle clearly recognize the teachings of Jesus to be counter to the habitual use of retribution, retaliation and revenge and favor redemption, restitution, rehabilitation and reconciliation. The attorney, Clarence Darrow, an agnostic, took much the same position and claimed Jesus influenced him. He wrote a book entitled *Resist Not Evil* taking the title from the words of Jesus in Matthew 5:38. Darrow was always against capital punishment and in one of his most famous cases, representing the malicious young murderers Leopold and Loeb he plead for their lives in an hours-long closing argument. These teenagers, from privileged backgrounds, planned the perfect murder as a matter of entertainment. After hearing Darrow, the jury came back with a penalty of life in prison not death. Loeb died violently in prison, while 18 years later, Leopold, who learned a medical skill in prison was released and devoted the rest of his life to saving human lives in Puerto Rico as a medical technician.[7]

There is no need here to recite an exhaustive list of innocent people who have been convicted and executed as a

---

[7] Bishon, William, and Stone, Christopher, "Darrow's Closing Argument in *State v. Leopold and Loeb*" *Law, Language and Ethics,* Mineola, NY (Foundation Press: 1972) pp. 670-713

result of cultural bias. One of the first plays I read in my freshman year at Syracuse University, appeared in my western literature and composition textbook. It was "Winterset," a dramatization of the trial and execution of Sacco and Vanzetti, Italian immigrants falsely convicted of murder, as anarchists and socialists. They were blue-collar workers, not speaking English well, who were put to death more over a fear of Soviet communism in the 1920s than the perpetration of crimes they were accused of that they did not commit.[8]

Today we hear of many innocent individuals released from death row on DNA testing, yet Americans still favor the death penalty two to one. Why is this subject included in the Right to Live or the Demise of Democracy? One reason is the death penalty threatens our own individual lives in at least one way. Once a defendant rationally understands that he or she has committed a capital crime, there is no incentive for him to refrain from enlarging upon it. One death is enough, the rest he gets away with. Let us not forget that "irresistible impulses" and "mental disease causation," were once justifiable arguments to prevent a person not responsible enough for his actions to be sentenced to death. We put more and more people to death who are legally irresponsible because they do not meet the only test remaining for legal insanity, which is the ability to know right from wrong. It is a scientific fact that some people

---

[8] Avrich, Paul, *Sacco and Vanzetti,* Princeton, NJ (Princeton University Press; 1991); Durland, William, "Sacco and Vanzetti in a Nutshell: Guilty or Not?" Class Guide, Trinidad State Jr. College Logic course. Trinidad, CO, 1998.

suffering from mental disease or defect cannot control their impulses, which have come under the compulsive sway of schizophrenia and paranoia.

In a recent case involving the insanity plea in Colorado, the prosecutor told the jury that the heinousness of the crime outweighed any plea of insanity. Obviously the degree of violence involved is not relevant to a determination of whether the defendant is insane. Several jurors, however, were impressed by the prosecutor's comparison and further influenced by the victims' families, who accepted the fallacy in the sentencing phase of the trial. Fortunately, one or more jurors realized the fallacy of that statement, i.e. the two are separate considerations and one cannot be used to overcome the other. More often, American jurors are less thoughtful and compassionate. A democratic nation can ill afford its citizens to be threatened by a barbaric device that has been proved not to deter those who resort to capital crimes. For one to do so he or she must think rationally and even if sane not be overcome by one's emotions or to believe that he can simply get away with it. For all these reasons: 1) it is inhumane, 2) it may kill the innocent, 3) it does not deter crime, 4) it is discriminatory, and 5) it is not taking into consideration the valid defense of mental disease or defect, it should be abolished. The right to live is an additional reason. Getting rid of the death penalty will enhance our quality of life, contribute to our moral evolution and make this country safer for all of us.

Torture and Assassination – Cultural Norms?

Why is this category included in a book about the decline of democracy? The reason for America's support of the use of these tactics is that apparently we believe they increase the security and safety of our nation. But, in fact their use creates circumstances that ultimately threaten our right to live, not to mention their immoral and illegal character. A majority of Americans since 9/11 have embraced torture according to several polls. In the Denver Post's "Readers Forum," a reader wrote: "It was so gratifying to read your article and to know a majority of right-thinking Americans finally appreciate the value of torture." She went on to suggest that we use it "in our prisons, jails and police stations on our own criminal classes." Her opinion is that we would save money so it is an economic expedient and that lawsuits and lawyers only get in the way with something called "innocent until proved guilty." Get rid of "the right to an attorney" she says. I rest my case.[9] Most recently, Americans have had second thoughts about the value of torture and whether it is consistent with American values.

Evangelist Pat Robertson, a Reagan favorite and Christian Coalition founder, called for the assassination of then President Hugo Chavez of Venezuela. "We have the ability to take him out. ...We don't need another $200 billion war to get rid of one, you know, strong-arm dictator. It's a whole lot easier to have some of the covert operatives do the job and then get it over with." This from a disciple of Jesus who claims he has been "born again" and given his life to God and to Jesus his Savior and asks others to follow him as

---

[9] Bowman, Jane, "Americans' Acceptance of Torture" *Denver Post,* December 23, 2014, in response to "Torture Justified" December 17, 2014.

their pastor. He is also a very outspoken republican conservative.[10]

The U.S. government disowned his statement and the National Council of Churches said that "it defies logic that a clergyman could casually dismiss thousands of years of Judeo-Christian law, including the commandment that we are not to kill." Well, that went out long ago but then Robertson called for his flock to pray for vacancies on the Supreme Court so they could be filled with conservative Christians. He joined with another conservative republican fundamentalist Christian, Jerry Falwell, claiming the 9/11 was God's punishment for "pagans, abortionists, feminists, gays, lesbians, the ACLU and the People for the American Way." So we see to this day republican presidential candidates leaning this way."[11] A justification for a much harsher domestic criminal justice practice has come at the same time as this international practice broadened.

Another part of this trend is detention instead of arrest, trial, attorneys and juries. First we resorted to detention by the CIA without arrest, whether U.S. citizens or not, assuming assassination wasn't resorted to first. The relevance of both domestic and foreign relaxation of the rule of law plays a part in the demise of representative government because we are denied information from the government upon which we can reach informed decisions. The States Secrets Act, and the Patriot Act are examples of congressional legislation obstructing that information.

---

[10] "Evangelist: Assassinate Hugo Chavez," *Colorado Springs Gazette*, September 2005.

[11] *Ibid*.

A question was recently posed: "Can America run a secret intelligence service under law in an open democracy?" Obviously it is a rhetorical one. Democracy is not based on lies, spying, kidnapping, and murder under the guise of "intelligence" gathering. But that is our direction and process now – kill them or kidnap them, detain them with no access to an attorney, no arrest, no trial. Instead we use extreme rendition to a far away location or confinement in a place such as Guantanamo.[12] The preferred process for gaining information now is what is euphemistically called "enhanced interrogation" – just plain torture. Before 9/11 torture was ruled out, if not morally, at least pragmatically. It was seen as counter productive resulting in false information. Why do we do it now – to retaliate, seek revenge, or just so our representatives can say they are tough on terror and are supporting the wishes of their constituents?

Eventually, human experimentation became a subject of CIA scrutiny, studying the impact on the human psyche of enhanced interrogation and detention. Two psychologists pursued this latest American study of the effect of torture on humans. It took place in "black sites," and was carried out by

---

[12] At this writing there seems to be no hope of closing this indefinite detention, offshore prison. Some detainees could remain there forever. It took years for the Supreme Court to recognize a common sense reality. That was that the prison, leased from Cuba, according to American law should be under the jurisdiction of domestic courts. Guantanamo is second only to Abu Ghraib in Iraq, in operating under undemocratic processes and in violation of international law. The Iraqi prison came to an end after much publicity, but it remains a symbol abroad of U.S. lawlessness. It has become "a defeat for law itself." Friedman, Noah, *Denver Post*, July 26, 2015, p. 5D; "Judge Rejects Guantanamo Challenge," *Guardian Weekly*, August 7, 2015, p. 2.

experimenters who did not have any expertise. Their aim was to produce "debility, disorientation and dread," a Senate Intelligence Committee report revealed. They concluded that "enhanced interrogation techniques do not themselves produce useful information, rather they produce the condition of total submission that will facilitate extracting actionable intelligence." The techniques studied were water boarding, rectal dehydration, months of nakedness in total darkness and isolation, among others.[13]

Soviet and Chinese techniques were adopted by the U.S. as early as 1953. They included hypnosis, sleep deprivation, hallucinogenic drugs, perpetual standing and isolation. They were considered "scientific." By 2012 we knew that torture "had lost its stigma" as morally reprehensible and criminal. But GOP presidential candidates continued to favor it and Vice President Cheney said he "would do it in a minute." No one has been held accountable. We have been told it has stopped, by the Obama administration but we are prohibited from knowing for sure by the Military Commissions Act and other security blockages. These techniques also became part of the curriculum of the School of Americas in a guide entitled "Human Resource Exploitation Model."[14] My wife and I demonstrated there against such activities in 2006.

---

[13] Hajjar, Lisa, "The American Way of Torture," *The Nation,* January 5, 2015, pp.4,5; Weiner, Tim, "The Audacity of Impunity," *The Nation,* January 5, 2015, pp. 3,4. Weiner is a Pulitzer Prize winning *New York Times* writer and author of *The Legacy of Ashes: The History of the CIA,* 2007 National Book Award winner.

[14] Hajjar, *Id.*

Senator Diane Feinstein (D.Calif.) and her committee worked diligently over several years to reveal the truth behind enhanced interrogation procedures. Her report on CIA practices was released on December 9, 2014. It confirmed the torture practices being used. It also put to rest CIA claims that these gross practices led to valuable information, saving hundreds of American lives. They were never substantiated. Feinstein received little help from President Obama or her close friend, Secretary of State Kerry. The New York Times editorial board, on the basis of her report, called for prosecution of "torturers and their bosses, starting with former Vice-President Dick Cheney." This never happened. The republicans on her committee refused to support her findings and responded negatively just as the CIA did. She did receive support from Senator John McCain and former CIA director, General David Petraeus. She states that she has not heard from Obama, but she and Senator McCain have introduced an amendment to the National Defense Authorization Act that would permanently ban these enhanced interrogation techniques.[15]

For those who believe that some of these techniques are minor and that they, or those like them, would not have a negative effect on a detained person, my own experience as a victim in a military environment has given me pause. I was

---

[15] The transition from torture to surveillance, our next topic in this chapter is aptly made by Feinstein's report, facilitated by Snowden's revelations on NSA surveillance revealing much about torture. Both these aspects threaten our way of life and our right to live. See Bruck, Connie, "The Inside War," *The New Yorker*, June 22, 2015, pp. 43-55 for a complete chronology of events.

drafted into the Army in May 1954 and told that after basic training we would be sent to French Indochina to replace the French, who were withdrawing in the face of the Vietminh. For a year prior to my induction, as a patriotic American citizen, I had been a top secret and cytological analyst for the National Security Agency. I had turned down a Navy Officers School commission in order to go to law school but the draft prevented me. So off I went to Ft. Dix for eight weeks basic training. At the end I was chosen one of two out of 500, to attend Army Counter Intelligence School. But when I arrived at Ft. Holabird Maryland I was sent back to Ft. Dix as a security risk having married a woman whose parents were Polish and Lithuanian born American citizens, with a number of relatives behind the Iron Curtain. I had not lost my intelligence, just my status as a result.

At Ft. Dix I was told that because I had "failed" intelligence school, I could not be assigned to another school and must continue a second eight weeks of basic training in an infantry outfit that would later be assigned to the Cold War battlefront opposite Czechoslovakia. I assumed that there must be a misunderstanding because I had not failed the school since I never started it. In fact, they used me for night guard duty to guard the top-secret files at this secret Counter Intelligence base. I had no time to wonder how this could be logical since I was declared a security risk. Anyway, I told the sergeant at Ft. Dix that I was just married, was a college graduate, and wished to be assigned to a school from which I could use my education to good effect. The sergeant said that I could go to any school I wanted if I would re-enlist for an extra year. And he added, if you're planning to go to law school you can get out three months early because the timing will be right. So after talking with my wife, we decided this was the lesser of two evils and off we went, with a few hundred dollars bonus and several weeks' leave.

When I returned I told the sergeant the school that I had chosen from the ones he listed for me. But he said: "I'm so sorry Pvt. Durland, that school is closed, pick another one." So I went through the list again and picked another. "I'm so sorry Pvt. Durland but that school is full. Pick again." I realized by this time that a little harassment was going on, but what could I do. I picked a third and was assigned to the Medical Service Corps School at Ft. Sam Houston, Texas. I was told, since I was attending a school, I could bring my wife, my car, my belongings and find an apartment off post; which I did. My orders clearly stated so. My wife got a nursing job at the local hospital and I reported for duty. When I did, a sergeant told me that I would not be assigned to a school and would be sent to medical basic training, which is everything basic training is, except no guns. I asked how could that be since I signed up for an extra year and was guaranteed a school, and he said "We don't care what Ft. Dix says and you are now under orders not to leave these company grounds, consisting of a barracks and grounds, and that I would spend the next six weeks in this restricted area and could not leave.

I asked to at least telephone my wife about this change of circumstances and the sergeant pointed to a phone across the street. I started towards the phone and the sergeant said, "You don't have permission to go outside the company boundaries, and that's where the phone is." My car was in the parking lot. After the sergeant showed me my bunk, I knew what I had to do, which might cause me even more trouble including courts martial. I had to drive the car to my newly rented apartment and have my wife drive me back after I told her my predicament. She was on her own but would at least know what happened and have use of the car. I pulled it off. But the next day, I was called out of formation and made to stand in front of Company Headquarters, at attention, in the sun at 118 degrees, except for lunch, each day for three days, before beginning medical basic training. After two weeks of no hope and no contact with anybody outside the company grounds, my wife and a young Lieutenant, who had the power to do so, visited me. He and his wife had moved in above my wife's apartment and he was attending the Medical Service Corps Officer's School at Ft. Sam Houston. He arranged to give me the opportunity to make good what the Army had already promised me. But to do so, I now had to pass a test to be transferred to the Medical Service School. I did just that and, thanks to him, I then attended the Medical Service School.

One last thing happened to me, as part of the initial military bullying, when I was at my lowest ebb after two weeks indefinite detention. I was ordered to go off company grounds to deliver a document for the company commander some distance across the military installation. As I walked, I cried, felt humiliated and harassed and wanted to run away, but knowing I could not do that. As I look back on these events, I wonder whether that was a set-up to entice me to go AWOL so that they could finally court martial me. Never had I experienced such treatment, and felt a victim of a power that could arbitrarily and abusively decide my every move. That is why I can appreciate, in very a small way, why the subtle abusive devices, both physical and psychological, combined together, can constitute torture. The right to live includes the right not to be treated in an inhumane manner, especially when one is simply, as an American citizen, serving his country. An American citizen should not lose all his rights simply at the whim of someone with captain's bars.

Surveillance: The Patriot Act and Whistle Blowers

The right to live also includes the right to be free from irresponsible and illegal surveillance of our every move as American citizens by our own government. Part of our constitutional freedom is taken away and it is just that lack of freedom we identified with the Soviet Union and NAZI Germany. With the advent of 9/11 in 2001, a new version of "big brother" emerged. Most recently after the passage of the Patriot Act, events like the National Security Agency gathering telephone and other records of U.S. private citizens here and abroad have resulted in just the opposite. Spying on ourselves became amplified in the Bush Jr. administration. Somehow the conservative pursuit of small government in Washington has never extended to this area of really big government.

The Congress we elected then as our representatives, presumably to protect our freedom to live, created the opening to such civilian surveillance. There is no need here to recap the Edward Snowden whistle-blowing event, but simply to show how the Patriot Act and the revelations from Snowden's leaks, have tied torture and surveillance together.

The Patriot Act was due to expire on June 1, 2015. A majority of Americans have voiced their negative opinion of continuing the provisions of section 215 of the Act. This section gives NSA its legal powers, which may have been used illegally to justify the bulk collection of telephone records of almost all Americans. An appeals court had earlier ruled that the law could not be used to support collecting domestic telephone records, but was put on hold pending Congress's action. This section has also been used to obtain business records, hotel bills, travel vouchers, and Internet data thought to be relevant to a terrorism investigation. The FBI claimed that collection is extremely useful, although a recent Justice Department report said the Bureau could not point to any terrorism cases cracked because of the program. In addition, section 206 authorizes roving wiretaps. Private companies have been coerced to cooperate with NSA in retrieving such records. In fact they have been paid taxpayer money, it is now known, to "play ball." AT&T is one of those companies that has been described as in "a partnership" with NSA. These procedures would have remained secret but for Edward Snowden's criminalized whistle blowing, letting us know what our representatives allowed NSA to obtain. The new republican majority leader, Mitch McConnell led the fight to re-authorize all Patriot Act provisions while libertarian Tea Party republican, Rand Paul, was outstanding in his opposition to section 215 remaining, joined by many democrats. Democratic Senator Patrick Leahy and republican Mike Lee led a middle-ground compromise, which became law.[16]

One on-going impact of the ever-enlarging spy and surveillance network has been in regard to public libraries.

---

[16] Davidson, Amy, "Unclear Dangers," *The New Yorker,* May 18, 2015, pp. 33-34.

As the disintegration of our democratic representative culture progresses, anything public becomes an open target. In this case it's the fight for privacy, as the story unfolds, and is updated by a recent report.[17] I remember speaking out publicly on this matter as chair of the Colorado Springs ACLU chapter, when local librarians complained about federal agents demanding library information and warning librarians that it was illegal for them to comment on this activity.

Under the Patriot Act the government has the authority to collect copies of library records by secret court order requested unilaterally by government officials without notice to the library and without probable cause required for a warrant. If a warrant is necessary, a secret court has been established whereby, merely by allegation and hearsay presented by the FBI concerning a suspected terrorist, the government may proceed with no other parties present. The end result of all of this is that the Constitution was apparently being used to legitimize the Patriot Act so that a person who stood in the way, for example a librarian, would be subject to felony charges and long jail time.

It was *The Guardian Weekly* newspaper of London that first published the Snowden documents that showed that the NSA was collecting the records of phone calls made by millions of Verizon customers on an "ongoing daily basis" and ordered by the secret Foreign Intelligence Surveillance

---

[17] Carpenter, Zoë, "Librarians vs. the NSA" *The Nation,* May 25, 2015, pp. 13-15. See also Flood, Allison, "John LeCarre Warns of Threat Posed by Secret Services to Democracy," *TheGuardian.com,* March 5, 2014.

Court "to build ... a comprehensive picture of who any individual contacted, how and when and possibly from where retrospectively." Section 215 made it legal. The justification, of course without the necessity of proof by the FBI, was that the high-jackers used public libraries in Florida to plan and coordinate with one another. Traditional subpoenas were available as a legal avenue but section 215 was quicker, easier and did not require a trial. Simply an allegation of the need for "any tangible thing" became a regular description of materials sought. When librarians resisted, they were described as "hysterical." (The majority of librarians are women, hence the stereotype.) In 2006 the Act was renewed after 30,000 national security letters to librarians were issued with no review from prosecutors, juries or judges, giving legal cover to NSA actions under section 215 for its several uses as described above. Moreover, along the way, section 215's interpretation was broadened to include "a telephone company's entire call record data base as a 'tangible thing' subject to collection and storage."[18]

On May 7, 2015 two years after Snowden, the U.S. Court of Appeals for the 2nd Circuit decided that the secret program had been illegal from its inception. It ruled that section 215 did not authorize the above-described intrusions into the lives of almost all of us. Yet against the will of the majority of Americans polled, conservative political representatives, including the present Senate republican

---

[18] *Ibid*, p. 13. The NSA has added a new "cyber command" agency. It claims it is for the "defense of U.S. computer networks, but the agency is built for assault, just like its parent." *Citizens for Peace in Space Bulletin.* Colorado Springs, Colorado.

majority leader, Mitch McConnell, continually supported those intrusions.[19] A life is something to live. To remain alive is our greatest possession. While doing so the quality of that life should be protected. In political, constitutional language, it is the part we honor as "the general welfare," lest we forget.

Detention, Prisons and Punishment

For those, such as myself, who have experienced more than a week in jail for conscience' sake, an inkling of what imprisonment is like is possible. Just as I experienced in several military versions, imprisonment carries a generally inhumane treatment of the incarcerated. Only recently with the advent of DNA testing, we have been able to show that a good percentage of those deemed guilty, sentenced and then treated, in some places, as less than human, is wrong. A person recently told me, when I was speaking about incarceration in America, that "its hard to get into an American prison." If so, why do we lead the world in imprisonment? There are ways to improve the humanity and responsibility of our prisons. A program known as the Milwaukee Experiment is one.[20] The Experiment is focused on limiting minimum sentences and has attracted the support of the National Association of Criminal Defense Lawyers, the ACLU, and the Koch brothers. It further aims to reduce prison sentences generally, providing statistics that support

---

[19] Cole, David, "Snowden's Vindication," *The Nation,* June 1, 2015.

[20] Toobin, Jeffrey, "The Milwaukee Experiment," *The New Yorker,* May 11, 2015, pp. 24-30.

the view that in doing so the prison system will be improved. Senator Rand Paul (R.Ky.) and Senator Cory Booker (D.NJ) support this experiment because it provides useful offenders more opportunities to expunge criminal records rather than being hardened into the system for nonviolent crimes.

Much has already been written about the increasing military-like security mechanisms of our prisons today. One example of the decline in this area is the privatizing of public prisons where motives of profit require no empty beds. Even retribution is secondary. This is another example of the disestablishment of government control of public projects. The Milwaukee Experiment is one alternative to the negatives described and an example of a program designed to halt the use of undemocratic and inhumane methodologies in the American prison process.

The right to live for Americans does not end when one is convicted of a crime. The idea that because a person is incarcerated and must pay the price of his or her crime does not mean that they may be treated as less than human. The notion that prisoners should be subjected to inhumane conditions and treatment while serving time is wrong. It is not only southern states that have been associated with this sort of thing. Northern states, with increased republican representatives, have been doing this as well.

Take Wisconsin for example, where most recently the state has opted for conservative republican representatives, on a local and state basis, and produced two presidential candidates. Wisconsinites are six percent of the U.S. population, but have 37 percent of state prisoners. This is a state that has eliminated union collective bargaining, imposed right to work laws and along with its bordering state, republican controlled Michigan, suppressed the minimum wage, and created a family situation where employment and occupation do not meet the minimum requirements for the right to live in some decent manner. The governor of Wisconsin, Scott Walker, has been most associated with these deprivations, and is a leading contender for the republican presidential nomination in 2016.

The most densely populated part of Wisconsin is Milwaukee County where half the men are African Americans in their 30s and have served time in prison. Statewide, thirteen percent of African American men are behind bars nearly double the average. Police officers imitate military practices and racial discrimination is evident. According to a study, thirteen percent of the state's African American men of working age are behind bars, nearly double the national average of 6.7.[21]

Since 1980 in Maryland, the prison population has tripled with racial disparity the same as in Wisconsin. The Black population is 30 percent, the imprisoned 70 percent with mandatory minimum sentences imposed by conservatives. Being "tough on crime" has become a popular stance with conservative representatives, causing democrats to try to keep up with them. The issue that plays a big part in prosecutorial decision-making does not seem to be over

---

[21] *Ibid.* p. 24. University of Wisconsin – Milwaukee Study 2010. For other efforts see Friends Committee on National Legislation project, "Mass Incarceration Massively Wrong," May 2015; Kelly, Bill, "Prison Revolt" *The New Yorker,* June 29, 2015, pp. 22-28. The first national activist organization to which I became a member was the NAACP.

violent or nonviolent crime, but the amount of pigment in one's skin.

The prison population in America has grown from about 300,000 in the 1970s to two million after 2000, the highest incarceration rate in the world, surpassing Russia and China. For most of our history, it has been about 100 in 100,000. Now it's 700 in 100,000. Although convicted criminals have a price to pay, the term of payment and the manner of treatment during that time is what distinguishes America from the rest of the democratic industrial nations.

There was a time in the 60s when there was a strong attempt to humanize the criminal system. We know there is no reason for any prisoner to be raped. Violent crime among prisoners, especially rape, has been going on, as long as there have been prisons. To me, that is the ultimate indication of the failure of our prison system to provide any positive outcome. In 1957 a federal rule was developed called the *McNabb-Mallory* doctrine to insure that when a confession was secured during a period of "unnecessary delay" i.e. detention, it was inadmissible under the exclusionary rule of the 4th Amendment. A young Black man was beaten with a rubber hose and confessed to a crime while detained in a D.C. jail. Subsequent cases, however, modified the rule out of which evolved what is today's permissive legal attitude and practice both domestically and internationally on indefinite detention.[22]

---

[22] *Mallory v. U.S.* 354 US 449 (1967). There is now proof that our domestic imprisonment system is taking on more and more characteristics of the military. 3,500 Americans have been indefinitely detained without access to an attorney for secretive interrogation in Chicago. Eighty-two percent are Black. Ackerman, Spencer, and

I was fortunate, when I was a young attorney in the nation's capital, in the early 60s, I took part in two new programs – pretrial diversion and the public defender program. Before a governmentally sponsored public defender program was established, attorneys, who were voluntarily moved to do so, represented indigent or unpopular defendants *pro bono*. For a while these two programs grew and were extremely beneficial. In the case of the public defender program, conservative politicians saw fit to diminish its budget and therefore its application and the expertise of its representation. In regard to the lesser-known pretrial diversion project, certain cases were taken out of the criminal trial procedure and diverted to psychologists or other avenues of correction, such as restitution and community service. Prosecutors changed it from pretrial diversion to pre-sentence diversion. Restoring the trial process but preserving an alternative to prison compromised this program, but it is still worthwhile, where practiced. These programs should be restored to what they were. Unfortunately there are many Americans who would like the system to remain as it is, enhancing personal suffering beyond simple incarceration. The practice of an eye-for-an-eye is expanded to revenge and retaliation. According to some conservatives, prisoners are not fully human anyway. They deserve all they get, whether legal or not, once they are locked up, apparently including sodomy and murder.

Stafford, Zach, "Vulnerable Get Lost in 'Secret' Chicago Prisoner Warehouse," *The Guardian Weekly*, August 14, 2015, p. A4.

The right to live needs to be extended to all human beings, regardless of how they have acted at any particular time in their lives. Our right to live has been attacked, not only for convicted criminals but for many innocent people who have suffered from various forms of abuse. Certainly we have a right to life, to be human beings. It is worthwhile that conservatives and liberals alike protect that right to life. But some of us forget that once we are born the right to life truly begins and, as it is ongoing, it is more aptly described as a right to live. And as we live that life, our right to live it in a representative, democratic society becomes more precious.[23]

---

[23] Recently, attention has been given to what is being called "moral injury." It is described as a psychological wound received from participation in war making. It is a condition similar but not identical to PTSD. It arises when veterans "feel extreme guilt and shame for something they did or witnessed in conflict that goes against their values or may even be a crime." Sufferers experience "suicidal thoughts, withdrawal, hyper-vigilance, agitation and nightmares. Often they are demoralized and behave in a self-destructive way, such as binge-drinking, doing drugs and destroying relationships." They find no relief from PTSD treatments, experts say. Treatment for moral injury focuses on acceptance and forgiveness. This is just another example of how the right to live is being irreparably damaged by war making orders that run counter to the way human beings, universally, understand and wish to practice a more neighborly life based on love and morality. Associated Press, "Learning About the War Wound, 'moral injury' " *Colorado Springs Gazette,* August 17, 2015, P. A4.

PART III – THE GENERAL WELFARE UNDER ATTACK

CHAPTER SIX

ECONOMICS AND THE ENVIRONMENT

"TRADE ... IS WHAT EVERYBODY TALKS OF BUT FEW UNDERSTAND."

A PLAN OF THE ENGLISH COMMERCE, DANIEL DEFOE, 1728

Introduction

Economics and environmentalism are subjects that always seem to be at odds with each other. For those who are concerned with economic regulation and environmental protection, that might not be the case. But in the economic system Americans have chosen, called variously free enterprise, laissez-faire, or capitalism, the question arises does one's freedom mean another's deprivation of it? The names themselves might give us a hint. Capitalists are defined as the private investors, employers; owners of the system and the rest – workers, consumers, and employees – are the cogs that produce the profits to those for whom the economic system is named. Environmentalism is not a private enterprise but a public one and is concerned about the protection of nature, open spaces, and historic sites. There are those who take the position that the two can complement each other and need not be in opposition. One of the stumbling points, however, is that every bit of land that is set aside and not utilized for profit making, either by governments or corporations, is a drag on the essential feature of economics – maximizing profits. The biblical declaration in Genesis 1:28 that the human race is free to have dominion over the environment has resulted in an imbalance between our economic life and our environmental well-being.

It took a while for me to see this dichotomy. When I was a young lawyer in northern Virginia in the early 60s, I was recommended to fill a vacancy on the Fairfax County Planning Commission. I thought that would fit in rather nicely with my new law degree, in that planning and zoning law was an interesting subject for anyone who was attracted to the designing of our living spaces. There was a time, even earlier, when the word "planning" had no political meaning for me. I was a student at Syracuse University, in my second political science course in my freshman year. The professor, at one point, attempted to elicit a discussion probably on some of our readings, on the word "planning." As far as I had developed at that point, planning meant what I was going to do on the weekend. The professor had a much deeper subject in mind. He wished to compare the extent and manner in which capitalists and socialists plan their economy over a five-year period. As it turned out for capitalists, planning had a negative connotation. It was seen as taking away individual freedoms in favor of governmental planning that smacked of a socialist system.

Fourteen years later, I had planning under my belt as well as zoning. So I was set for my interview with the Chair of the Fairfax County Board of Supervisors. Her very first question to me, as a democrat, was what was my view on "open spaces?" I might as well have been back in the professor's 1950 class, for I didn't have a clue what she meant. Open spaces meant spaces that were open. Well, who could be against that, so I said I was for it. Unfortunately, State Senator Scott, who recommended me, was not one of her favorites. I remember one of his favorite words when describing how the Virginia poll tax was used against African Americans to buy their votes. He called the victimizing process "invidious." He was the first southerner that I had ever met who took a strong stand against racist discrimination. The poll tax was abolished in 1966. Unfortunately, Senator Scott failed to get re-nominated. I didn't get the job, but I did my homework. Those two events were seminal in launching the detailed knowledge I gained in the fields of economics and the environment over many subsequent decades.

The Economic Evolution

This Chapter will be devoted first to economics and then to the environment. A fair economic system must truly be a fair enterprise system. Opportunity within it must be available not only for the capitalist enterprisers but the worker, consumer, employee, homeless, poor, or disabled. Recent statistics have informed us that several attributes of the system are no longer in progress and others have sharply reversed their previously progressive trends. This is not well known to the American electorate. Time and time again, when polled, they call for improving our condition. The polls, as we shall see, are on specific subjects, such as minimum wage, collective bargaining, equality of income, etc. They do not deal directly with the more fundamental problem that each illustrates, i.e. that modern capitalism is intrinsically calculated to invest money and power in the hands of a few, thereby replacing economic competition with capitalistic consolidation; but they do initiate the negative effects on human beings.

The capitalist sees the national government not only as a private competitor but also the opposition. When the government provides public services and initiates public projects such as environmental projects, that take that arena out of private realm, it reduces the amount of power corporations may consolidate as their own. So naturally, multi-national corporations are anti-government since they seek to control all aspects of the economy. There is one exception. The U.S. military is America's thoroughly socialist enterprise and is supported to provide protection for our chosen economic system. The public is told that the only reasons private corporations oppose the government is because it is too big, it is "socialist" and they can do the job better. Private corporations also look favorably upon state governments because each is in competition with the other to attract business. States offer corporations incentives that they would never think of offering to private citizens, to operate within their boundaries. This works in two ways, first it gives tax breaks that normal citizens will never see and then it regulates corporations' activities, much less than it regulates private individuals. Corporate capitalists also combine globalized free trade privileges and state incentives as their power base, and attempt to remove the national government from the playing field, all in their own interest and not usually in the public interest. One side effect is that power is removed from government and shifted to a globalized economy where the economy of one country now has much greater effect on other countries' economies, as we saw with the latest economic downswing in China and its effect on the U.S. stock market in August 2015.

Most Americans were not aware until recently that a corporation is a person under the law. They only became aware sometime after the Supreme Court decision in *Citizens United*. When this was first done legally, at the turn of the 20th century, the idea was not really that a corporation was a person with First Amendment rights, but was only an artificial, fictionalized entity created to benefit political and economic business and bookkeeping. As our discussion progresses, we will see how this legal fiction has impacted general economic fairness and has greatly expanded in our own time.[1]

Where does the power come from to create such illogical and unreasonable characteristics of privilege? When more power is concentrated in economic business leaders, the end result becomes that the top one percent gains control of the system and the wealth it generates, at the expense of the other 99 percent. One side effect of all of that is currently CEOs are making some 400 times the amount of money their workers are paid by them. Is this new? The words are; the facts aren't. An economic system called mercantilism emerged from medieval feudalism in western

---

[1] *The Oxford Guide to the Supreme Court*, 2nd ed., edited by Kermit Hall states under "Corporations" that the "person" fiction originated from an "off-hand dictum of Chief Justice Morrison Waite" in *Santa Clara County v. Southern Pacific Railroad* (1886) Corporations became "persons" under the 14th Amendment, but with the limited intent as described above. It wasn't until 1978 in *National Bank v. Bellotti* that the 1st Amendment was included. On this basis *Citizens United* broke the dam and made corporations identical to human beings, who eat, sleep, copulate or possess physical functions that as yet corporations have not practiced.

Europe when, at the same time, political nation-states were emerging and setting up autocracies and oligarchies in the form of kingly monarchies. They constituted the same one percent of that population. The remaining 99 percent had other designations. Whereas the one percent included emperors, kings, lords, nobles and bishops, the 99 percent was made up of vassals, serfs, peasants and slaves. One could say that roughly today the lords are comparable to our capitalists, the vassals to our merchants, the serfs to our employees/workers, and the slaves to our poverty class or "under class." The material wants and needs have a different twist and the standard of living under capitalism, in a material sense, is quantitatively higher for some of the 99 percent. There is more material comfort provided today in the lives of the 99 percent, and a minimum income to give the life of the lower middle class and below some semblance of basic quality. But the one percent tops it all with CEOs paid an average of $16 million a year.[2]

But another common thread runs through the ages where the greedy resort to dominating violence and the downtrodden respond through nonviolent, resistance organizations such as guilds or unions, and when hard pressed, resort to violence. The emergence of democratic institutions and principles was going to be the instrument that would set the common person free. As a matter of fact, Adam Smith's form of free enterprise attempted in part to produce that outcome. Smith has been criticized for his empirical judgment that economics works best if it is motivated by self-interest because better products are produced, and the consequence is a more free and democratic society. But economics was not primary then because the power of economics was vested in the monarch, who at that time in England, controlled not only politics but religion and economics as well. That concentration of power would now be vested in one person, while there was at the same time a slowly developing democratic institution resisted by the powers that be.

By 1900, in its march to progress over the centuries, the middle class was stabilized and became the largest economic segment in the industrialized western democracies, with a small percentage of rich and poor on the extremes. But in our present day, the move backward has been evidenced by the diminution of unions and collective bargaining, as well as the failure of minimum wage legislation nationally to keep up with the cost of living. At the same time there is a massive increase of the wealth of the top one percent. Somebody loses, somebody gains. It doesn't go away simply by changing the name of the elite under capitalism.

How wealth is distributed is the determining factor in whether the economic system is equitable. In our own society there has been a successful conditioning campaign to negativize social economies and raise up capitalist ones. A very plausible third choice to capitalism and socialism is little known and goes under the name of cooperativism.[3] The

---

[3] An excellent summary of cooperativism is Dr. Richard Williams' *The Cooperative Movement*, Hampshire, England (Ashgate Publishing Ltd.: 2007). I first learned about alternatives to capitalism in a course I took at Bucknell University in 1951. The text was *Comparative Economic Systems*, Loucks, William and Hoot, Weldon, 3rd ed. New York (Harper Bros.: 1948), pp. 723-752; The article was entitled "The Consumers' Cooperative Movement," and began my lifelong study of economic systems as they affected human life.

very people harmed most by a capitalist economic system are workers and consumers, the middle class, not to mention the poor. Yet because this privatized system is described as free this same group of people seem to be persuaded that it benefits them as well as the capitalists for which it's named. The fact that it is not based on a social equality does not seem to deter Americans from favoring this form of economics. To say this in another way, it is psychological or political reasons, rather than economic factors that convince the same middle class Americans to support democracy in politics and more recently in religion, but to continue not to do so in economics. The economic system of capitalism would need to be a much more participatory system, which is just what it is designed to suppress. Much of the lower 99 percent vote to empower the one percent in political elections, or how else could the one percent gain a majority of voters on economic issues? It must be that the fear of so-called "big government" is always greater than fear of a multi-national corporation maximizing its profits at the expense of the rest of the community.

Other psychological beliefs have reinforced such conclusions. Unions are mobsters, the poor are ignorant, the dark-complexioned are lazy, women are weak, and homosexuals are sinful. And as for the democrats you might say they spend all their time maliciously passing laws to facilitate the killing of babies by, let us say weak women.

Workers are convinced that requiring the payment of organizational dues by minorities is a violation of their freedom. To unionize is to collectively organize workers to balance the organization of their employers. In the absence of unions, the employers' power is strengthened and wages kept low. Recently, such traditionally progressive states as Wisconsin and Michigan have obliterated their unions by voting in right-to-work laws.

Statistics establish that there is a greater disparity of the distribution of wealth between the one percent and the 99 percent, as argument and evidence for either a fundamental correction in the economic system or a complete change to another. But this has been around now for a period of years and did nothing to prevent the republican victory in November 2014. This could only mean for the one-third of Americans that voted most recently in that off-year election, that equality of wealth, or even a greater opportunity for more citizens to gain a comfortable living, was not seen as a way to love one's neighbor. As a matter of fact, it may be seen by many that sharing the wealth with "the mobs," the ignorant, the lazy, the weak and the sinful would be the consequence. One hopes this is not true, for if it is, there's nothing in this book that will persuade people of that mind set to change their minds in the 2016 presidential election. The hope is that the other two-thirds who have been acquiescent or oblivious will heed this wake-up call to them and move to make the difference. Most Americans claim they believe, as Christians, in loving their neighbor. Now is a chance to do it.

Apart from efforts to raise the minimum wage and develop more equity between employer and employee power, there are other abuses that need to be terminated. American jobs go overseas and capitalist profits are hidden away in off shore accounts or Swiss banks. At the same time the rich pay fewer taxes and the corporations nearly none. Employee rights are eliminated and unions are destroyed. When the predator banks are caught, no person physically goes to jail, even though we know that the corporation is a person and human persons go to jail all the time, in this country, more than anywhere else in the world. Those that we elect to represent us are primarily millionaires and for the most part they vote their own self-interest while we, the citizens and the majority, become collectively forgotten unless we exert our rights as a community of citizens.

Persons, Pawns, and Plutocrats

The capitalist system, as we know, conscientiously designed by Adam Smith was openly based not on altruistic or social principles but on individual self-interest. The motive is to maximize profits at the expense of everything and everyone else. It was to be self-regulated and free of governmental interference. Instead, it would be regulated as described by Smith by "the invisible hand." As it evolved, other philosophical attributes were attached to its workings and it was eventually described as based on a morally or ethically free philosophy known as Positivism. That is, it cannot be criticized for air or water pollution, for that would be attaching a moral value to its operation. This morality-free characteristic of capitalism grew out of the work of Hayek and Friedman.[3] The original self-interest

---

[3] See Friedman, Milton, "The Social Responsibility of Business is to Increase Profits" in Abelson, Reziel and Friquegon, Marie-Louise, *Ethics for Modern Life,* 4th ed., New York (St. Martin's Press: 1971) p. 313-318; Durland, William, *The Price of Folly: A Layperson's Guide to American Plutocracy,* Colorado Springs, Colorado (CreateSpace: 2013) pp. 43-46.

characteristic is not an ethical principle to begin with. But Smith claimed that the consequence of that motivation was. That is because, as each individual or organization is left free to make its product, an atmosphere of "perfect competition" will emerge so that each business in competition with the others will strive to make the best quality product. The product will sell and the workers will raise their standard of living as the capitalist maximizes his profits and the consumer receives the best quality product. In this competition the makers of poor quality will fail and so employee and employer will go down together and consumers will no longer support the business.

Adam Smith was a philosopher. Modern economists, like Friedman and Hayek and others we will meet, vary in their philosophical insights. In any case, where we see an economy in the hands of a few, we find that competition is not preferred. Rather the elimination of competition through concentration and consolidation, eventually establishing a completely different and undemocratic economic structure, is. This was certainly not what Adam Smith had in mind when one of his strongest motivations was to take the concentration and consolidation of economic power away from the king and a few of his chosen and re-distribute it freely and democratically into the hands of an emerging middle class entrepreneurship.

Instead a movement towards inequality, fostered by powerful capitalists, created an inequality of the middle class resulting from its morality-free and competition-free characteristics. The Darwinian theory was also used to justify the concentration of economic power in capitalist hands, as they were seen as the result of the survival of the fittest. This became known as "social Darwinism." Hence governmental regulations only protect the weak from the strong, and aid the mediocre, whose weakness is demonstrated by their having less wealth, from producing an inferior product.

By the turn of the 20th century, this concentration of power was known by names such as "trusts" and "monopolies." It was not the Democratic Party, in those days, which did the trust busting of the Gilded Age, but rather a resurgence of liberal Lincoln republicanism under the likes of Teddy Roosevelt. The Democratic Party, the majority of which resided in the south was still recovering from the stresses of the Civil War. That would all end when Roosevelt was out and his disappointing buddy, Taft, became the father of the modern conservative Republican Party. The resulting power vacuum was slowly filled by a moderate democratic President, Woodrow Wilson, who after eight years in office had progressively evolved to a point when he was driving not only republicans but the Prime Ministers of France and England so crazy that they were calling him "Jesus Christ." Conservative Republicans Taft through Hoover drew the political trends into the 1930s. Their party, during that time, advocated privatization, de-regulation, elimination of taxes and scarce employment in order to keep wages down. But it would all end.

The economy was based on ever-expanding growth. Americans with a capacity for intelligence might easily surmise that growth may expand, but not forever and one day the bubble will collapse and the boom will bust. It's built into the system. It is only natural that other participants in the economy, workers and consumers and environmentalists, would want a system with full employment, collective bargaining, the right to strike for higher wages and better conditions. The capitalist system was not created to produce that. The bubble burst, the Great Depression came, but Franklin Roosevelt's New Deal created a truly equitable economic system that embraced the protection of public services such as transportation, housing, jobs, and healthcare. Necessary programs like social security, Medicare, Medicaid, affordable healthcare, adequate minimum wages and working hours, unemployment insurance, and a healthy environment were anticipated as well. The right to live with an acceptable quality of life should be universal, not simply for those whom the economic system was essentially benefiting. The threat to diminish full employment has remained to this day, because that human necessity may be sacrificed in order to enhance a domestic and global privileged economic structure.

A wise man, I am told, once said that the Jews gave the world three persons that were each rejected, although eminently wise – Moses, Jesus and Marx. I would differ about Moses, and substitute Abraham or Isaiah, but certainly Jesus and Marx fit the bill. All are relevant to economic considerations, even though the first two are primarily religious personalities. Marx criticized capitalism, in the 1850s, writing that workers are held to a subsistence wage in order to maximize corporate profits and given just enough compensation so that they would not revolt but simply feel alienated. The so-called productive part of the emerging middle class separated from the unproductive part, as Adam Smith described them, to form, in our own time the top one percent, replacing the kings and lords of old. Income inequality, we will see, has worsened in our own time. The richest one percent of Americans are still expanding over the 99 percent in 2015.[4]

A political revolution had taken place earlier than Marx, in the late 18th century in France, where the top one percent – kings, nobles, and bishops – became the target for the *bourgeoisie*, a newly developing middle class, and their allies, known as *sans culottes*, or the poorer peasant class. The former convinced the later that if they were successful against the elites, they would remain together and form a strong majority in a democratic republic. Instead, history shows that the *bourgeoisie*, who were attracted more to the rich than to the poor, once the revolution was successful, deserted the poor class. So it was that by the 1850s Marx was criticizing the *bourgeoisie* for deserting their poorer friends for the rich and powerful one percent. The middle class, as well as the poor, will find out from that time on to the present day, that their break-up would empower those above them under the new economic system to subdue them more easily.

---

[4] Lawhead, William, "Surveying the Case for Marxism," *The Philosophical Journey,* Boston (McGraw Hill, 2006) pp. 599-603; Adam Smith distinguished between productive and unproductive work and said that those groups that would not qualify as engaging in a productive enterprise were 1) the military, 2) public servants, 3) the clergy, 4) orators, 5) lawyers, 6) physicians, 7) "men of letters" 8) actors, 9) musicians, because their work "perishes in the very instant of its production and therefore is 'unproductive of any value' like 'menial servants.'" Arendt, Hannah, *The Human Condition,* Chicago (The University of Chicago Press: 1958) p. 93.

In America from then clear up to World War I, workers were putting in up to 16 hours in mines and factories and women and children in sweat shops, all working for a subsistence wage. Money had replaced estates and titles, but the same dichotomy persisted. The only question today is: has this split been ameliorated or is it on the increase? The obvious answer, based on statistical political and economic evidence, is that it is becoming ever more divergent. Naturally, that conclusion is evidenced empirically and runs counter to the nature of democracy wherein sovereignty lies with the people. These people are not capitalists but they are workers and consumers and constitute the rest of society.

Eventually, the *bourgeoisie* class that was once comprised of the guilds, artisans and merchants, rose above farmers and peasants, who tended, in the industrial age, to be absorbed into the new factory system. The lucky ones, lawyers, doctors, artisans, merchants become more comfortable than their predecessors, leaving a lower middle class in a less desirable situation. The *bourgeoisie*, it could be said, were actually the ones who replaced the kings and bishops as the CEO's of giant corporations, the new nobles. Even Marx admitted that capitalism might foster an economic materialism but at the expense of a favorable quality of life. A recent publication of *The Nation*, on its 150th anniversary, contained a reprint of an editorial written in 1873. This is what it said in its entirety:

Some thirty or forty years ago American society discovered that this country lies remote from European complications. In this safety of isolation American society said: "We will lay aside the responsibilities and sacrifices of citizenship, and religiously ascribing all virtues and all growth and progress to a republican form of government, will allow our own to go to the dogs, devoting ourselves meanwhile to the business of getting rich." The broadest views of duty were covered by the word "industry," and of elevation by the word "wealth." These ideas were flung about by the press, and caught up and adopted by society, so that every philanthropist who addressed a public school generally summed up his moral teachings in the prediction that all the good boys would work hard and get rich.

Such sayings as, "The world is governed too much," "The less government you have the better," "Individual enterprise will accomplish everything, if you will only give it a chance," were adopted as incontrovertible maxims, and society set itself to giving individual enterprise all the chance it asked. At the same time, the science of government, which had received so much attention from the earliest statesmen, was allowed to die out in this country, and the business of governing was gradually abandoned to a class of professional politicians contemptuously called office-holders and office-seekers, and the task of serving one's country fell into general disrepute.

In a country so undeveloped on the one hand, and so rich in resources on the other, there were innumerable fields for individual enterprise – and fields of such vast extent as to be beyond the powers of any single fortune. Hence it was inevitable that individual enterprise should seek the aid of combined capitalists, and that these combinations should take the form of corporations. Such corporations were manifestly too small, too weak, and too local to control legislatures, or seriously conflict with the interests of the community which created them. They were practically, as well as theoretically, the creatures of the legislature, and created for the public convenience. In time, however, these several corporate links, with others of the great chain, became welded together, and since then consolidations here and "giant enterprises" there have brought great corporations upon the whole country. The immense power of great and concentrated wealth, which is actively employed, made itself almost immediately felt.

With such new forces springing into existence in every State, more numerous, if not intrinsically greater, than was ever known before in the history of corporate bodies, and growing rapidly into a magnitude that could never have been anticipated, and with the efficiency of American government constantly lessening, it is apparent that a time might, indeed must, come when Government would be really too inefficient to maintain the rights of society by duly restraining their aggressive powers. Such is not far from the condition of American society at the present moment. Corporations to a certain extent take the place in American society of the privileged classes in aristocratic Europe; for they constitute a feudal system which exacts service, if not homage, from an influential portion of every community, and which carries off a disguised warfare with the Government, sometimes in Congress, sometimes in State legislatures, in which warfare concentrated wealth and power are arrayed against the wishes and, in some case, the interests of society at large.[5]

The 2008 Great Recession

A comparison with the events of more recent years will show the extent of our modern aggression. Let's focus on 2008 forward. It all started with the Reagan administration and culminated in the Great Recession of 2008-2010, certainly with the help of both Presidents Clinton and Bush, Jr. By 1970 lower real income was replacing the progressive economic steps made since 1945. Balance comes about when all segments of the economy are advancing - capitalists, workers, and consumers - and minimum wage is on the increase, and full employment becomes a reality. But when the balance of these economic participants is upset, all segments of the economy, including the capitalists, will eventually pay the price. The reduction of unions and collective bargaining is the primary culprit. Unions went down from 44 percent to 12 percent during this period. In August 2010, when the Great Recession was nearing its end, and a Financial Reform law, the heavily compromised Dodd-Frank bill, was passed by Congress, I composed my own understanding of what was going on for my regular column

---

[5] "The Growth of Corporate and Decline of Governmental Power," *The Nation,* May 15, 1873, reprinted in *The Nation,* April 6, 2015, p. 25.

in a local Colorado Springs newsmagazine. (Colorado Springs, my hometown, according to *Forbes* Magazine is the 4th most conservative city with over 200,000 population in the U.S.) Following is a general summary of what I said at the time.[6]

Most people are at a loss to understand the underlying causes of the 2008 economic crisis or the attempts made to avoid another such crisis in the form of a major federal reform law. Some knowledge of the implications of our economic system helps. Capitalist practitioners fall into two distinct groups, as I see it: the social capitalists who possess a conscience such as Keynes, Galbraith, Volcker and Krugman, and the self-interested capitalists, such as Hayek, Friedman, Rand Paul and Reagan. The latter, in place of a social conscience, possess capital.

In the political world of economy, privileged capitalists influence privileged politicians through their privileged lobbyists to propagandize the less privileged majority to purchase their products with the minimum ethical regulations in order to maximize their ethically shady profits. The majority, that is the consumers, employees, workers, small businesses, etc. are necessary in order for the system to work. But the majority benefits the least and when a crisis occurs due to the risks taken by venture capitalists (as part of the system) social wounds occur and someone must be held accountable. The entire system needs reform. The treatment

---

[6] Durland, William, "2010 Financial Reform Bill Needs Understanding," *Active for Justice* newsmagazine, Colorado Springs, (Pikes Peak Justice and Peace Commission: October 2010).

of these wounds with Bandaids becomes the only perceived remedy. As a result the same crisis and collapse repeats itself cyclically as greed and power repeat themselves. What did the crisis look like this time and how did we go about bandaging the wounds instead of applying major surgery?

After the Reagan deregulation years of the 80s, perhaps the most fundamental change of the 90s was the repeal of the Glass-Stegall Act in 1999, which had prohibited banks from conducting activities in two conflicting realms at the same time, commercial banking – issuing credits (loans, mortgages, etc.) to households and firms, and investment banking – issuing and trading securities. We learned that this was a bad conflict of interest combination as a result of the Great Depression and passed legislation in the 30s in order to end that crisis. Henceforth commercial banking would be separate from investment banking. Commercial would be limited but protected by government. Investment was free to speculate but was on notice that "too big to fail" coverage would never be forthcoming. Obviously this was FDR's democratic lawmaking, naturally opposed unsuccessfully then by republicans. After all, Harding, Coolidge, Hoover and the self-interested capitalists were then, as now, the essential causes of the crisis.

But then Glass-Steagall was repealed, one major cause of the 2008 downfall. One solution to avoid it after 2010 was that commercial banks should be protected but not allowed to engage in such risky activities as proprietary trading and sponsorship of hedge funds ever again. (City Group and Wells Fargo were examples.)

A few definitions would be helpful at this point: Proprietary trading: describes banking firms which actively trade stocks, bonds, currencies, commodities and their derivatives or other financial instruments such as hedge and private equity funds, with their own surplus money and that of their customers in order to maximize profits for themselves. Banks engage in this non-commercial banking activity because it offers more volatile profits but at greater risk to itself and to its commercial customers, which suffer when the bank is in crisis from risk speculation. Private Equity Funds: refers to equity capital not listed on a public exchange, which is invested directly in private companies or in buyouts of public companies; leveraged buyouts are those where large amounts of debt are issued to fund large purchases and when thereafter companies are resold, to maximize profits. Hedge Funds: are instruments for limited investors who undertake a wide range of trading activities such as debt commodities or paying a performance fee. Such funds "hedge" risks by short sales and the use of derivatives as a trading strategy to maximize profits. Derivatives: are agreements that have a value linked to the expected future price movements of an asset such as a share or a conveyance, e.g. swaps, futures, options. Subprime Mortgages: are non-conventional mortgages sold to borrowers with low credit ratings, and high risk of default, charging a higher interest rate to maximize a risk profit.

In 2007, with such commercial and securities trading banking unregulated and intertwined, a crisis similar to the depression occurred and caused, in part, the recent recession. The fall of investment bank Bear Stearns in the spring of 2008 marked the beginning of the direct causes of the recession. Nevertheless, the feds agreed to take over any loses on $29 billion worth of Stearns' mortgage assets. Six months later Lehman Brothers and A.I.G. collapsed. The Bush Administration and Congress then brought $700 billion to the rescue of the banking system, and granted Goldman Sachs and Morgan Stanley, investment banks, commercial banking licenses with access to federal loan guarantees and federal emergency lending facilities. These banks, which were primarily engaged in trading, were made bank-holding companies. Thus the financial floodgates were opened in an attempt to quell the panic.

It became obvious that one of the first major reform recommendations should have been to restrict system-wide banking institutions from undertaking high risk and conflict of interest proprietary activities. In the case of Sachs, that amounted to ten percent of its reserves. Bush's Treasury Department, however, took no action to curb these unregulated banking activities, including hedge fund investments. Bush executives suggested that to stem the tide, banks should hold more money in reserve, but enacted no such legal regulations. So bad risks continued to be taken. Of course risk is the lifeblood of Wall Street capitalist "enterprise" and the burden of Main Street taxpayers. In spite of the first Bush 2008 bailout legislation for big republican banks, the system itself began to collapse, or that at least was the perception.

Most Wall Street and government elites believed that the big banks were too big to be allowed to fail or the entire economy would collapse. The majority was warned that they also would go down if the banks were not saved. So the privileged big corporations were saved and the common folks' jobs sacrificed as illustrated by, but not limited to, the automobile industry and its related contractors.

It was only when Obama took over and offered a second bailout and then a Stimulus bill, that we heard the republicans take on as their own for the first time the position that banks should be allowed to fail. After all, that was only consistent with classical conservative "free enterprise" theory. But, of course, it's a fiction, for the conservatives always look for the government for protection as well as tax breaks.

Obama's first steps were to appoint as his economic advisors, Summers and Geithner, who were chief operatives causing the creation of the crisis and to look to Bernanke and the elder Greenspan for continuing advice. Former Federal Reserve Chair, Paul Volcker, who retired in 1987, and Paul Krugman were ignored initially when they called for significant reform of bank commerce and trading. Independent analysts agreed that excessive commercial borrowing and sub prime mortgage market investment destroyed Stearns and Lehman trading banks. Volcker felt that if banks are too big to fail, the responsible thing to do was to ensure that they would not act in such a way as to require another bailout to avoid failure. His proposal became known as the Volcker Rule. Volcker opposed Reagan's massive deregulations of the 1980s, which were a main contributing factor of the 2008 recession. There were several warnings before the 2008 big crash. A major one was the 1999 Savings and Loan scandal in the Senior Bush Administration involving a Bush son of the then President and brother of George W. It resulted from the Garn-St. Germaine Law giving Savings and Loans power to make commercial loans. It cost the main street taxpayers $180 billion. Financiers were motivated by the prospect of short-term gains. For years Volcker had warned, "financiers motivated by the prospect of short term gains – traders, investment bankers, quantitative analysts, hedge fund and private equity managers – have been exacting outsized monetary rewards." That helped in 2007 to begin to bring down the entire economy.

The Bush unregulated approach to bailing out firms gave them new huge profits by laying off employees and paying big bonuses - $16 billion for Sachs executives. Unemployment, never a concern for the Hayek-Friedman conservative school of economics, rose and the public became furious. Jobs were gone. The Obama White House, on January 21, 2010 invited Volcker back. A year after Obama essentially copycatted Bush's bailout solution, which again proved inadequate for the job, a stimulus program was added that made modest improvements. Together they publicly urged Congress to enact simple and common sense reform which included "the Volcker Rule." (To republicans it was as threatening as single-payer and "public option" were in the Health Bill program.) As the Obama administration and the democratic congressional majority began serious moves toward financial reform, the lobbyists were on the path to causing its defeat, the same people and their political cronies such as Senator McConnell, Republican Minority Leader, who fought healthcare reform.

The Volcker Rule was defined as "barring banks from speculating in the markets" i.e. the end to proprietary trading and operating and investing in hedge and private equity funds. Volker believed that if effectively enforced it would separate commercial and investment banks, which would go a long way toward removing the cause of a "too big to fail" crises in the future and create stable reform.

The democratic Dodd-Frank Bill was offered as a comprehensive solution and included a robust Volcker Rule. But quickly it was compromised due to the perceived need for republican votes. That meant pleasing their big financial firms and lobbyists. The perpetual rub! The democratic Merkley-Levin amendment was offered, designed to preserve the "essence" of the Volcker Rule. It would have removed vague language for more explicit terminology. However, it allowed banks to invest three percent of capital in hedge and private equity funds. But it contained specific restrictions on the three percent such as a specific investment dollar limit. But then Dodd and Frank agreed to drop that as well. This was followed by more republican "watering down" demands, which were accepted, increasing the three percent to forty! An amendment by Senator Lincoln would have forced big banks to move derivative trading to subsidiaries, creating some needed separation. But Volcker thought the Merkley Amendment was enough. Then, by clever parliamentary maneuvering, the republicans dropped an amendment of theirs to which the Merkley amendment was attached, thus removing it from consideration. Brown and Kaufman wanted size limits, the essence of the problem, which would force big banks to split up and thus directly deal with "too big to fail" – a crucial approach. It was soundly defeated by both democratic and republican votes and Volcker's approval. Nevertheless a weakened version of the Volcker Rule passed. The "remains" of the original bill has been described as the most far-reaching finance reform law since the 1930s. Why?

To answer, it was because there were provisions to: 1) establish a new, not the first, Federal Consumers Bureau (which I introduced for state legislation as a Virginia Legislator in 1966), this time to protect against predatory financial companies, 2) force derivatives trading into the open exchanges, 3) give the federal government power to seize control of stricken non-bank financial institutions such as Bear Stearns, Lehman and A.I.G., and 4) ban most proprietary trading practices.

Volcker's assessment was that the law "provides a constructive legal groundwork for reform but we could have done better." At the outset three areas needed reform: 1) reducing "leverage," i.e. for every dollar of capital investment, 20 or 30 should go into markets, 2) raising cash amounts banks would be required to hold in order to survive sudden losses, and 3) breaking up financial firms so they are never too big to fail. The Dodd law contains elements of the first two but not the third. It orders firms to hold more capital for derivatives and other risky trading but doesn't provide for enforcement. If there is another recession, businesses will be taken over but the law doesn't rule out bailouts

The Obama Administration was willing to agree to many republican and "moderate" democrat concessions for Wall Street. Volcker was happy with bans on proprietary trading and some safeguards on hedge and private equity funds, forcing big banks to reform. The crack down on derivative trading and a new Federal Reserve Vice Chair, specifically accountable for financial regulation, were gains.

If the stricter version of the Volcker Rule contained in the Merkley Amendment had passed, Sachs and Stanley would have been forced to give up their banking licenses in order to protect their trading operations and a stricter dividing line between banking and trading activities based on who is or isn't government protected would exist. Notice for the future and fair warning would be in place. The weaker version allowed banks to retain to some degree, their current operations of proprietary trading and hedge fund sponsorship. J.P. Morgan and other big commercial banks would hold on to both commercial and trading operations but in a smaller regulated version. None of this would go into effect for two more years and during that time firms would try to skirt around the rules by a process of their own redefining.

The law should have required the banks to hold on to a greater amount of capital in perpetuity. It did not reform the following practices which led to the crisis: 1) extravagant Wall Street compensation practices, 2) misleading accounting practices, 3) incompetent credit rating, and 4) "too big to fail" bailouts. The law was essentially a Band-Aid approach. Given the perpetuation of essential flaws in the capitalist structure and governmental processes more cannot be expected. The day when the 99 percent are equal to the privileged one percent is still far away. This unjust and undemocratic system could collapse again. However, the solution to the crisis, the Reform Act, was better than none, but just barely. Making our economic system a democratic and not a plutocratic one was never contemplated. It most likely will not be until social sharing is considered morally valuable and self-interested wealth accumulation not so, in our predominately "Christian" nation.[7] Recently four banks

---

[7] My 2010 analysis ended here. It was inspired by an article by John Cassidy in the July 26, 2010 *New Yorker* magazine, and was published in

pleaded guilty to market rigging and agreed to pay over five billion dollars in penalties. Federal prosecutors also extracted an admission of criminal wrongdoing. The Justice Department has been criticized for its reluctance to take on financial misconduct. In the past year prosecutors have brought criminal cases against banks accused of tax evasion and sanctions violations and their roll in the 2008 financial meltdown. They will all continue to do business as usual.[8]

This apparently has made no impression on business interests represented by the Republican Party since they have introduced a bill to further water down Dodd-Frank, now that the voters have given them control of the U.S. Senate as well as the House of Representatives. In November 2014, the American voters put back into power the party that has consistently supported and passed legislation that creates such recessions. This new republican bill would exempt banks from the type of oversight the democratically passed Dodd-Frank bill envisioned. Democratic Senator Sharrod Brown, the top democrat on the Senate Banking Committee, now controlled by the republicans, called the bill: "A sprawling wish list of Dodd-Frank roll backs." Dodd-Frank was never very strong in the first place.[9]

---

the Colorado Springs *Active for Justice* news magazine of August 2010 under the title "The 2008 Economic Crisis and the 2010 Financial Reform Law: An In-a-Nutshell Summary." A Senate bill to put the guts back into the Dodd-Frank law was introduced by democrats in March 2015. See Taylor, Andrew, "Senate Bill Would Re-do Dodd-Frank, *Denver Post,* March 13, 2015.

[8] Sweet, Ken, and Tucker, Eric, "Four Banks Plead Guilty to Market Rigging, $5B," *Denver Post,* May 2, 2015.

[9] Taylor, Andrew, "Senate Bill Would Redo Dodd-Frank," *Denver Post,* March 3, 2015. Our founding fathers had something to say about banks

The American Corporation

As may be evident by now, one of the basic flaws in our economic system is the American corporation. Corporations were opposed by our founding fathers, especially Madison, in the early 1800s. Recently, I wrote a paper analyzing the dichotomy between corporate self-interested principles and religious altruism in American denominations such as the Religious Society of Friends (Quakers) of which I am a member.[10] This dichotomy could (and perhaps should) give serious pause to church organizations.

Over half a century ago a French immigrant who devoted his life to helping those who were harmed by our corporate structures and whose religious calling was to the Sermon on the Mount (Matt. 5-7) had this to say:

> Modern society has made the bank account the standard of values.

---

and corporations. John Adams: "Banks have done more injury to the religion, morality, tranquility, prosperity and even the wealth of the nation, than they can have done or ever will do, good." Thomas Jefferson said: "The end of democracy and the defeat of the American Revolution will occur when government falls into the hands of lending institutions and moneyed corporations." And he added: "I hope we will crush in its birth the aristocracy of moneyed corporations ... the selfish spirit of commerce that knows no country and feels no passion but that of gain."

[10] Durland, William, "Of Quakers and Corporations: Are Governmental Privileges and Duties in Harmony With Quaker Testimonies and Values?" May 2014. (Presented to the Pendle Hill Quaker Study and Retreat Center, Wallingford, PA.) President Madison's veto of a congressional attempt to incorporate a religious institution in 1811 is discussed. The powers invested in American corporations, both for profit and non-profit are an invitation to practice such indulgences as cause recessions without consequence to them and as we see the 2008 recession illustrated.

When the bank account becomes the standard of values the banker has the power.

When the banker has the power the technician has to supervise the making of profits.

When the banker has the power the politician has to assure law and order in the profit-making system.

When the banker has the power the educator trains students in the technique of profit making.

When the banker has the power the clergyman is expected to bless the profit-making system or to join the unemployed.

When the banker has the power the Sermon on the Mount is declared unpractical.

When the banker has the power we have an acquisitive, not a functional society.[11]

Infrastructure Derailed

Much has been in the news on the disintegration of our national infrastructure. One of the reasons, some have said, is because of the failure of the republican Congress to authorize budgeting expenditures to make us safe. Just the

---

[11] Maurin, Peter, "When Bankers Rule," *Easy Essays,* (New York) Catholic Worker Reprint, May 1, 2010; Peter Maurin and Dorothy Day founded the Catholic Worker Movement in the early 1930s, and its houses of hospitality, for the poor and homeless. Catholic Worker houses still exist today and carry on "round table discussions" on current subjects, originally created and organized by Peter Maurin. My wife and I participated in the Catholic Worker Movement from 1975 to 1993.

opposite has taken place in recent years, where government shutdowns, defaults, by republicans, and the like have enhanced the problems. For example, Amtrak has not been adequately funded for decades, in general because the rich class fly and the poorer class take the train or the bus. Those who are either on a voluntary or involuntary small income along with disabled and overweight people are found there. My wife and I, over the past decade, have chosen domestic travel by coach train across the country. It is pleasant and civilized (while domestic air travel becomes more tedious and uncivilized) and deserves better treatment by our elected officials. It is an integral part of our infrastructure. Recently, derailments have occurred due to failure to install new technologies that have not been adequately budgeted, a national embarrassment. Amtrak has fallen $21 billion behind what it has needed during that time, with the money going elsewhere. John Nichols, in an article entitled "Our Derailed Infrastructure," gives a detailed report on this and other examples of slashes in infrastructure budgets.

U.S. transportation funding, including highway bridges, has fallen even behind third world countries. The *New York Times* reported, on May 13, 2015, that, "spending on transportation infrastructure in the U.S. sunk to 1.7 percent of our gross domestic product in 2014, a 20-year law." And finally infrastructure studies show that our aquifers are in danger. This will serve as a transition, as we move now from economics to the environment. Infrastructure is a necessary link of the two.[12]

---

[12] Nichols, John, "Our Derailed Infrastructure," *The Nation,* June 8, 2015, p. 3; "Studies Show Aquifers in Danger," *Denver Post,* June 17,

Conservation and the Environment

The Christian Bible, by appending the Hebrew Bible to it, includes the declaration of the God Yahweh stating clearly, "the earth is mine."[13] Fundamentalist Christians claim to worship this God more devoutly than anyone else, but when it comes to the protection of the earth, its environment and its resources and the freedom of its people to voluntarily migrate, as did Abraham, they don't seem to have heard.

The activist movement called "environmentalism," at least as far as that word came into common usage, began in the 60s, when so many other such new things originated. The same state senator friend who recommended me for the County Planning and Zoning Commission, when running for re-election in 1963 made air pollution an issue to be addressed. A friend of mine who was on his campaign committee with me, brought the subject up, perhaps for the first time in Virginia politics. Even so the word "environment" had not replaced what was previously known as conservation, but only added other things to it. President Teddy Roosevelt was associated with it and the word was still in use when I founded the Conservation Committee for Mason Neck in the spring of 1965. By then I certainly was familiar with the preservation of so-called "open space," for that idea signified that not all taxable, viable land should be

2015, the studies were conducted at the University of California, Irvine, at its Jet-Propulsion Laboratory.

[13] "Indeed, the whole earth is mine," Exodus 19:5, *The New Revised Standard Version* of the Bible, London (Harper-Collins: 1993)

transformed from forest to high-rises just to increase the tax base.

In my first campaign to be elected a member of the Virginia Legislature, my attention was directed to an area less than 15 miles from the nation's capital on the Potomac River called Mason Neck. I lived fairly close to this peninsula, which was named after George Mason. He lived in the 1700s and became the first representative to the Virginia Legislature from the area where I was now living. George Washington also held that seat from his home in Mt. Vernon only a few miles north. Five thousand acres were threatened by developers to be changed from a wildlife area for American eagles, egrets, herons and other beautiful animals into a rich private estate for well-to-do Virginians. I had experience already in forming citizens' committees out of nothing. First it was the Greater Springfield Civic Association, then the first Gun Control committee and following that the Virginia Citizens' Consumer Council. It was amazing, in those days, what ten people and a title could accomplish rather than ten individuals going at it alone.

It took over three years to save Mason Neck for a national, state and local wildlife refuge and park. My location where only 100 miles separated the state capitol, the national capitol and my local government, afforded the opportunity for me, as the spokesperson to bring together all three necessary entities to create this environmental blessing in place of a rich subdivision, a deep sea port or a southern Disneyland, all of which were being pushed by developers.[14]

---

[14] Durland, William, *The Battle to Save Mason Neck,* Raton, New Mexico (Markus Printing: 1999)

153

As I ran my first campaign, making Mason Neck an issue, another candidate, mocking the effort said, "y'know Bill, bears can't vote," a silly remark but one which I've always remembered as a perfect illustration of how people value commerce and profits over preservation of nature.

Apparently there was another misplaced reaction to what we had done, but it all worked out well in the end. In Virginia, the words "conservatism" or "conservative" were sometimes confused with conservation. I was never able to know whether that was the case when the Mount Vernon Daughters of the American Revolution chose me for their annual speaker and "conservationist of the year" in 1966. One thing was certain they were southern conservatives. It was not until the late 60s when citizens' committees began using the new designation - environmental committees - for these worthy endeavors. I was one of the first state board members of the Virginia Committee for the Environment.

Global Warming and Climate Change

In 1998, the most current issue of the environment raised its ugly head – global warming – we were warned by respected international scientists that we had ten years to change this trend or it would then become irreversible. The environment should never have become a threat to practical economics. The two can complement each other. Nevertheless, to take a strong environmental position to reverse global warming, or as it is now more commonly called, climate change, requires that maximizing profits, economically, must give a little bit to protect the earth and its humans from serious harm. In the long run, global warming can be economically devastating.

However, two Bush presidents acted as if the issue doesn't exist and two democratic presidents have not given much more than lip service to this emergency. It took more than ten years for the scientific community to uniformly declare the empirical reality of the danger and emerging evidence of its presence in our oceans and arctic areas. Conservatives continue to profess the belief that CO2 levels, created by humans, have nothing to do with global warming, if they admit such a change at all. It is rather seen as God's will and will pass, or be of no concern when the end times come, which is always just around the corner. Fortunately a small body of conservative Christians recently began to see that if the earth is God's, it needs to be preserved and not demeaned and over-exploited.

In the 1960s, when the issue of air or water pollution was first raised, it was denied to exist and then when admitted was justified as business waste necessary for profit making. The waste, however, was toxic and lives were lost. So some economists, who had taken up the philosophical idea of positivism tried to convince us that air and water pollution could have no moral value since economics, as a discipline, was moral value free. There are poorer third world nations already injured by colonization of western elites and are now recognizing that climate, jobs and justice are interdependent.

A group called "The Labor Network for Sustainability" is rallying unions and labor behind climate change. A ten-point platform of unions in New York under the title "Climate Works for All: A Platform for Reducing

Emissions, Protecting our Community and Creating Good Jobs for New Yorkers" worked on reducing emissions and creating energy efficient entities by installing solar collectors in schools and other public centers. In California, a project entitled "Movement Generation, Justice and Ecology Project" attacked fracking and promoted the state's "Global Solutions Project" and a new law requiring that 25 percent of the state's cap and trade program be spent to benefit low income, high unemployment, heavily polluted communities. In Connecticut climate and labor activists formed "The Round Table on Climate and Jobs."[15]

President Obama, in his final years in office, with no more elections to worry about, stepped up his vocal calls for global warming mitigation in the face of rising sea levels. It was only a few years ago, at the Copenhagen Conference on this subject that the U.S. was anything but a leader. Although voters and scientists have called for action, our representatives composed primarily of the same combination of confederate, corporate, military and Christian conservatives have failed us. The Copenhagen Conference of 2009 declined to commit the U.S. to a binding target for reduction of emissions.

In 2014, the National Audubon Society, an organization no longer known for progress, issued a press release declaring climate change "the greatest threat to

---

[15] Brecher, Jeremy, "How Climate Protection Has Become Labor's Solidarity," *The Nation,* May 25, 2015, pp. 17-18; Brecher is co-founder of the Labor Network for Sustainability and author of *Climate Insurgency: a Strategy for Survival.*

American birds" and warning that "nearly half" of North American bird species are at risk of losing their habitats by 2080. It is we who will do it to them. We are deforesting the planet and poisoning the oceans. Human beings are the "universal killers of the natural world."[16] That sounds like a sin. Middle class urban citizens have found pollution to be their leading concern. The ten-year limit I mentioned earlier has been extended once and now we are in simply another extension. We are thwarted from rising, as a united community against global warming because of the opposition of the same coalition. Sixty percent of Americans polled believe climate change is harmful. The earth is our parent, says Jonathan Franzen, with terminal cancer. It is time to cure it.[17] Meanwhile, conservatives call for "freedom for fracking."

Most recently, Obama announced the Federal Clean Power Plan proposed by the EPA, which calls for a 32 percent reduction of carbon pollution caused by CO2 emissions by 2030. Its effect will save the average family 85 dollars a year and prevent up to 3600 premature deaths and 1700 non-fatal heart attacks, and 90,000 child asthma attacks. The White House estimates it will create tens of thousands of jobs. Republicans immediately opposed it.[18]

---

[16] Franzen, Jonathan, "Carbon Capture," *The New Yorker,* April 6, 2015, pp. 56-65, at p. 56.

[17] *Ibid*, p. 60. Franzen writes "a good democracy, after all, acts in the interest of its citizens, and it's precisely the major carbon-emitting democracies who benefit from cheap gasoline and global trade while the main costs of our polluting are born by those who have no vote poisoning countries, future generations, then species."

[18] Anleu, Billie, Stanton, "Clean Power Plan to Affect Utilities," *Colorado Springs Gazette,* August 4, 2015, pp. 1-6.

My wife and I have lived for 35 years in view of the Colorado Springs' Martin Drake coal-fired Power Plant, emitting visible clouds of nitrogen oxides.

Immigration and Indigenous Peoples

There is a poster published by the American Friends Service Committee that says, "No Human Being is Illegal." It is a reference to immigration restrictions on the right of human beings to migrate. There is no doubt, because of the manner in which nation states have been created, that they may claim a legal right to govern immigration into their countries. When nation states, for whatever reason, become threatened from the outside their concerns for security tighten up on the number and origins of people who can legally immigrate. These would be legitimate steps except for the fact that it is well known that nation states discriminate on what otherwise might be legitimate reasons to prevent the coming of certain ethnic groups. When this is taken in its context and a nation state has, in other ways, harmed such peoples through other foreign policy considerations or colonial domination, movements arise to justify the laws that regulate such migrations.

In the United States, for decades, people have crossed our borders without documents believing that because American laws claim to welcome those whose lives are threatened in their own country, they would be considered welcome in our own. Nevertheless they were imprisoned in camps on our borders. As an attorney, I visited such places in the 80s. After illegal American activities in Guatemala and

El Salvador forced refugees to seek sanctuary in the United States, several of us, locally, joined the Sanctuary Movement and became the 12th announced church opening its doors to such victimized people. More recently, a new sanctuary movement has taken form. We have been inspired by language written years ago, appearing on the Statue of Liberty, advocating migration here. It was from the poem written by Emma Lazarus: "Give me your tired, your poor, your huddled masses yearning to breathe free, the wretched refuse of their teeming shores, send these, the homeless, tempest tossed, to me, I lift my lamp beside the golden door."[19]

In the Obama administration, we've had two messages going forth. One has been to tighten the borders. The Obama administration has deported more undocumented refugees, many of who have children who are American citizens, than ever before. Innocent children, must stay here without parents because they are citizens, or leave their country of citizenship with their parents. At the same time his administration and democratic senators have supported what's called The Dream Act, is an attempt to provide a way for children, brought here as infants or very young innocent

---

[19] See Lo, Puck, "Inside the New Sanctuary Movement," *The Nation*, May 25, 2015, pp. 20-24. An article written by J. Adrian Stanley in the *Colorado Springs Independent* describes how Hispanic veterans who served their country years ago, at this writing, are under deportation orders to be sent back to their "teeming shores" of Mexico as undocumented. They have never been offered citizenship as a result of their military service, which others have received. August 19-25, 2015, pp. 17-24.

children, to stay in the only country they have ever known, many of whom cannot even speak their native language.[20]

My wife and I, for the better part of the last 15 years, have been members of a Quaker group working to humanize immigration laws and practices in the "four corners" states – Colorado, Arizona, New Mexico and Utah. My legal practice in the same period helped many Hispanic individuals, some to gain citizenship and others to avoid deportation. We also witnessed to the need for reform as we highlighted the number of deaths of those crossing the border in what is known as The Migrant Trail Walk through the desert from Sasabe, Mexico to Tucson, Arizona. The republican opposition claims to be truly Christian, but apparently they have yet to incorporate Jesus' examples of universalism when he asked, "who is your neighbor?" and gave his own answer that neighbors include not only your friends but strangers and even your enemies.

Obama finally took the conscientious and necessary step with an Executive Order in 2015 staying present and future deportations in order to grant the opportunity of earning citizenship. But the political opposition effectively brought a case to court, which resulted in staying that Order pending a Supreme Court decision on its merits. Citizens

---

[20] See for a specific chronology of current events, Toobin, Jeffrey, "American Limbo: While Politicians Block Reform, What is Happening to Immigrant Families?" *The New Yorker,* July 27, 2005, pp. 30-35; In August 2015 leading presidential candidate, Donald Trump, said if he were elected he, all by himself, would deport the children with their parents. Most republican candidates are absolutely in favor of protecting "innocent fetuses" but once they are born, they have no qualms about deporting "innocent children."

polled have favored Obama's actions and these new steps towards reform and a more neighborly relationship with those suffering under untenable economic and political conditions. Republican presidential candidates have stated their support for lowering the number of people south of the border who may become eligible to legally come to this country, a country originating on the backs of immigrants from Europe. Certainly, insecurity over consequences of Middle Eastern aggression plays a part.

Several national organizations have taken up the call for immigration reform. It certainly seems to be favored by Americans who want their representatives to follow that call. The Interstate Immigration Coalition listed the root causes of immigration and called for Congress to recognize and address this problem by implementing values in relation to our neighbors that will help: 1) to reduce the need for people to leave their homes, 2) invest in sustainable development in immigrant-sending countries, 3) reshape international financial institutions' policies and practices, and 4) link policies to address root causes to any immigration reform bill. Causes identified by this organization are poverty, food insecurity, violent conflict, militarization, persecution, environmental destruction, political insecurity of their home country, inequality, lack of opportunity and loss of hope for a better future. Members of this coalition include The American Friends Service Committee, the American Jewish Committee and several more. We've also become familiar with the recent statements of Pope Francis I of the Catholic Church, both on climate change and immigration.[21] In spite

---

[21] Kirchgaessner, Stephanie, "Pope Speaks Out on Climate Change," *Guardian Weekly*, June 26, 2015, p. 6; The U.S. Conference of Catholic

of polls demonstrating American majority support for the resolution of this problem and such stalwart organizations working so hard for that to happen, in November 2014 American citizens, at least 37 percent of them who voted in the off-year election, took power away from the political party that supports their views and gave it to the one party that clearly obstructs them. In the context of this study, a most perplexing question is why such a thing would happen. One good reason for such an interdisciplinary rather than a specialized study as this book is, is that it more easily clarifies why such a thing is possible.

Chapter Three of this book has already discussed the dismantling of American representative government. These are the issues that government is supposed to resolve as representatives of the people. But when the people who vote are not even vigilant, naturally the popular will cannot be the result, but rather the wishes of the power brokers in control.

When taking in all the foregoing, it may seem that we as a people are a bit hypocritical when we remember that our first ancestors were European immigrants from Spain, France, Germany and England and that, although we were welcomed here by indigenous people, we treated them abusively. Our almost religious call to "manifest destiny"

Bishops released a report and policy recommendations in which they urged Congress and the administration "to build a system that affords due process protections, honors human dignity, and minimizes the use of detentions. It is time for our nation to reform this inhumane system ..." "Vulnerable Migrant Groups Should Not be Detained," Houston Catholic Worker, June-August 2015, p. 3; The American Friends Service Committee and the Friends Committee on National Legislation both of which have made it a priority to bring justice and mercy to an understanding of the wrongs taking place.

seemed to require us to "civilize" the "savages" and relegate them to reservations after taking possession of their land.

In the fall of 2014, my wife and I were fortunate to attend a commemoration of the massacre of Cheyenne and Arapahoe at Sand Creek, Colorado on November 29, 1864. Our Governor on that occasion took the opportunity to formally apologize for the violence used against these First Nations peoples. We, as a people, could also improve our relationship with those whose country we violently occupied and now wish to hold secure from immigrants who would migrate here as well. When we take time to reflect over the manner we have treated and occupied this earth, it's hard to argue that we haven't, as dominant people, been as neighborly toward the more vulnerable as we should have been. It's unfortunate that I could say to myself and my wife that "this world is not for everybody: its for some bodies." A Colorado newspaper headline says that the Sand Creek deaths were inexcusable. Today, our border deaths are also inexcusable. Our treatment of the earth, which is not ours to own but only possess has also been inexcusable.[22]

---

[22] "Sand Creek Deaths are Inexcusable," *Denver Post*, December 4, 2014, p. 3A. That statement was made by our present Governor in Colorado, John Hickenlooper, to tribal members gathered at Sand Creek on this 150th anniversary of the massacre.

CHAPTER SEVEN

RELIGION, SCIENCE, SEX AND SANITY

"FOR BETWEEN TRUE SCIENCE AND IGNORANT BELIEFS, TRUE SCIENCE IS IN THE MIDDLE." THOMAS HOBBES, *THE LEVIATHAN* 1651

Religion

The subject of religion has crept into many of the discussions in earlier chapters. Now I want to expand on that with particular examples of how a preferred religion finds a place to exercise its beliefs and practices in a secular nation. Let's take a look at religion, science and sex and see how these particular fields influence each other and government.

In America, from its birth, influences of fundamentalist Christianity have played a huge part as pilgrims and Puritans arrived here to escape the strictures of an established (national) religion. These colonists came with grandiose ideas of a new Jerusalem replacing or enslaving an indigenous people. This concept eventually came to be known as "civil religion." Here was a group looking for a sanctuary in which kings, emperors, bishops, lords and nobles would no longer possess absolute and particular religious, economic and political dominance over its common folk. Would a great wall of separation emerge, protecting both the church and state from each other and providing fairness? These questions, or ones similar to them, have been pondered for a long time.

Civil religion is defined as patriotism grounded in the spiritual symbols primarily of Exodus and the idea of manifest destiny, to be discussed in depth later. In my opinion, ever since the Reagan era, we have been moving from that position to a more comprehensive, religiously dominated "secular theocracy." A secular theocracy is an enlargement of civil religion, viz. a movement hell-bent on incorporating specific laws and doctrines from religious origins into the fundamental secular operations of the nation. In this case those laws and doctrines arise from the Torah of the Hebrew Scriptures made part of the Christian Bible.[1]

In my own state of Colorado, in the spring of 2015, we experienced yet another example of this thrust to replace representative constitutional democracy with another spoke in the wheel of secular theocracy. In this case the target was public education. A federal lawsuit was filed over religious activities at the Florence Colorado High School concerning the 1st Amendment's meaning of the free exercise of religion and the establishment of one religion over others. A former teacher, Robert Basevitz, in his suit, claimed that the school and district officials permitted a fundamentalist, far-right version of Christianity to have a dominant presence there. It caused me to remember that when I was in junior high school, my Catholic Church held its Sunday school on Wednesday afternoons after school. I never could figure that one out, but I never questioned what happened next. Instead

---

[1] Secular and theocratic are direct opposites. Yet there are nations, other than our own that have been practicing this combination successfully for decades. Israel claimed to be a "Jewish state," and a politically "democratic" one in its Declaration of Independence in 1948. America has never made the claim in its Constitution that it is a Christian state and a democratic one at the same time.

of my having to go to the church on Wednesday afternoon, the church received permission from my public school to hold "Sunday school" on Wednesday afternoon in the public school rather than the church, where Catholic dogma and doctrine could be taught to its public school Catholic kids. It didn't last long, for whatever reason, I don't know. Jefferson's post-constitutional interpretation of the 1st Amendment that a great wall of separation should exist between the public and the parochial has been the traditional stance in America until the latter half of the 20th century.

In the case of the Florence school the issue was prayer circles organized at the school to precede the beginning of classes, religious-themed pizza parties during school time and all-school assemblies featuring the Gospel of St. Matthew for the entire school population in addition to normal academic teaching. An organization called "the Cowboy Church at the Crossroads" coordinated these goings-on. Members of the school staff were direct participants. The principal of the school was one of those listed as a contact on a flyer publicizing the prayer circle at school. Voluntary student gatherings and prayers, the distribution of religious literature, and extra-curricular religious groups with access to school facilities were taking place daily.

Churches had been previously allowed to rent school facilities for a Sunday session only. That's okay. What isn't permissible under Supreme Court rulings are administrators, teachers and staff, i.e. the school's public employees, personally soliciting and encouraging religious activities of a particular denomination or faith and with student membership distributing religious materials. At the all-school public assembly, students dropped to their knees and prayed. Basevitz, who is Jewish, felt ostracized and was offended when such activities took place.[2] The 2016 presidential election includes numerous fundamentalist Christian candidates, such as Huckabee, Santorum and Cruz, who seem to believe that such a twist on public education is right for America.

Tolerance of all religions or of no religion in a multi-religious and non-religious nation is a requirement of our representative, constitutional government. It is done equally to protect and free both church and state from each other. The reason why religion is an issue to be highlighted here is just because this, more than ever has become prevalent, perhaps partly in response to fear of Islamic extremism and terrorist activities.

Recent Supreme Court decisions have taken a trend towards politicizing, the effect being that it has lowered the barrier protecting church and state from each other. In 2014 corporate personhood took another giant step forward in *Burwell v. Hobby Lobby Stores, Inc.* where our corporate non-human counterparts are now deemed to have a religious conscience without the benefit of physical or spiritual bodies or minds. The manipulation here by five majority Catholics of the Court was to prevent Hobby Lobby's human employees from exercising their own constitutional rights of

---

[2] "High School Broke Rules on Religion," *Denver Post* editorial, May 28, 2015. Abraham Lincoln in his Gettysburg Address said that this was "one nation under God" but he did not say it was "one nation of God." He was not a disciple of organized religion, much less of any established religion but was generally religious.

conscience as they may differ from far-right Protestants and pre-Vatican II Catholics. Employees were denied a free choice to use contraceptives under the Obama healthcare plan. Many years ago there were those who attempted to prevent married couples from purchasing contraceptives that they sought to use in their own private homes. Conservatives, then, tried to interfere with that right, but were unsuccessful in *Griswold v. Connecticut*, (1965).

McCullen v. Coakley, also in 2014, allows only far-right Christian - "right to lifers" - a right to be free from restrictive barriers, freeing them to confront strangers with words and leaflets. Such restrictions remain in place for those of us who witness on issues of war and peace. We have gone to jail instead. These cases illustrate how corporate and non-human rights are replacing the right of human beings to keep their constitutionally guaranteed place in American representative society.

What is civil religion all about?[3] The phrase was coined to indicate that there are set traditional policies and beliefs that bear a resemblance to religious ritual and

---

[3] The term "civil religion" was created by Jean-Jacques Rousseu in *The Social Contract* (1762) to identify that part of the emerging democratic nation-state from which its moral and spiritual principles emerge. It is not as over-reaching as an establishment of religion or a preference for a religious faction under the "free exercise of religion" clause. That is where the line is drawn and "secular theocracy" picks up. I wrote about each under "civil religion" and "secular religion" *God or Nations* at pp. 167-173. See also Bellah, Robert, and Langhlin, William, *Religion in America,* New York, (Houghton-Mifflin Co.: 1980) pp 5-6, 14-20; Kruse, Kevin, *One Nation Under God: How Corporate America Invented Christian America,* New York, (Basic Books: 2015).

ceremony but in a secular context. National patriotism is colored by religious belief. We are raised, from a very early age, to take a strong position in favor of our national heroes. One of our rituals is the Pledge of Allegiance. I was between the ages of ten and fourteen in junior high school when World War II was going on. On a weekly basis we would have our school assembly in the auditorium, which would begin with the Boy Scouts bringing in the flag and our saluting and taking the Pledge of Allegiance. My girl friend at the time was seated just in front of me. When it came time to take the pledge, she did not do so. I can't express how odd that seemed to me, raised as I was in the civil religion that is part of the culture of American life. Was she a communist? A Nazi? It turned out not so. She was a Jehovah's Witness, a Christian sect that believes its members should not only be pacifists (at least till the end times) but that it was idolatrous to salute or pledge allegiance to a piece of cloth. This was her right. That's what the 1st Amendment and Jefferson's great wall were all about, not much known to me at the time.

Another thing took place in my high school that went by unnoticed and did not seem at all out of the ordinary to me. At Christmas we would all gather in the auditorium and go through the same patriotic process and then the Superintendent of Schools would read to us from the Christian Bible book of Luke about the birth of Jesus. The school would be decorated with Christmas ornaments and symbols, a crèche, a Christmas tree, wreaths and so forth. That seemed perfectly normal to me. I was a Christian, the same symbols were in my home, my church, why not my school? I learned why not from my best friend, Henry Shuldener, when he stayed at my house overnight. As we made small talk in bed after the lights were out, somehow we got on to the subject of these public declarations of Christianity at school. He was Jewish, as were some others of my closest friends. So I learned from him what it felt like to be an American citizen who is not a Christian but a student at the same school. Fifteen percent of the students at Scarsdale High School at that time were Jewish. Their rights were being infringed in the name of what I later came to know as civil religion. There were other times of the year when similar events took place.

It could not be said that civil religion progressed to the extent, at that time, of what I have earlier described as a "secular theology." That is much more serious. There have been calls for the Supreme Court of the United States to apply laws taken from the Hebrew Torah as it is formulated in the Christian Bible's "Old Testament" to interpret the Constitution. This has not been a call from Jews but from far-right Christians. The Hebrew Scriptures, more than the Christian Scriptures, seem to attract such people, apparently because this is where they find the justification for their priorities of "God, guns and country." The violent nation and the violent god come together and justify each other. For some time the 10 Commandments of the Hebrew Scriptures, in more simplified form, have been placed in public, political locations. In some of the parts omitted, one could read that slaves are permitted and wives are property, but those parts were taken out. There are many more examples that have emerged from conservative Christian representatives presently in Congress, seemingly bent on turning America into a theocracy. One good example is Huckabee's declaration, while visiting Jerusalem, that Palestine belongs to Israel.

The American nation was founded in direct opposition to its parent, Great Britain, and its unity of religion, economics and politics all bound together in the monarchy, with a king at the head of an established church. We would do well to remember that we declared our independence from monarchial control of religion as dangerous in its implications, emerging from the economic or political world of the past.[4]

Science

Science is another area where we are threatened with the degradation of established truth and facts. Issues such as global warming, evolution, stem cell research and use, vaccinations, and homosexuality find divergent views of their truth depending upon how influential religious beliefs effect scientific understanding. When critical thinking, logic and scientific processes are used, rather than what some call "blind faith" a more exact understanding comes about as a more open mind is applied. Where religious statements are accepted on authority only, without studious investigation, the conclusions may be *prima facie* believable, but when centuries have passed and intelligence evolved and new information is available, would it not seem implausible to

---

[4] See also Stewart, Katherine, "Church and School: A Christian Movement Seeks to Plant a Place of Worship in Every Public School," *The Nation,* February 2, 2015, pp. 17-22. An excellent book offering more positive Christian alternatives is Dr. Linda Seger's *Jesus Rode a Donkey,* revised 2nd ed. North Hollywood, CA (Havenbooks: 2014).

cling to original views based on faith when scientific reality runs overwhelmingly counter? For example, some of the same political and economic conservatives who are also religiously conservative retain literal biblical views about how old the earth and the human species are, and where we came from. Such believers claim that our species was created, just as we are today, only some 5,000 years ago and lived at the same time as the dinosaurs, when empirical, scientific evidence discovered in the earth proves that to be absolutely false.

It is natural for human beings to try to reconcile new information with sincerely held foundational spiritual beliefs and practices. Christians, Jews and Muslims all may try to equate newly available historical and scientific information with what was written thousands of years ago. When others claim it doesn't, the natural reaction is that science and other disciplines, that supply such information and conclusions, are simply temptations to apostasy. In the case of those who have extreme views in this regard, whether Christian, Jewish or Muslim, it becomes a religious duty to deny the truth of such facts, and use extreme measures to eliminate the apostate or the "infidel."

Global warming has already been discussed but I will use it as an example here to illustrate my point. The relevance of this is that the same people who have embraced a conservative, confederate, corporate and militaristic Christian identity are the ones who take anti-scientific positions when in power. They diminish the importance of science and logic in political and economic power in the name of religion. This, of course, acts to also diminish the existing sensitive balance of representative democracy and valid religious conscience by representing only one faction. For example, the republican leadership, in 2015, influenced by this faction, was reflected in House Speaker Boehner's words on global warming and carbon dioxide emissions. He said that the harm claimed by scientists and elected representatives is "almost comical." John Boehner resigned in October 2015.

Recently, a discussion was held at the University of Colorado entitled "Science Denied."[5] Four panelists and a moderator provided a packed room with an intellectual conversation on why some of our population has a hostile view towards scientific conclusions and method. Global warming was included in the discussion. Three of the four panelists were Christians. They were emphatic that as religious and scientific people they did not find it necessary to deny the scientific method in order to uphold their faith. My own experience has been that science complements and is of value to religion and not a hindrance. The Catholic Church has not been threatened by "evolution" as some Protestant "creationist scientists" have been. Much religious study in the past 100 years has utilized scientific methods that have proved extremely valuable in determining the context of the statements found in the Bible.

Certainly there are distinctive religious ways to understand some propositions presented in biblical texts that

---

[5] Annual World Affairs Conference, April 8, 2015. Participants – Dr. Tom Blumenthal, University of Colorado Medical School, Dr. Richard Alley, Penn State University, Chip Berlet, Investigative Journalist, Michelle Maller, Assistant Director, NASA, and Leonard Pitts, Jr., Miami Herald Journalist and Author.

run counter to "common sense." These are called revelations and may not come rationally to a religious person. One of the reasons is that if a biblical pronouncement runs counter to a political, economic or social worldview, then for those who are not religiously oriented, it seems untrue. For example, world relationships historically, from emperors to individuals' have been based on a principle enunciated in the Hebrew law and even before described by Moses as "an eye for an eye." But when Jesus came along, he took some of the Hebrew laws to task and declared that there was a higher spiritual path for humans to follow. In that case, he said, "of old it was said an eye for an eye, but I say unto you resist not the evil doer,"[6] and then he followed with examples of alternatives based on nonviolent activism. The secular world, and even most Christians, have found that pacifism and nonviolence, as a lifestyle, is beyond their spiritual or political capacity. After all, they reason, if you lay down your arms, your enemy will not. But most Christians have, as well, given up following Jesus, even though they claim to do so, and are more influenced by Old Testament violence and law (the Torah or the first five books of the Bible). In so doing a large segment of modern Christianity renounces Jesus, his teachings and life experiences.

I would criticize nothing about the stance of Christians who find a morality that is more spiritual and does not harm others that they must practice in their faith. It is not a more spiritually devoted activism, but a more materially devoted violence that we are concerned about. To deny

---

[6] The Gospel of Matthew, *New Revised Standard Version,* 5:38-48.

scientific discoveries on faith alone is dangerous both religiously and politically. The evidence overwhelmingly demonstrates that the world is under a great threat from the actions of human beings hasten global warming by increasing carbon emissions.

The Colorado University panel discussed the scientific truths, which have been denied by far-right fundamentalist and evangelical Christians and described their views as "false is true and true is false." They recognized that it is a dominant minority of a far-right Christian faction only that takes these positions, but further recognize that it is that group that possesses the type of power that can be extremely harmful to scientific discovery and acceptance of its truths.

During the panel discussion, Michelle Maller of NASA, presented evidentiary proof accumulated by NASA spacecrafts, of the drying up of aquifers on earth. It may be too late to reverse such situations that we have created. Richard Alley talked about the impact of global warming on big cities not designed for it. Chip Berlet provided the history behind the modern beliefs that humans have been here for only 5000 years and were created just as we are today. He presented evidence that people who take such views have, at the same time, stated that they see scientists as "agents of Satan" and that government's support of them is evil. The same group believes that only "rugged individualism" allows a Christian to have a direct relationship with God. So scientific organizations, or any kind of collective effort, such as unions or governments only stand in their way. The panel concluded that what they had to say was not new. The current level of global warming remains an immediate threat to civilization and is enlarging in the face of such denial by contrary religious views backed by political and economic power.

I should note that perhaps the majority of Christians don't share these views. The words we mentioned in Genesis about God giving human beings dominion over everything else have been interpreted to mean to do what you want with creation. The idea of stewardship of the earth came much later in Christian theology and drew support only by the 1960s. A poster published by the Episcopal church some years ago might be appropriate here. It says: "Jesus came to take away our sins, not our minds." It is no sin to think cognitively and critically and to apply it to all our human responsibilities. The new Catholic Pope, named after the great St. Francis of Assisi, certainly is an advocate of the gentle treatment of our environment, and has emphatically supported efforts to reverse global warming and for each of us in rich, developed nations to live a more simple life, taking care of the earth, not destroying it.

National Geographic magazine is not a bastion of radical liberalism. But it has also chimed in, commenting about the rise and popularization of people called to doubt reason.[7] I too, am urging a wake-up call for both church and state, in a democratic representative society, to apply the scientific evidence that proves that our planet is imperiled. Polls have shown that American voters believe this is so.

---

[7] Achenbach, Joel, "The Age of Disbelief," *National Geographic Magazine,* March 2015, pp 30-41.

This has not moved their republican conservative representatives to actively represent them on this matter.

NASA Space Exploration

We should not forget the national government programs that educate us scientifically, such as NASA space exploration. It has been in full swing in regard to the moon, Mars and exploring other planets in our solar system as far away as Pluto. Unfortunately, the space budget has been curtailed from five percent at the time of the moon landing in 1969 to 0.5 percent of the federal budget today. Presently, we must piggyback Russian space vessels to get to the International Space Station. For far-right factions of Christianity, space exploration is unnecessary when if one's spirituality is concentrated only on a heavenly reward after life, rather than spiritual activism in this life on earth. A similar example can be found in some Muslim thinking that rewards violence in the name of religion with martyrdom and paradise. Such thinking came to us first in the Hebrew Scriptures in the book of Genesis where "the tree of knowledge" was off-limits for the first humans by command of the gods (they were multiple) and who feared that humans, gaining too much intelligence, would replace them.[8]

Exploring space can't hurt if it turns up a better and more livable world. Space exploration basically enlarges our intellect and our humanity. We, as physical and spiritual beings are greatly enhanced by constantly increasing our

---

[8] Kochbert, Elizabeth, "Project Exodus," *The New Yorker,* June 1, 2015, pp. 76-78.

knowledge of the universe. It is God's creation and God surely does not expect or want us to remain in ignorance. Knowledge is freedom and gives us the tools with which to improve our world and ourselves.

Sex and Sanity

I've combined a few issues together under a buzzword – "sex" – here, and attached a calling for us to exhibit some sanity as we look at the substance of this category of threats to representative democracy. These issues revolve around abortion, homosexuality, same-sex marriage and stem cell research. Each one of these is related in some way to sexual politics.

I am old enough to remember how the abortion issue became transformed into political power, starting with Ronald Reagan, as the diminution of representation in our political system sped up. It was centered on how to get conservative democrats to be conservative republicans. It began in the late 60s before Reagan came to power and concentrated on the solid south. The south had always been democratic, the republican party an anathema to it as a result of the Civil War. By the time of the late 80s, the south had aligned itself with the more conservative Republican Party of Reagan.

With that base Reagan began to work on northern democratic conservatives to convince them that now the Republican Party might be a better home for them. The Civil War wouldn't do as a reason, but issues such as abortion would. Southern prejudices against Blacks and Jews helped that region to leave the Democratic Party, which had been their political persuasion for some time. The next step would be for the republicans to switch another powerful minority group, the Catholics. The way to do it was what the issue of abortion offered.

When I was in the Virginia State Legislature from 1966 to 1970, as a Catholic, I was wined and dined by the Catholic Bishop to take a strong political stand against abortion. I was morally against it, as I had been against capital punishment, because of the violence in both cases. But whereas capital punishment laws were mandatory, there were no mandatory laws forcing someone to have an abortion. There were also other rights than the mother's involved in the abortion issue. Not only the mother's rights, but the father's, family members', as well as the rights of the fetus were at issue. Neither the rights of the fetus or the mother could be absolute, when there were other rights involved concerning life and health.

Nevertheless, I did not actively support any side in the legislature, believing it was a moral more than a legal issue. I admired Catholic priests who came each year to express their views when committees held hearings on whether to liberalize existing statutes. The statutes operative at that time, in many states, provided a right to an abortion with medical approval and only to save the life of the mother. The liberalizers wished to enlarge that to include a threat to the health of the mother or if a woman was pregnant as a result of a rape or incest or if the fetus was suffering from demonstrable defects that would make its life untenable. The Catholic church had already approved a D&C, which in effect terminated a pregnancy, if the fetus were lodged in the fallopian tube – an ectopic pregnancy - where, if it was not removed, 99 percent of the time both mother and fetus would die. The church employed the principle of "double effect" where if one intended consequence led to another, not intended but obviously possible or even probable occurred, the Church considered that to be a sinless act.

Many state statutes were liberalized in the late 60s to allow for a woman to choose to have an abortion in the case of rape, incest or where the life or health of the mother was threatened. The early 70s brought on a constitutional interpretation in the case of *Roe v Wade.*[9] That case took into consideration the three trimester periods with an almost absolute right to an abortion in the first trimester, and very qualified rights in the last trimester. Reagan took up the banner for right-to-life groups and proved successful in switching Catholic votes from democrat to republican. The same followed for Catholics on the issues of homosexuality, same-sex marriage and the use of fetal stem cells from legally aborted fetuses for saving lives medically. Not to be outdone, the Reagan administration approached Jews claiming that the Republican Party now supported Israel more than the Democratic Party did. Reagan was called the great communicator and apparently he was as more Jews and Catholics became "one issue" republicans

As we have stated earlier there are no absolutes in American constitutional law when several rights are in conflict. This is certainly true in the tension between the women's right to choose and the right to life of the unborn. So *Roe v. Wade* specifically laid out how these rights applied

---

[9] *Roe v. Wade*, 410 U.S. 113, 1973.

in determining if, when and how a pregnancy could legally be terminated. Not only the mother's life, but her health could be considered, but certainly no such thing as abortion-on-demand could take place because the mother simply wished to divest herself of an unwanted pregnancy.

It's interesting to note that although the conservative party talks much about the termination of the life of the fetus as a violent act, when it comes to violent acts committed against the living such as killing the innocent in capital punishment and war making, the logic and moral consistency don't seem to stand up. Nevertheless, citizens, when polled still favor capital punishment, but support the right to choose and are less moved to support war making since 9/11.

Regarding the issue of homosexuality and same-sex marriage, there is strong evidence that our national sanity is still intact. Within the past 20 years there has been a sea change in public attitudes toward homosexuals as citizens with full civil rights as well as in the acceptance of the need for loving homosexual couples to have access to the rights and duties associated with legal marriage. There are hold-outs among extremely right wing Christian groups, but generally churches as well as other public institutions have moved steadily forward in terms of acceptance, with full recognition of the constitutional rights and inclusion of homosexuals in society's functions.[10] The Supreme Court in 2015 followed suit, including same-sex marriages as a political right under the Constitution, even though it might

---

[10] *Obergefell v. Hodges,* (June 2015) A 5 to 4 decision decided in favor of a constitutional guarantee to such marriages based on "equal dignity under the law."

not be considered religious or moral under some understandings of the Bible. Homosexuals have a political and natural right to be threated the way they are. That doesn't necessarily change some people's minds that it is not the way to be. There is significant scientific evidence that people are born with a particular sexual orientation, just as Downs Syndrome babies and lefthanders are. We must be politically free to live according to the way we are even though some have religious or moral beliefs to the contrary.

We, as Americans, have the duty to educate ourselves on how science, morality, sex and politics relate, as we, as sovereign people are called to be virtuous and to elect representative who are virtuous and educated as our founders directed us. We have not only a right but a duty to elect representatives who truly represent what our founders understood to be in the best interests of American democracy. We haven't been doing this. As a result we have lost control over this great gift that we live out in our public world, and which affects our private lives as well. The next chapter will touch on two ways we can keep our eye on this. One is how we educate people and the other is how we seek, in our representatives that which is virtuous or which we might, in modern language, more normally call moral or ethical.

CHAPTER EIGHT

HEALTH, EDUCATION AND WELFARE

"TO SUPPOSE THAT ANY FORM OF GOVERNMENT WILL SECURE LIBERTY OR HAPPINESS WITHOUT ANY VIRTUE IN THE PEOPLE, IS A CHIMERICAL IDEA." JAMES MADISON, JUNE 20, 1788

Introduction

Three major public issues remain to be discussed – health, education and welfare. The first, healthcare, has been in the headlines throughout the last eight years, and like religion and science issues, particularly global warming and the preservation of our church-state relationship, it is perhaps the best known public concern of the American people. This chapter will discuss these issues before we get to the final ones on the rule of law and the pursuit of justice, which are dependent directly upon them for a stable democratic representative democracy. I take my authority from Madison and Jefferson.

It was Madison who stressed that his structure of federal government would help to thwart stark, overt attempts to replace this new form of government with the extremes around it then and now. His structure set up a representative form of government but was dependent upon the electorate to choose representatives who possessed the necessary level of integrity and reliability. When Jefferson returned home from his work abroad, he added his strong voice not only for virtuous representatives but also for a well-educated electorate to obtain them. Madison and the constitutional drafters had presented their magnificent document replacing the weak and dangerous Articles of Confederacy - the new Constitution, which Madison orchestrated and Jefferson endorsed. These events called for education and virtue in American politics, and that call has never diminished.

Perhaps the long history in which we as Americans have suffered from inadequate healthcare, one of the major necessities of life, will demonstrate why virtue and education are so important. It will also serve as another example, along with the many issues we have already considered, that we are in a state of democratic disintegration. We have seen how religious factions threaten our sensitive community balance and our scientific progress. We will see that historically religion has also often served as an advantage in offering a moral and ethical foundation for public affairs. Finally I hope to make clear how all the considerations are dependent upon the rule of law and the pursuit of justice.

Healthcare

Healthcare, as a right of all American citizens began to take shape after World War II when Roosevelt made his famous "Four Freedoms" speech to Congress, including freedom from want and fear.[1] Healthcare, a universal right, became a reality not only for the United States military, but also for our elected officials. But what about the rest of us? Harry Truman and Richard Nixon made some moves, but it

---

[1] State of the Union Address, January 8, 1941

was not until the administration of John Kennedy in the early 60s that a comprehensive community mental healthcare program was proposed. It began to take effect nationally in various states after his death by the creation of local mental health clinics replacing state "insane asylums."

I was elected to the Virginia Legislature in 1965 at the age of 34, the second youngest there. Six other people also represented the area that I represented; seven seats for Fairfax County, Falls Church and Fairfax City, under the new "one man, one vote" Supreme Court decision, *Baker v. Carr* (1962). The case called for a redistribution of representation, the effect of which gave northern Virginia more seats needed by the growing population there. Southern Virginia districts, less populated, wound up with fewer seats. This helped to make the districts more balanced and thus more democratic. No candidate represented his own single district, however. Some of the candidates running for election had staked out their own areas of legislation. Some believed association with certain topics brought them more votes. Mental health was not one of them. I was told when I ran that since only ten percent of the voters had any relationship to mental health issues, such areas as education and roads were much better issues to emphasize. So why would I be interested in healthcare? I had my own personal connections with the medical field. I served my military time in the U.S. Army Medical Service Corps as a medical technician and my wife then was a surgical nurse. While in the army I took various detailed on the job training courses in medical techniques including a stint on a mental health ward at Valley Forge Army Hospital.

What I was to find out when I ran for office was that no one in my group seemed to be interested in medical issues. So I took that area under my wing. My first healthcare legislation was in the field called at the time "mental retardation." The Commonwealth of Virginia had a unique program in which it took its newly elected officials on a week's tour around the state to visit public institutions, including a state mental hospital.

While a youngster, at camp in Maine, over evening bonfires, I had heard stories about "the crazy house" in the state of Massachusetts called the Danvers Insane Asylum, where a "monkey man" resided. That was scary. Virginia's state hospital was not as eerie. It was just like the army mental health ward at Valley Forge Army Hospital, a very sad place where only a few of the mental health patients exhibited any form of violence. Most seemed to be suffering mentally because, as diagnosed psycho-neurotics, they were still in touch with reality. Only the psychotic ones seemed to be set free to express another more pleasant alternative "reality." Many had feelings of low esteem from their childhood relations with their parents.

Kennedy's new law was caused by the inaccessibility of large state hospitals wherein personal treatment was not often administered. The moving of personnel and patients, to smaller community centers initiated the Comprehensive Community Mental Health program. I supported this legislation on the state level and introduced bills in the area of mental health, mental retardation and new laws on compulsory child vaccinations. About the same time, Senator Ted Kennedy picked up his efforts, little as they were able to be, when he, in the 60s and 70s campaigned for universal healthcare in America. If his suggestions were enacted into law, America could catch up with other democratic and industrial states in the world, which had had universal healthcare for some time.

When I ran for Congress in Virginia in 1972 I made healthcare a central issue in my campaign. But I was not elected and Kennedy became less than popular for a while. By 1995, Senator Kennedy was making some progress but it was not until 2008 when Barack Obama picked up Hillary Clinton's earlier failed attempts and carried them on against republican opposition that anything substantive happened. In 2010, the Affordable Care Act was passed and became a huge step forward in increased coverage and lower costs for healthcare participants. Unfortunately, personal attacks on Obama took precedence over what Obama proposed, and what came to be known as Obamacare was constantly under attack until finally conservative groups were able to bring it before the U.S. Supreme Court, which many expected would kill the Act outright. I wrote a summary of the Supreme Court decision in 2012 and what I said at the time is paraphrased below:

The Health Care Law was upheld almost entirely, not the way politicians or the media expected, but certainly in a manner within the bounds of constitutional law. Officially, it was a 5 to 4 margin, with Chief Justice Roberts writing the decision, joined by the four "liberals" – Ginsburg, Breyer, Sotomayor and Kagan in most of it and where not, by the four "conservatives" – Scalia, Kennedy, Thomas and Alito, thus making all of it a majority.

In *National Federation of Independent Business, et al v. Sebelius*, Secretary of Health and Human Services, Justice

Roberts raised two constitutional challenges to the Patient Protection and Affordable Care Act: 1) the requirement that all individuals participate in a minimum program or be penalized a sum of money unless excused or subsidized (called "the mandate"), and 2) the expansion of state Medicaid services that provided for the cost covered by the national government and only later with 10 percent state payments. Failure of a state to expand the program would result not only in the loss of the expansion payments but all payments made to a state by the national government. (The reason for this, I suspect, is that loss of national money for an expansion program the states don't want anyway is no loss at all, so that a coercive "incentive" to participate is needed.) Nevertheless, two liberals joined five conservatives to invalidate this part, 7 to 2, Sotomayor and Ginsburg dissenting.

Roberts wrote that our national government (he incorrectly calls it "federal") is a government of enumerated powers with the remainder left to the states or people except those that additionally may be assumed as "necessary and proper." He decided that the individual mandate could not be sustained under the Commerce Clause because failure to participate in a minimum program or otherwise be subject to a "tax penalty" is not a commercial activity on the part of individuals who opt out. Four conservatives joined him and four liberals did not. The liberal dissent argued it is part of a huge national and local commercial activity, the health care industry, and the act not to participate is, in fact, a commercial activity.

 Roberts said that if it is a commercial activity, "the government's logic could order everyone to buy vegetables."

(A very conservative British court made a similar interesting statement in 1903 where the issue before it was parliamentary legislation limiting excessive working hours. The court argued that if the government could limit a work day to eight hours, which eventually it did constitutionally in America, it could "control the use of a man's leisure hours.")

But Roberts decided that the individual mandate could be upheld under the taxing power since taxes may penalize, and because the penalty is administered under the Act by the IRS as a tax even though the congressional intent was not that it was a tax but a penalty. And it was here, that to support this position, Roberts left political considerations and justified his decision on the basis of traditional Supreme Court statutory construction rules. A premier one requires that if there are two ways to uphold congressional legislation, even if the first one is not constitutional and the second one was not intended, it may be used "to save the Act." The four liberals joined and the four conservatives dissented. (The media went off on a heyday arguing with itself whether the tax penalty was a tax or a penalty.)

The final matter to be resolved was whether the remaining legislation upheld could be severed from its unconstitutionally declared parts or that the entire Act must fail as a result. Roberts and the liberals said it could, and the conservative four, no. He also had to overcome the Anti-injunction Act, which prohibited the Court from hearing a case involving taxes before a taxpayer is actually affected by it, which wasn't until 2014. Roberts circuitously decided it was a tax but the Court could hear it anyway because the Anti-injunction Act doesn't apply. Neither side raised the issue that because the Act did not become active, in its entirety, until 2014, the Court could not hear it because the case was not "ripe," i.e. cannot be heard, until then. The reason why the Court agreed to hear it is probably because part of the Act affected people's decisions now.

Although *The Nation* wrote this up as "a huge victory for liberals" I was concerned that Roberts may have pulled a fast one in the long run since this decision on the interstate commerce clause could be used to limit existing social projects and services promoting the general welfare on the grounds that the interstate commerce clause is no longer broad enough to cover them. This could become the means whereby conservative anarchists and libertarians successfully dismantle the national government's power to so legislate, and effectively privatize all interstate commerce power to private corporations already employed as persons with constitutionally protected rights by previous Court decisions

Recently, Obamacare's success was summarized, five years since the Act's passage. The writer discussed its affects in the state of Texas:

> .... The cost of a Medicare patient has flattened across the country, El Paso, included. U.S health-care inflation is the lowest it has been in more than fifty years. Most startling of all, McAllen has been changing its ways. Between 2009 and 2012, its costs dropped almost $3,000 per Medicare recipient.) A total saving to taxpayers is projected to have reached almost half a billion dollars by the end of 2014. The hope for reform has been to simply "bend the

level." This was savings on an unprecedented curve.[2]

Lester Dyke, a cardiac surgeon in Texas had this to say: "Medicare has become a pig trough here. We took a wrong turn when doctors stopped being doctors and became businessmen."[3] Most doctors and businessmen are conservative republicans and healthcare has been, since Reagan, an increasing business for profit first and patient care second as insurance companies and big pharma practice medicine and doctors are relegated to being mere technicians.

Let me give you a personal example. In the early 2000s the Bush administration passed what is known as Medicare, Part D, a drastic change advertised by republicans to help Medicare patients who found pharmaceutical costs prohibitive. In many instances the patients' rights to access reasonably priced medications dropped as the prices rose forced by the new regulations. On top of that, community health centers' distribution of low cost medications was prohibited. I was taking two blood pressure pills at the time. One called Atenalol had basically been around for years and its cost would not change. I was able to get the other, Darvan, from the community health center for less than $60 a year. The effect of Bush's law was to close the community

---

[2] Gawande, Atul, "Overkill," *The New Yorker,* May 11, 2013, p. 49. See also Eubanks, Virginia, "System Failure: The High-Tech Way to Slash Public Benefits," *The Nation,* June 15, 2015, pp. 31-33. Therein it was reported that the Texas Health and Human Services Commission participated in a venture that terminated 6,000 children's medical cases. One child died as a result.

[3] *Ibid.*

health center's pharmacy and require me to get the medicine on the open market, where it cost, for the same amount $800 plus per year. Fortunately, I am a veteran and reopened my veterans account, where I was able to obtain a generic Losartan for $96 per year.

Why do most conservatives oppose universal healthcare and reasonably priced pharmaceuticals? For exactly the same reason I mentioned earlier. Their policy and practice is consistent and they are steadfast in their loyalty to the people they represent. Medicine is a business, it's incorporated, and it only makes money if the prices stay high. What's the incentive to eliminate a disease when to be able to continually treat it, perpetuates the security of a maximized profit, even if not the health of the patient.

In 2013, with conservative urging, conservative states went to court before republican judges to bring down Obama healthcare. If they were successful, 8 billion people would be deprived of new healthcare, as well as many others enjoying Obamacare healthcare improvements. For example kids could come under their parents' healthcare program up to age 26, and insurance companies could not turn sick people who had a pre-existing condition away. Nevertheless, it was expected that in June 2015, Obamacare would be dead by a 5 to 4 vote of the conservative U.S. Supreme Court. Healthcare became one of the few lights at the end of the tunnel for American citizens, in spite of congressional politicians and states' rights officials trying to make it otherwise. The last chapter in the chronology of the human right to healthcare was registered when the U.S. Supreme Court made its surprising decision in June 2015.

The six to three ruling stopped a challenge that would have eliminated subsidies in at least 34 states for individuals and families buying insurance through the national government's online marketplace. Otherwise coverage would have been unaffordable for millions and created price spirals for those who kept their policies. Chief Justice John Roberts wrote the opinion for the Court, joined by frequent swing voter Anthony Kennedy and Ruth Bader Ginsburg, Stephen Breyer, Sonia Sotomayor and Elana Kagen, the "liberal four." The opinion states: "Congress passed the Affordable Care Act to improve health insurance markets, not to destroy them, ... The combination of no tax credits and an ineffective coverage requirement could well push a state's individual insurance market into a death spiral. It is implausible that Congress meant to operate in this manner."[4]

Republicans controlling Congress are likely to advance new legislation amending or repealing the law, although it is even more likely to be vetoed by President Obama if it gets to his desk.

Tax credits created by Congress help middle-income consumers buy insurance through online marketplaces, known as exchanges. The subsidies are "established by the state," according to the law. Thirty-four states did not set up their own exchanges and relied on the federal government website. Plaintiffs' attorney argued that millions of consumers in those states should not receive tax credits to pay premiums. "Pulling the subsidies would have undermined the insurance market in those states to the point

---

[4] *King v. Burwell*, decided June 25, 2015

of likely failure. Unable to afford the coverage, many consumers would have dropped out. Those remaining would probably have been older and sicker, driving up premiums to unsustainable levels, according to healthcare experts. ..."

Eighty-five percent of those who bought insurance through healthcare.gov qualified for subsidies averaging $272 per month. The Department of Health and Human Services predicted 6.4 million people would have lost subsidies if the court ruled for the plaintiffs. Those subsidies effectively constitute revenue for hospitals and health insurers, financing premiums and the cost of care. Both industries are relieved they were upheld.[5] But republicans continue to seek power to repeal and replace the law.

Education and Welfare

Here we will discuss in more detail the necessary ingredients that Madison and Jefferson singled out for this nation to develop in this new kind of government based on a federal structure, separating and balancing the powers that it would wield, and calling for its new electorate, which was ever expanding, to be sufficiently educated to be able to elect the kind of people who could perform the tasks of voting and representing with integrity and responsibility. The virtue required to ward off the temptations of money or fame was to be the fundamental characteristic of representatives. This

---

[5] An excellent summary of the case from which the above quotation is taken from Hancock, Jay, "Supreme Court Upholds Obamacare Subsidies" published on line by Kaiser Health News. By August 2015 the number of uninsured Americans fell below 10 percent, another million signing up in the first 8 months of that year. By 2016, 20 million were covered that had not been previously.

would ensure that the general welfare called for in the Constitution would become a reality. If these characteristics envisioned for the government came into reality through a new structure and educated moral participants, then it would succeed. It is my position that this fundamental basis of representative democracy evolved and progressed but has now stalemated because of our failure to preserve that structure and elect representatives with those characteristics. Of course such failures took place in the past as well. History shows that there were always fortunate corrections. My hope in writing this book is to raise the alarm that new corrections are urgently needed now.

The issue of public education alone currently stands on its own and may be examined just as all the other specific issues have been. But it is also, as we have pointed out, a foundation for the well being of the entire system. Today we have threats, serious ones, to the continuation of public education by religious and private factions that wish to provide a more narrow privatized foundation, based on their own specific beliefs than a comprehensive one suitable for a public community such as the United States of America and its fifty states. And we have already seen how a narrow religious intrusion can damage a public school in the Florence case.

Public schools have become sites of violence as they are easy targets for people taking advantage of the permissive nature of our gun culture. Public schools serve everybody, the rich and the poor, geniuses and handicapped. Private schools are designed for making profit or spreading propaganda. They have a place in American society but they are not a replacement for the breadth and necessity of a public system. Advanced education must be affordable to all, unlike private schools; both secondary and college level, that often are available only on a more selective basis. College education in general has become unaffordable except for the rich and has burdened those who graduate with excessive debt and interest. The important and outstanding exception of this trend is community colleges, still usually affordable and available to everyone.

The disadvantage of private schools, except perhaps traditional ones, which were generally priced beyond common availability, is found in the new private factional schools that present a curriculum based on specific religious and/or political agendas. Such schools may produce graduates who enter the electorate without open minds able to grasp all sides of important issues. American students over many decades have failed to include political science and American government courses in their choices, preferring more "personal" courses such as psychology, not realizing how politics affects their lives personally.

Republican leaders have targeted the Department of Education as something not worth spending taxpayers' money on. Strangely inconsistent is the greater reliance of privatized schools on public money. Charter schools can play their part for the less fortunate, for those who need a second chance, or those with disabilities who cannot cope in a regular public environment, perhaps even special education needs. But they are frightening to people like myself who went through a period here in America when state laws prohibited minorities from attending public schools by providing tuition grants, similar to current "voucher" programs, from state public education funds to allow their preferred constituents to seek private education elsewhere.

When I graduated from high school, I received a journalism scholarship to Syracuse University. One of the first activities of new students in those days (this was 1949) was to rush fraternities and sororities. My first roommates were Jewish, so we visited the fraternities together, but not for long. My Jewish buddies were more street-wise than I was. They knew that the fraternities discriminated and Jews, African Americans, dark-skinned people, those with smaller incomes were not acceptable. That proved to be the case at the fraternities we visited. They were not welcome.

When I transferred to a smaller, liberal arts school, Bucknell University in 1950, one of my closest high school friends was already there, the same person who had educated me about the Christian decorations at Scarsdale High School. He joined the only Jewish fraternity there and later became its president, with such famous fraternity brothers as Philip Roth. When I was chosen by one of the fraternities located "up on the hill," Hank told me that they offered him a membership until he told them he was Jewish and then they politely reneged. When a friend of mine and I transferred to Bucknell, we were too late to get a dormitory room and lived for the first semester in a private home. This home happened to be down the street from the only Jewish fraternity. On the other side of the street, facing the Jewish fraternity were some of the Gentile fraternities that were located "down the hill." It never occurred to me why my friend and I were rushed by most of the fraternities "up the hill" but by none of the fraternities "down the hill" which were in view of the Jewish fraternity house. That house had been kind enough to provide us with breakfast each morning. It wasn't until a couple of years later at a party I attended at one of these fraternities that a friend there told me that the reason we were not rushed by the fraternities "down the hill" was because we had breakfast at the Jewish fraternity, and assumed we were Jewish.

These are the kinds of incidents that were taking place in private American institutions that were affording an education to a future electorate that would then be called upon to vote for representatives to serve the American people. The great calling of the public community exercised in the form of its governing institutions is to treat each citizen equitably. It is called the "equal protection of the laws" in our Constitution. Some say those that added that phrase to the Constitution in the 14th Amendment, were influenced by their Christian principles, primarily to love your neighbor as yourself and to do unto others, as you would have them do unto you.

All of this brings us finally to how education, among other things can create virtue (today we would more aptly describe virtue as integrity or honesty) in our representatives and ourselves. Thomas Jefferson believed, as did the Greeks before him, that people are basically good and education, goes a long way to helping them gain knowledge and apply that knowledge with critical thinking and logical understanding to make unbiased, unprejudiced decisions in their lives.[6] There are other institutions that can join with our

---

[6] See Aschwanden, Christie, "A Users Guide to Rational Thinking," *Discover Magazine,* July/August 2015, pp. 44-49; Martin, Clancey, "Playing With Playdough," *The Atlantic,* April 2014, pp. 35-37. Philosophers still provide answers science cannot, he writes. Philosophy

government and with public education, such as the family and religious institutions to do this. Each so-called faction or specific group, whether it be the American Civil Liberties Union, the American Friends Service Committee, the Jewish Anti-Defamation League, the Southern Christian Leadership Conference, the Ku Klux Klan, the Republican Party, The Freethinkers, the Baptist Church, the list could go on and on, claims it has a lock on what morality and ethics is all about, whether they tie it to Christianity, Judaism, Islam, the White Citizens League, the libertarians or a public interest view.

Somewhere along the line our ethical moral path and philosophical study should cause us to open ourselves sufficiently to take in numerous ideas and to develop a balanced and fair and mostly objective way of arriving at our life decisions and how they affect other peoples' lives, beneficially or detrimentally. But we must be trained to resist temptations of personal and group interest for the common interest. Public education is a democratic way of providing an opportunity to engage our public community in a fair representation of us all. In this way we may also create an educated electorate who then are able to pick virtuous and intelligent people as representatives. That, then, empowers the general welfare. When one agrees to be a representative of the people, he or she takes on the moral responsibility to effectuate the public interest. He or she must then put aside his or her own private self-interest. This is the first call of

---

in the modern sense began with Socrates. Ethics, Logic and critical thinking is today an essential part of it. I taught philosophy from 1973 to 2014, when I summed up some essential thoughts in my play, "The Dead Philosophers' Society: Does Morality Matter?"

objectivity and consideration for those one has the duty to represent.

Let me give you a personal example. When I was elected to the Virginia Legislature in 1965, my major concerns were healthcare and consumer and civil rights. At the last minute it was suggested that I introduce legislation, already made law in 33 states, whereby mandatory testing would be required for all newborns in Virginia to determine whether the baby had a condition called phenylketunria. Only three percent of newborns had such a condition, but there was no mandatory test to determine that. Without such a test, a baby born with that undiagnosed condition, which is an reaction to a particular protein, phenylalanine, would over a period of a year and a half, become irreversibly "mentally retarded." It seemed to me a simple as apple pie to pass into law in Virginia what so obviously would save approximately 23 babies a year from a life of mental disability and parental anguish. I was astonished that medical professionals opposed such legislation, but pursued it on my own anyway. The test would cost 50 cents and the condition averted by providing the baby with a diet that would avoid the damage. One afternoon, in a dimly lighted hallway of the state capitol, I was approached by one of the Governor's representatives who told me that if I didn't vote for the Governor's tax bill, they would make sure that my "baby bill" was killed. The choice I had to make was between following my conscience and voting against a tax bill that inequitably harmed poor people and thereby exposing my own bill to this powerful threat; or to relax my principles and ensure that my "baby bill" would become law. I chose to represent my constituency and risk the consequences. My experience has been that almost everyone who becomes an elected official faces, at some time, a test of his or her integrity. In this case there is a happy ending. My bill, called the PKU Bill, passed by my own efforts and the efforts of my constituents, even though I voted against the Governor's tax bill, which also passed by a huge number.

The worry today is that we have not been vigilant about making sure that we have representatives that have the education and virtue to act for the general welfare.[7] The thesis of this book is that our lack of vigilance must come to an end. There are ways to begin to reverse that situation. One is to adhere to the very foundations of representative democracy that Jefferson and Madison enunciated. If we do that, and in the process maintain a rule of law that reflects those ethical and moral principles and rights and duties that we all need to have and exercise, we can continue our journey in the pursuit of justice and peace.

We now approach my concluding chapter with this warning, that there has been a chronological, historical development in what is known as the rule of law and the pursuit of its goal - justice. We will take an overview glimpse, moving quickly from Greek and Roman foundations to the English countryside of the 12th and 13th centuries when such initial developments as *Magna Carta* began the long trek to the guarantees found in the American Constitution, e.g. the Bill of Rights amendments, the free exercise of religion and free expression and the equal

---

[7] See Bosworth, David, *The Demise of Virtue in Virtual America,* New York (Front Porch America Publications, 2015).

protection of the laws for all persons. After that, we may reflect together on what has gone wrong and how we are to make it right. But consider many of the clues and hints on how we can do that have already been touched upon in these first eight chapters.[8]

---

[8] Limitations on free speech have been criticized recently, justified "in the name of emotional well being. College students are increasingly demanding protection from words and ideas they don't like." Lukiandoff, Greg, and Haidt, Jonathan, "The Coddling of the American Mind," *The Atlantic,* September 2015, pp, 41-52. This trend has caused educational presentations to be vetted as "neutral" and not "one-sided." Consequently, challenging and controversial ideas are less and less a part of higher education. At the other extreme, as we've seen in this chapter, there are those who wish to take away the protection of the 14th Amendment – the equal protection of the laws – to all "persons," thus including the innocent human beings born to undocumented immigrants, giving them the rights of citizenship. Republicans Trump, Carson and Huckabee has expressed views favorable to the elimination of the 14th Amendment to the U.S. Constitution and at the same time are critical, in some cases hypocritically, of others exercising their right of free speech because it offends the doctrines and dogmas informing the religious beliefs of such as Huckabee, Cruz and Santorum.

CHAPTER NINE

WILL WE LET THE AMERICAN DREAM DIE?

THE RULE OF LAW AND PURSUIT OF JUSTICE

"MAN IS BORN FREE, AND HE IS EVERYWHERE IN CHAINS" JEAN-JACQUES ROUSSEAU, *THE SOCIAL CONTRACT, BOOK I, CH. I (1762)*

A Call to Action

To conclude this study, we'll take a quick review of the evolution of the rule of law and pursuit of justice as it unfolded in the common law countries of Great Britain and America. This will give us a reminder of what we have to lose.

At this, the conclusion of the book, and having spelled out the consequences of acquiescence or oblivion to the rapidly eroding democracy in America, I suggest there should be a call to action for a new birth of freedom in America, which will culminate in the restoration of the American experiment and its progress forward. Democracy, the rule of law, and the pursuit of justice are the highest virtues that the structure of a nation-state can offer. They are necessary attributes that come from a world controlled by political power. The highest value of the secular state is justice. It can offer no more. I am not advocating, in this study, that we should glorify government and nations beyond what their natural limitations are. My point is that our government should be true to what it claims to be. It has not yet evolved to that level and, in fact, my concern is that it is presently backing off. Those who seek the state, as an end in itself, are not the ones to which this study is directed. The political culture is best expressed in a form of democracy, but as then Prime Minister Winston Churchill said in 1947, and is much quoted: "It has been said that democracy is the worst form of government except for all the others...." He prefaced that with: "no one pretends that democracy is perfect or all wise."[1]

What we are working on here is the culmination of the American experiment as the earliest founders aptly described it. So the question before us is – is the American experiment over? There has been a downturn in interest in American government in colleges as more individualistic courses such as psychology have been on the upswing among today's youth. There is also the perennial statement that most Americans are turned off by politics, especially when politicians squabble over things that don't relate to the average citizen. Meanwhile, we have had a newfound interest among young people in this country and several others, we are told, in the freedom to kill others or capture them and enjoy taking their heads off.

Are we to believe then that much of what we have been concerned with in the confines of this study is not that

---

[1] An interesting comparison of spiritual contemplation and political action may be found in Hannah Arendt's *The Human Condition*, London (The University of Chicago Press: 1958), as she discussed what she calls "the vita contemplativa" and "vita activa."

important to the average young American? For many of us who have been around for a while, particularly those like me who majored in political science and history in college and had the benefit of a legal education not confined to the techniques of practicing law to make a profit, but including the logic and critical thinking so necessary to a legal education and so needed by the general population in times like these. A knowledge of the history of law is also a key ingredient since history contains all the seeds of the future. We have moved across history's spectrum, some say, in a steady but shaky progression from old systems of extremes of lawlessness or the tyranny of one ruler, i.e. anarchism and autocracy, to the people finally becoming the center of sovereignty in their own national community.

Philosophers have had a lot to do with this – Socrates, Plato and Aristotle in Greece and Cicero and Seneca in Rome - to name the most prominent. The creation by them of a natural law and a "social contract" conceived by Hobbes, Locke and Rousseau helped the movement of the rule of law to be pursued in a climate of justice. As Augustine of Hippo said, "an unjust law is no law at all."[2]

---

[2] From *On Free Choice of the Will,* Book I, section 5, written at the turn of the 4th century. Rousseau had this to day in detail: "The passage from the state of nature to the civil state produces a very remarkable change in man, by substituting law for instinct in his conduct, and giving his actions the morality they had formerly lacked. ...Although, in this (civil) state, he deprives himself of some advantages which he had from nature, he gains in return others so great, his faculties are so stimulated and developed, his ideas so extended, and his whole soul so uplifted, that, did not the abuses of his new condition often degrade him below that which he left, he would be bound to bless continually the happy moment which took him from it forever, and instead of a stupid and unimaginative animal, make him an intelligent being and a man." *The Social Contract,* Book I, ch.viii.

The phrase "rule of law" is garlanded with the flowers of justice and does not sanction law by command that is held out as value-free and power-centered. It may have been that way at one time but it progressed from Hobbes' "state of nature" and preference for monarchy, in the direction of what Locke was anticipating in his political philosophy, and upon which Montesquieu and Madison built.

There has been a movement towards creating a balance, not that of Aristotle's "golden mean" dealing essentially in quantitative terms, but rather in qualitative terms, a balance between the extremes of lawlessness and legal oppression where the people's sovereignty rests comfortably. A further development has been that where this balance subsequently gets out of whack, the sovereign people have an inherent right to nonviolently and conscientiously object in the form of civil disobedience, war tax resistance, conscientious objection, protests, demonstrations and vigils against their elected executive and legislative representatives, who may have imposed upon them a civil religion that is too heavy.

Madison carried out another unique aspect of the development of this democratic institution when he wrote the 9th Amendment to the U.S. Constitution. When people choose a social contract, as formulated by Hobbes, Locke and Rousseau, they enter into a "state of society." Under their chosen form of government, they retain their innate and inalienable human and natural rights. These are not delegated to their new public community without their agreement. Sometimes they are codified as in the American Bill of

Rights and sometimes they simply remain inherent in humanity. "Unalienable," Jefferson called them. They cannot be taken away and it becomes the duty of the government, the reason for which it is instituted, to protect those rights. All of this has come out of this evolution of the rule of law.

In the United States of America we are well aware that the greatest barrier in our own history towards a democratic society, was slavery, which resulted in the explosion of a war by a faction of Americans who wished to continue to benefit by the unpaid labor of others as slaves, enthusiastically prosecuted. The slave states seceded from the Union on their own accord and set up, for the second time, the political institution that usually identifies them, the second Confederacy. By the time that I graduated from law school in 1959, this country was still in the throes of its attempts to provide its citizens with their civil rights, still as yet segregated from a minority of them.

To be acquiescent to the values of this historic movement called the rule of law, or oblivious to its worth has been a perennial problem. The rule of law in respect to the United States of America has been called the American experiment. So the question is, will this experiment continue or is it now over, due to the abuses and practices we have heretofore highlighted?

The Rule of Law

For some, the phrase, rule of law, might simply mean, literally, law rules. Whatever the law is, good, bad or indifferent, it will be enforced because it rules. As we have said earlier, this is not its substantive characteristic. It is more than that, and if it isn't it is less than what we strive for.

When did the quest for representative democracy activate? When as in Europe, kings, lords and nobles held sway over vassals, serfs and slaves. But a slight crack was evident just beneath the king where the lords and nobles, played second fiddle. They decided that sufficient power was not distributed to them. *Magna Carta* was the result. A strife between the kings, lords, nobles and bishops was also apparent, as church and state, with King Henry II and Archbishop of Canterbury, Thomas Becket, each vied for a piece of this power the other wished to retain in total, beginning as early as the 12th century.

Events such as the Renaissance and Reformation shifted the balance of power in favor of the secular nation-states and away from the long ruling Papacy. Thomas More's attempts to protect his religious conscience ended in his execution by King Henry VIII, who became Supreme Head of the Church in England.

A turning point can be found in the year 1610 when King James I of England, the very same for whom the *King James Bible* was named, received a petition from the English House of Commons, in its development towards democracy having begun some 500 years earlier. It could be more directly called British. The petition said that: "Amongst many other points of happiness and freedom, which Your Majesty's subjects of this Kingdom have enjoyed under Your Royal progenitors, Kings and Queens of this realm, there is none which they have accounted more dear and precious than this, to be guided and governed by the certain Rule of Law, which giveth both the head and members that which right belongeth to them, and not by an uncertain and arbitrary form of government."[3]

In 1607, the English Chief Justice Edward Coke, quoted *Bracton*, "That the King ought not to be under any man but under God and the Law."[4] As Becket and More earlier argued for God and attempted to protect the Church from the King's intrusion, Becket told Henry that the church would be with the king in all that prevailed "save for the honor of God." Later, Locke and Coke argued that the law was common to the people as sovereign and legislated for their protection. In America, such patriots as Tom Paine, the Adams's, Ben Franklin, Thomas Jefferson and James Madison pursued the enlargement of the common law to be progressively more democratic. John Adams authored the Massachusetts Constitution in 1780 and wrote there that we were now: "A government of laws and not of men," meaning that the rule of law is not arbitrary, as men would have it, but objective in its equal protection for all. Unfortunately, the stage of evolution at that point included only white people of some property.

George Mason, was my ancient predecessor in the seat I held in the Virginia Legislature for four years (while there I had the opportunity to insert new language in the Virginia Constitution at only its third Constitutional Convention). Mason wrote the Virginia Declaration of Rights in 1775. In 1776 Jefferson incorporated some of his

---

[3] Hallan, Henry, *The Constitutional History of England,* Vol. 1, London (Dent and Sons: 1827) p. 441.

[4] In *The Case of Prohibitions* (1607)

language into The Declaration of Independence, as well as the new Virginia Constitution. Mason said, "A Declaration of Rights made by the good people of Virginia in the exercise of their sovereign powers, which rights do pertain to them and their posterity, as the basis and foundation of government." Its first three sections specifically stated the following:

1. Equality and rights of men.

That all men are by nature equally free and independent and have certain inherent rights, of which, when they enter into a state of society, they cannot, by any compact, deprive or divest their posterity; namely, the enjoyment of life and liberty, with the means of acquiring and possessing property, and pursuing and obtaining happiness and safety.

2. People the source of power.

That all power is vested in, and consequently derived from, the people, that magistrates are their trustees and servants, and at all times amenable to them.

3. Government instituted for common benefit.

That government is, or ought to be, instituted for the common benefit, protection and security of the people, nation or community; of all the various modes and forms of government, that is best which is capable of producing the greatest degree of happiness and safety, and is most effectually secured against the danger of maladministration; and, whenever any government shall be found inadequate or contrary to these purposes, a majority of the community hath an indubitable, inalienable and indefeasible right to reform, alter or abolish it, in such a manner as shall be judged most conducive to the public weal.

Mason was one of the first to say that judges "could declare an unconstitutional law void." [5]

The international value of a rule of law based on constitutionality and justice spread henceforth until, by our own time, we would have an evolved international organization with legal principles from treaties such as the Fourth Geneva Convention, The Universal Declaration of Human Rights, U.N. declarations, Security Council pronouncements, and International Court of Justice rulings arose. Our international sphere of existence has lagged far behind the development of nation-states. It might have been over 500 years or more ago that such keen political thinkers as Grotius, William Penn, and later Immanuel Kant called for an international form of government. But it was not until 1918 that a proposal from President Woodrow Wilson would initiate the League of Nations. Even though Wilson's proposals in part were adopted by the European nations, the American Congress, led by republican Senator Henry Cabot Lodge, Sr. killed U.S. participation in such progressive international formations. And the same party has consistently

---

[5] Snowiss, Sylvia, *Judicial Review and the Law of the Constitution,* New Haven, Connecticut (Yale University Press: 1990) pp. 41-42.

taken that stand up to the present time with a few notable exceptions after World War II.

This concludes the summary of argument and evidence I have offered to highlight the crisis of collapse that we are experiencing. Some say threats to our form of government are not from ourselves internally but only from our enemies abroad. But I hope this compilation indicates that it's not only our external enemies that threaten us so much as our own acquiescence to the factions within our government and country that seem determined to eliminate many of our sacred rights and freedoms under government in favor of a gun-ridden, individualistic corporate state where community well-being has no importance. The forthcoming 2016 presidential election could e the vehicle to do it. I reach this conclusion if not on expertise then on experience as a former member of town and city governments, a state legislator, member of presidential campaign staffs, and professor of philosophy, history and government, and for a while, theology and pre-law. In addition my legal practice has focused on civil and human rights and I have been a half-century participant in nonviolent social activism. With the unique opportunity in my life to observe the changes in American democracy over more than half a century, my conclusion is to sound the alarm that we are in a crisis, but that we can do something about it.

The Conservative Case

It would not be fair to end this prolonged essay without a word said of the conservative view as they see it, often severely criticizing their liberal opponents as a principle cause of our present crisis. I have accentuated the pluses of our national government, at least in respect to the way it has tried domestically to represent all of it's electorate by providing public benefits for the general welfare. My fear has been that power is being taken away from the national government and transferred to states, mostly confederate in character, and to corporations that are purely private. To vote in a corporation, one must be a shareholder and individual states may do well enough taking care of their own, but such a country would have no community continuity. Christian factional policies and practices, and militia-like organizations have also been participants in support of this reorganization of power. These, I named once before, in my first Edwin Mellen publication,[6] and they don't seem to have gone away, but rather have become an increasing problem.

Even more conservative Americans than those who fit into the above four categories, see national government as a "big government" threat to their freedom and security. Moreover, we are told that all things being equal, private corporations do a more moral and efficient job than our national government does. Therefore, the consistent republican position domestically has been to be a watchdog to the extent that, as they see it, an increased power in the

---

[6] Durland, William, *William Penn, James Madison, and the Historical Crisis in American Federalism*, Lewiston, NYC (the Edwin Mellen Press: 2000), pp. 210-213. In regard to corporations, a voter put it this way, "We elect our representatives by one person, one vote. In theory the representative reflects the views of those represented. In many cases, especially at the national level, this theory no longer holds. The rule is: one large donation, one representative vote. The representative's vote is being bought, so that large campaign costs can be covered. This is not democracy." Doug Telford in the *Colorado Springs Gazette*, of August 14, 2015. I would add that not only republicans but democrats are guilty of this corporate influence.

national government is an unnecessary evil. Just in one day, in my local newspaper, two editorials summarized succinctly why republicans can govern better and given the opportunity, a year or so ago, have done just that. Now, in 2015, they control the 114th Congress, which according to Colorado Springs' only daily newspaper (in a city singled out as the fourth most conservative one in the United States) the republican Congress "has been surprisingly productive." The areas that it uses as examples are: "free trade, criminal justice reform and tax reform." We mentioned that free trade was an Obama bill supported more by republicans than democrats. Criminal justice reform is touted as being tougher on crime and tax reform will favor the 99 percent as the tax brackets for the top one percent are relaxed. But it adds that the number of laws Congress enacts is a "classic but misleading characteristic. " It claims republican leadership has been "less autocratic" than the democratic Senate leadership was. It criticizes former democratic Senate majority leader Harry Reid for trampling on republican minority rights by eliminating in some voting matters, the Senate requirement that, rather than a majority vote, a 60 vote margin would be necessary to end debates and vote on bills.[7]

One of the major criticisms of republican conservative policies has been their practices of allowing "income inequality" to enlarge to the greatest extent this

---

[7] Editorial, "Productive Congress had Better Leadership," *Colorado Springs Gazette*, 2015, p. A8. Presidential candidate Ben Carson says "the U.S. is in decline" agreeing with my thesis, but for other reasons.

century. Another *Gazette* editorial, on the same day, claimed: "they mistakenly assume growth in top incomes comes at the expense of those at the bottom." They cite their own data to prove this is a fallacy. There is no income inequality in America, they say. That is "nonsense." Presidents such as Calvin Coolidge, back in the 20s, during the period just preceding the Great Depression, presided over economic growth and almost full employment in a period of prosperity under republican rule.[8]

Another editorial in the same paper lists many firsts for the GOP. It starts off by saying that it is untrue that the Republican Party is the party of the rich, white male. To counteract that they say the Republican Party has a rich history of "promoting freedom and opportunity for all." They cite the same little-known fact in support. The first woman to be elected to Congress was a republican. The first African American governor was a republican. The first Hispanic U.S. Senator was a republican. The first Asian-American U.S. Senator was a republican. Abraham Lincoln, who signed the Emancipation Proclamation, was a republican. It was a republican Congress that passed the 13th Amendment to the Constitution abolishing slavery, and later passed the 14th Amendment providing "equal protection of the laws" to all citizens. A republican Congress passed the 19th Amendment to allow women's suffrage and in 1924 passed the Indian Citizenship Act, which granted citizenship to Native Americans.[9] All of these events, however, took place no later

---

[8] Ibid. A 2nd Editorial, "The Fallacy of 'Income Inequality" followed.

[9] Editorial, "Many Firsts Belong to GOP," *Colorado Springs Gazette,* August 3, 2015, p. A6.

than the 50s and are not typical of the period beginning in 1980 that this book claims as the start of the demise that is my subject of contention.

I was a republican from 1940 to 1960. My first political act, at age nine was to throw Roosevelt buttons in our local lake. What my local newspaper has to say in support of republican, conservative policies and practices is being said nationally by a large number of republican candidates for the U.S. presidential nomination. So it is fair to say that their statements can be taken as a valid sample of widespread conservative views at this time.

The Pursuit of Justice

It is now time to bring a close to this effort and rest our case. When John Kennedy highlighted in his 1960 presidential acceptance speech that "the torch has gone forth to a new generation of Americans," he had in mind the new representative leadership then emerging, many of whom were as young as he. Today it is not so much a new leadership but a new electorate that will hold the key in the 2016 election. The message must now go out to the new electorate that politics permeates everything, and whether one takes part in it or not, for reasons such as "politics doesn't interest me," it is always interested in you and it will affect you whether you like it or not. And that effect you can multiply by the millions. And if the effect is allowed to stand unopposed either through acquiescence or lack of interest, a dramatic change can certainly take place and we could all be saddled with an American democracy we no longer recognize. Recently someone wrote "in this age of disinformation the pursuit of evidence is probably the most pressing moral imperative."[10] We will be inundated, in the forthcoming election year, with much disinformation, allegations, assumptions and much of it unsupported by anything reasonably resembling evidence or proof. Regardless of what transpires in the presidential election of 2016, the compilation presented here will remain as a permanent agenda before the American people, available as an opportunity to overcome the threat of a demise in our democracy and the efforts to pursue justice in the American experiment to its fullest.

I offer this study to contribute to the effort in the search for objective evidence, rather than reliance on authoritative doctrine. This year is the 800th anniversary of the passage of *Magna Carta*. As I have said, this is where it all started and as we have further said, we have experienced a progression of the rule of law in its pursuit of justice since that time. *Magna Carta* may be more radical than is our contemporary understanding of it. That is, even though it was simply a conflict between nobles and king, common folks were also affected. The document contains an enforcement clause to prosecute violations by a representative assembly. The legal effect of this was that the king was not above the law and subject to punishment by the law, enforced by the common people in a representative

---

[10] Drager, Alice, *Galileo's Middle Finger,* review in *The New Yorker*, June 11, 2015, p. 75; She is a professor of clinical medical humanities and bioethics with an interest in science and social activism. She is alarmed when research clashes with doctrine.

assembly. Nevertheless, it took 400 years for that to begin to become a reality in 17th century England. It would be fitting to end where this progression began in its common law home country in England. *The Guardian Weekly* published its own editorial about that anniversary and it seems proper to repeat what it said:

> Even with the benefit of a legible version and a modern translation of *Magna Carta* it is sometimes difficult to see what all the fuss is about. The charter that King John signed at Runnymede on 15 June 1215 is, as the master of rolls, Lord Dyson, said this year, a curious hotch-potch. A ringing – or any other kind of – declaration of modern liberties it most definitely is not. It did not expressly endorse trial by jury. It states no overarching theory of rights. Most of what it contains is pragmatic rather than principled. Look at chapter 50 of the charter, for example, in which the king pledges to "entirely remove from our bailiwicks the relations of Gerard de Atheyes, so that for future they will have no bailiwick in England." This part of the document is all about brute power, not grand statements.
>
> Especially on the 800th anniversary of the charter, it is also a mistake to imagine that the road from Runnymede has been a smooth one. The charter was reissued, amended, reasserted and changed from the moment it was signed. Yet, for all that, *Magna Carta* matters in 2015 in some of the same ways it mattered in 1215. Partly that is because there is continuity and principle in the text. "To

none will we sell, to none will we deny, or delay, the right of justice" – chapter 40 of the charter and still in force today – is as resonant and succinct a statement today as it was eight centuries ago. The doctrine of proportionality between offence and sentence in chapter 20 echoes through the centuries too. The principles that judges must know the law and that only judges shall sit in judgment speak to the rule of law in the 21st as much as the 13th century.

An even more important continuity, though, is not so much the substance of *Magna Carta* as the idea of it. It is this created and imagined version that illuminates the national self-congratulation of the anniversary. F.W. Maitland, father of modern English legal history called *Magna Carta* a "sacred text." David Cameron has called it the "foundation of all our laws and liberties." Historically speaking, this is bunk. But in so far as it supports the idea that individual freedom is precious and must be defended and passed on, it is ennobling. Myth it may be, but a virtuous national myth that speaks to the belief that the timeless and magisterial law stands above the flawed ruler. The charter may or may not be an embodiment of British freedom or human rights. It was not a proto-constitution, yet to an extent, in popular imagination, it stands in as one. And while, in an age of globalization, it also points to our national failure to find ways, say, of bringing international business within the law, it recognizes the importance of trying.

We are free in part because we believe we are free and because we are determined that we should be free. We have *Magna Carta* and its history to thank for that but history is not enough: after 800 years, we may now need a comparable feat of farsighted courage.[11]

In fact, that farsighted courage might be found in one of our own Americans. It is fitting that it was a republican President, Abraham Lincoln, who summed up at a tragic moment what the American experiment meant to him. He said at Gettysburg on November 19, 1863: "Four score and seven years ago our fathers brought forth on this continent a new nation, conceived in liberty and dedicated to the proposition that all men are created equal.... It is for us the living, rather, to be dedicated here to the unfinished work ... the great task remaining before us ... that this nation, under God, shall have a new birth of freedom and that government of the people, by the people, for the people shall not perish from this earth."

This country is in a state of silent emergency and it is threatened by a coalition of confederates, Christians, militarists and corporations. Let us meet this threat with a new call to action by the American people for the restoration of its representative government. Although I have in mind a major grass-roots movement comparable to the 1960s, the

---

[11] Editorial, "Magna Carta, The Magic of Myth," *The Guardian Weekly,* June 19, 2015.

presidential campaigns of Senator Bernie Sanders of Vermont and former Governor Martin O'Malley of Maryland could provide the kickoff. (Sanders' positive progressive campaign energized the liberal left while Donald Trump's negative, reactionary campaign attracted the conservative right.)

Perhaps "a comparable feat of farsighted courage" will be called for to counteract the strong powers and principalities that stand in the way of what transpired from *Magna Carta* to what we have been blessed with in modern times – an ever more diverse and universal representative democracy moving ever so slowly in the direction of its full application to all human beings on earth. After all, we are becoming more and more each other's neighbor, as the world shrinks. Beyond the opportunity of the state to pursue its intrinsic responsibilities of justice and peace in the secular world are the moral values of love and mercy that transcend the secular to the spiritual. It is not only the secular political social democrats that must rise up; it is also the religious leaders and their faith communities that must add their voices and let their lives speak for the majority of Christians and others in America who wish for democracy to prevail. It is my hope that one day these two worlds – secular and spiritual - may coalesce under the connecting principle of the love of one's neighbor as oneself.

ABOUT THE AUTHOR

Dr. Bill Durland is a retired professor of Philosophy, History and Government and a civil rights attorney, playwright, educator and activist. He holds a B.A. from Bucknell University, M.A. from the University of Notre Dame, J.D. from Georgetown University Law Center and a Ph.D. from the Union Graduate School, formerly at Antioch College. He is a member of the Bars of the United States Supreme Court and several states and is a member of Phi Beta Kappa. Dr. Durland is the recipient of the State of Colorado's 1999 Martin Luther King, Jr. Humanitarian Award and Bucknell University's 2013 Service to Humanity Award. He has served as an elected legislative representative in the Virginia House of Delegates, the Trinidad Colorado City Council and Cokedale Colorado Town Council. He is a legal specialist in International and Constitutional law and legal counsel on five cases reaching the Supreme Court of the United States. He is married to Eugenia Smith Durland, who edited his ten books and eleven plays. He is the father of four – William Patrick, Michael Stephen, Jenifer and Christian Durland and lives in Littleton, Colorado. Dr. Durland and Genie are members of the Religious Society of Friends (Quakers).

AFTERWORD:

THE TRUMP ERROR

"POWER TENDS TO CURRUPT AND ABSOLUTE POWER CORRUPTS ABSOLUTELY," Lord Acton

Introduction

It's no mistake. Instead of "The Trump Era" this Afterword is entitled "the Trump Error." More specifically we voted in the Trump era, which was an error and the following pages will explain why as they relate to the original text. The Afterword is a chronological reflection on how, during the period since the publication of the first edition, the further demise of American democracy has taken place at a more rapid pace since its beginning with the Reagan administration in 1980. "Government is not the solution; government is the problem." So said Ronald Reagan as he ushered in a generation conditioned to believe that the government was no longer "us" but "them." In its place, he preached, we would be better governed if the functions of government were transferred to private corporate institutions controlled by the market and manipulated by CEOs. The power of government would remain in the hands of one party and removed from the people who would be trickled-down upon from time to time like the serfs were with handouts from the nobility in the monarchies of old. He would entice political strongholds of the Democratic Party, Jews with Israel, and Catholics with so-called "right to life" rhetoric.

From Reagan's retirement to Obama's election, the movement to a more perfect union was slow, spiraling and consequential, until the Great Recession, which had its roots in Reaganomics. Eight years with Obama increased the momentum once again, but nevertheless the voters, for many reasons, yearned for a strong man, a new man, an inexperienced man that spoke his own mind and unabashedly proclaimed that if elected he would move us back to a time before Franklin Roosevelt. He did so by beating fourteen other republican candidates while alienating at least as many factions. But in the end he could not do it with a democratic majority, but was elected instead by 538 unknown state Electors, even though his democratic opponent, Hillary Clinton received three million more popular votes. Winning only forty-six percent or less than half of American registered voters who actually voted. Clinton would have won the Electoral College save for Stein's votes. The polls showed Clinton in the lead by two to three percent on Election Day and that proved to be very accurate in regard to the total vote. Her election was certainly influenced by the FBI announcement eleven days before that it had reinstated an earlier investigation into her use of emails. Russia's intrusion, from the time of the Democratic Convention until the release of Wikileaks documents, obtained from Russian hacking, contributed as well. Trump had what he needed to chant "lock her up." He called on his new friend, Vlad Putin, to commit more illegal acts of hacking against his opponent. Interestingly, unknown at the time, the FBI had begun an investigation of Trump campaign surrogates as their actions on behalf of Trump revealed involvement with the Russian government already known to be influencing the election.

Trump's tweets, promises and contradictory statements were deciphered by the media essentially to mean the immediate end of the Affordable Care Act, "a disaster," building a border wall at Mexican expense, ending the movement to end global warming, "a hoax," and removing restrictions on coal, oil and gas pollution. He attracted a minority of Americans whom he encouraged to believe that he would bring jobs home, even while his own businesses were operating abroad and their profits were being stored offshore tax-free.

At the beginning China and Iran were the major enemies and other dictators emerged as friends, if only temporarily for some - Assad of Syria, Dutarte of the Philippines, Turkey's tough guy Erdogon, Egypt's el-Sisi, Arabia's Al Saud, and good old Vlad. The North Korean issue "would be solved." Blue-collar workers in Pennsylvania, Michigan and Wisconsin were under the impression that the coal industry would be restored by increased steel production for the multi-billion dollar wall, which would be built in "day one," preventing job hungry immigrants from entering the U.S., undocumented immigrants in the U.S. being deported, and killer Muslims from gaining entry through visas from war-torn countries.

Trump promised to "drain the swamp" of Washington establishment cronies and replacing them with experienced capitalists, inexperienced in democracy, but right thinking people. He would fill his government with America-first White supremacists, many of them military generals. A good number would come from what I call the "third confederacy" – southern racists. They would eventually be led by Steve Bannon, Trump's last campaign manager and his side-kicks Stephen Miller and Kellyanne Conway.

The Election

The eventual Election Day vote was influenced and manipulated by long-time republican state gerrymandering, voting restrictions and *Citizens United* uncontrolled millionaire cash. It was reported that eight individuals world wide, six in the United States, have as much money between them than fifty percent of the world's population. As it turns out, even so, Trump's electoral vote superiority came from four states where he won by one percent or less, giving him a surplus of electoral votes. The fix was on and the shock about to set in.

One of the chief characteristics of what has come to be called "Trump time" is the contradictory statements Trump has consistently made. It is as if he read, as another of his campaign guides, George Orwell's *1984*. As he tweeted about his struggles, not aware of the German translation of *Mein Kampf,* Trump time was being described as motivated by "Trumpthink." In Orwell's book "doublethink," "reality control," and "newspeak" were the terms used. As voters looked for a strong man in *1984,* Big Brother was his name.[1] Anyone who has ever taken a class in logic or critical thinking has learned that since the time of Socrates, twenty-five hundred years ago, that *homo sapiens* realized that it was not possible for contradictory statements to be true. But no matter, doublethink, as we are now experiencing through Trump twitter and Spicer spontaneity sounds like its right out of that book.

---

[1] Orwell, George, *1984,* New York (Signet Classics: 1980)

To know and not to know, to be conscious of complete truthfulness while telling carefully constructed lies, to hold simultaneously two opinions which cancelled out, knowing them to be contradictory and believing in both of them, to use logic against logic, to repudiate morality while laying claim to it, to believe that democracy was impossible and that the Party was the guardian of democracy....[2]

Trump, over eight months before the election, had attacked hedge-funds, promised to tax big corporations for benefits made overseas, and chastised government for not lending to small businesses.[3] He claimed he was for democracy and since the election has lent his support to several dictators. He was against the use of military force in Iraq and Syria and then for its use. He called NATO "irrelevant" and the European Union "obsolete," and now supports them. Hillary and Bill Clinton and Barak Obama were bad people and China's President Xi Jin Ping was also. The Trans Pacific Partnership was off and now it's on. Obamacare was to be immediately repealed and replaced and a wall built on the southern border at Mexican expense. And now there is no such urgency. Millions of undocumented persons would be gone and now, less than were deported in Obama's first year, is the case. The first hundred days of his administration were important and unimportant at the same time. Of course, there are many more examples of our current doublethink in Trump Time.

Sixty million Americans voted for Trump, some angry and afraid, others bored and indifferent, and many

[2] *Ibid*, p. 35.
[3] "Notorious Big," *The New Yorker*, March 28, 2016, pp. 72-75.

wanting to vent their antagonistic feelings against Hillary Clinton, perhaps thinking there would be no consequences. Democrats lost control of states as well. On the international scene, there was fear abroad. The Baltic States interpreted the shift to "isolationism" and the end to "interventionism" coming from his support for America first White supremacy proclamations led by Bannon and company.[4] Trump's negative comments on NATO and his declared friendship with Putin's Russia fanned the fumes. Russia's moves in the Ukraine seemed to have been forgotten.[5] The *Guardian Weekly* wrote about the "big epochal change in the Asian realm." Trump desired to dialogue with Kim Jong-Un, North Korean dictator, whom he described as "smart." Now, as we write, that has all changed. China was accused of raping the U.S. economy and tariffs were threatened. Now its leader is our close friend in partnership with America in subduing North Korea.[6]

After the Election

Days after the election it became evident, according to Trump, that climate change was a "hoax and it might be game over with climate change."[7] Trump has stood firm on such "false science" and currently holds the same position as an international summit later confirmed. Domestically seventy-six thousand coal miners out of a job were lured to vote for him as he promised to restore their industry in spite

---

[4] "Baltic States Fearful of Shifts in U.S. Priorities over NATO," *The Guardian Weekly,* Nov. 18-24, 2917, p. 5.
[5] "Trump's Unstoppable Rise," *Id,* p. 1, 8-9.
[6] "A Big Epochal Change in Relations with Asia Pacific," *Id,* pp. 6-7
[7] "Disaster for the Planet, Warn Climate Scientists," *Id,* p. 7.

of four million new jobs in clean air industries. It worked in three states giving Trump a one percent advantage there.

Forming a new administration began to take shape with such people as Christy, Giuliani, Bolton, Perry, Palin, Priebus, Bannon, in the news. Some of those didn't make it and many new names, primarily drawn from the military and multi-national corporations, that caused the recent recession, filled the bill. The eagerness of these secondary characters swarming around the President-elect, could remind one of Hannah Arendt's "Eichmann syndrome." Many of the touted appointees, even though described as such, disclaimed that they were bigots, misogynists, or just plain cons. All they were looking for were favors from a man obtaining complete control. [8] In return, they were willing to support his shortcomings if only they would move up the ladder to cabinet appointments.

The vote was not all it was supposed to be. Even though Clinton won by about three million, fifty-three percent of White women voted for "the self proclaimed groper ..." coming to Trump rallies in t-shirts that said things like "Hillary couldn't satisfy her husband – can't satisfy us" and shouted "lock her up."[9] Even before the election, books were coming out about the characteristics of American voters. One such book reviewed in April 2016, *American Amnesia,* put it this way: "The country has been brainwashed by a powerful alliance of forces hostile to government; big business, especially Wall Street, spending unparalleled lobbying dollars to advance its narrow self-

---

[8] "To Serve or Not to Serve," *The New Yorker,* Nov. 21, 2016, p. 29.
[9] "Muslim Sisterhood," *Id,* p. 30.

interest; a new wealthy elite propagating wrong-headed Ayn Randian notions that free markets are always good and government always bad; and a Republican Party using a strategy of attacking and weakening government as a way to win more power for itself." Matthew Bishop, writing the review, closed with persons who might lead America away from this election year alternative, people such as Bernie Sanders. Interestingly, Sanders and Trump in the primaries highlighted "wide spread anger" towards the American establishment and that there was "good reason to be angry." Bishop closed with "perhaps the unexpected strength of Donald Trump will provide a wake-up call if it isn't too late – to the republican establishment, reminding it that if all you ever do is bash government, you risk creating a vacuum that may be filled by something you really want to forget."[10] That cryptic prediction appeared to come true as the republicans first rejected Trump for insulting his fourteen republican presidential opponents but many others, one by one came to adopt him as the conduit for their own conservative programs, hungry after eight years to do so. So we were forewarned that he could be elected even though he discredited women, immigrants, people of color, unions, environmentalists, gays, military and many more. The angry voted for Trump, the comfortable ones did not, even though Clinton was their favorite. Others believed he could not win so wasting a vote for principle on Green Party and Libertarian candidates wouldn't hurt anyone but would preserve their own integrity.

---

[10] Hacker, Jacob and Pierson, Paul, *American Amnesia,* New York (Simon and Shuster: 2016); Bishop, Matthew, *New York Times,* April, 2016

Hillary Clinton was the sixth democratic presidential candidate in the past seven elections to win the popular vote, but only two of them, Bill Clinton and Obama became President. Madison was insistent that educated and virtuous Americans should be the backbone of the electorate. One weakness in that regard is that seventy percent of working Americans still don't have a bachelor's degree.[11]

Famous writer, Toni Morrison, commented on the impact of the election, "So scary are the consequences of a collapse of White privilege that many Americans flocked to a political platform that supports and translates violence against the defenseless as strength.... On Election Day, how eagerly many White voters – both the poorly educated and the well educated – embraced the shame and fear sowed by Donald Trump, the candidate, whose company has been sued by the Justice Department for not renting apartments to Black people.[12] Some Blacks voted for him and many in the South, with the citizen's right, privilege and duty to vote in a democracy, did not, including Hispanics. Others voted on their favorite and long-time single issue such as Israeli expansion or embryo protection. Capital punishment and war making were also issues popular with those inclined to vote for Trump. Christian corporations were strong supporters of recent conservative Supreme Court rulings, *Hobby Lobby*, *Citizens United* and enemies of *Roe v Wade,* along with Obamacare and climate change opposition. In so doing, they voted against many of their own self-interested needs thinking they were doing otherwise. They sacrificed the least of their brethren for their greed, lust and other deadly sins

---

[11] "Aftermath," *The New Yorker,* Nov. 21, 2016, 48; "Health of a Nation," *Id,* p. 50.
[12] "Mourning for Whiteness," *Id*, p. 54.

that surely Jesus would not advocate. Jill Lepore, in the same series of *New Yorker* articles, wrote these ringing words: "The end of a republic begins on the day when the heroism of the struggle for equality yields to the cowardice of resentment."[13]

By November 28, literary and political commentaries were coming down to earth as the reality of non-reality sunk in more deeply. "Today we woke up feeling like strangers in a foreign land," shades of William Stringfellow.[14] About the same time, *Time* magazine opened up with "Trump's presidency could mean the end of a livable climate.... Climate change is only one of the many areas where Trump could set back the progress of the Obama era."[15] He would "drain the swamp" of establishment people who believe such things.

It also became clear that he had no intention of draining the swamp even though, in the first days of his new transition team, Kellyanne Conway, Jared Kushner, Michael Flynn and Steve Bannon were prominent and inexperienced. Business-oriented cabinet choices would follow. Experienced establishment politicians would be in charge, such as Mike Pence and Reince Priebus. Initially, establishment cronies Chris Christy, Rudy Giuliani and Sarah Palin, none of who wound up in the administration, joined them.

---

[13] "Wars Within," *Id*, p. 60.
[14] "State v. Trump," *The New Yorker*, Nov. 28, 2016, p. 31; See, *An Ethic for Christians and Other Aliens in a Strange Land;*
[15] "Trump's Presidency Could Mean the End of a Livable Climate," *Time*, Nov. 28, 2016, p. 17.

In early December liberal commentators were still more taken up on the election itself. Ari Berman, writing for *The Nation* in "How the Republicans Rigged the Election" pointed out that fourteen states, including swing states had put into operation new minority voting legislation restricting that class of voters during the election year. Without the protections of the Voting Rights Act of 1965, for the first time in fifty years, these predominantly democratic voters would become less able to perform their duty as citizens.[16]

The Guardian Weekly chimed in with: "As the Trump era begins global turmoil rises. The election of the unpredictable and truculent U.S. President adds further volatility to an already complicated geopolitical situation."[17] As commentators began to see Trump examples of autocratic tendencies, the President-elect was adamant in refusing to criticize Putin, for whom he appeared to have great respect.

Around this time, unhappy with the coverage, Trump described the media as his "enemy," among others around him and in the world. Flexing his power, he tweeted that the United States "must greatly strengthen and expand its nuclear capability until such time as the world comes to its senses regarding nukes."[18] While Henry Kissinger was excusing Trump by saying he shouldn't be responsible for

---

[16] *Op Cit,* Dec. 5/12, 2016, pp. 12-14.

[17] "As Trump Era Begins Global Turmoil Rises," *The Guardian Weekly,* Dec. 12-16, p. 10.

[18] "Christmas Blessings Appeal," *Bethlehem Peace Community,* Dec. 25, 2016; "Not Our President," *Via Pacis,* Dec. 2016. "We cannot now more than ever, allow ourselves to be contented with our charitable acts and pious posturing even if we believe that our treasure is in heaven. Now is the time for drastic, risky and effective action to avoid hell here on earth.

positions he took during the campaign, I was reminded of Kennedy's "One man can make the difference and everyone should try" in the face of "what couldn't possibly happen was exactly what had happened."[19]

Inauguration

Next came the inauguration in late January to be followed by the traditional singling out of the first one hundred days of the presidency. Trump had already claimed "the greatest election win in history," which was not true, and now he imagined that before him was the largest crowd ever at an inauguration. Those who thought his inauguration would end his propensity to commit great lies, beginning with Obama's citizenship fiction, would be denied. As he reorganized the Oval Office, he gave Andrew Jackson, southern slaver and Indian bully, a premier spot behind his usually clear presidential desk. Day one arrived and prior claims of removal of Obamacare, building of a border wall, and proposals for tax reforms and budget drafts did not. The slowness of filling administration vacancies was delaying his campaign rhetoric from becoming reality. On board with confirmation was Steve Bannon, Steve Mnuchin, Todd Rickells, Gary Lohr, Walker Ross, Andrew Puzder, Elaine Chowi, Rex Tillerson, Linda McMahon, and Betsy DuVos, a collage of Wall Street executives, lobbyists and major donors. The process of draining the swamp looked like it would be fulfilled.

People were still suing him for their negative Trump University experiences while he was transforming the historic Old Post Office building into his latest profit-making

---

[19] "Kissinger and Kennedy Profiles," MSNBC, Jan. 16, 2017.

venture. I was particularly upset by that since I got my first job offer after college in that building on the first floor by a National Security Agency representative hiring college graduates to become intelligence analysts with top secret and cryptologic clearances.

The first of many bombshells had already exploded on January 11 when a *Washington Post* article reported that information had been delivered to both Obama and Trump of alleged claims that Russian intelligence had compromising material on the President elect and, as the report would unfold later, also involving several of Trump's campaign surrogates and soon to be appointees in complicity with Russian hacking and Wikileaks memos intended to disrupt the Clinton campaign and positively affect Trump.[20] It turns out that the FBI investigation had begun in July 2016 and at the time of this writing was still proceeding with numerous new revelations, almost a year later.

Shortly after the inauguration, Trump made clear his call "from this day, its America first."[21] Dissension within the staff was leaking as well as disparities between overt facts and Kellyanne Conway's claim emerging from Press Secretary Spicer's comments, that there were such things as "alternative facts." The progression of doublethink continued.[22]

Democrats were trying to stabilize their party and claimed the election, apart from Trump, was positive with Clinton's popular vote margin and its picking up two Senate

---

[20] "Trump Briefed on Claims," *Washington Post,* Jan. 11, 2017.
[21] "From This Day, America First," *The Guardian Weekly,* Jan. 27, 2017, p. 4.
[22] "White House Spat over 'Alternative Facts,'" *Id,* p. 5.

and eight House seats. But the general public was beginning to come alive, not only with street demonstrations, but well respected articles such as one in *The Atlantic* by James Fallows. He wrote as a former Bush republican: "I view Trump's election as the most grievous blow that the American idea has suffered in my lifetime.... For a democratic process to elevate a man expressing total disregard for democratic norms and institutions is worse," referring to the Kennedy and King assassinations and the wars in Vietnam and Iraq. Fallows ended by saying that American democracy is based on rules and norms and Trump disdains them all. Those who voted for him acted from "distorted, frightening and bigoted caricatures of reality."[23] "Trump think" is here to stay.

Planned Parenthood, during the campaign, had also been on the agenda for destruction as a result of a well-publicized and universally refuted claim that the organization had sold "body parts" referring to aborted fetuses. Twelve states conducted an investigation of these allegations in 2015 and all twelve found no evidence of the veracity of this claim. Nevertheless, Trump has continued, through the campaign and during the first one hundred days, with this "alternative fact" remaining the basis for his executive order eliminating Planned Parenthood from his proposed budget.[24]

Obama's farewell address expressed his concerns about the threats of economic inequality, racial divisions and

---

[23] Fallows, James, "Despair and Hope in the Age of Trump," *The Atlantic*, Jan. 1-Feb. 6, 2017, pp. 13-15.
[24] "Once Again This Week, an Investigation into Planned Parenthood's Alleged Sale of Fetal Tissue Came Up Empty," Internet, Sept., 2015.

disintegration of democratic institutions.[25] Ads appeared at the same time comparing Trump and Netanyahu in respect to their advocacies of walls, voter restrictions, deportations and attitudes of White supremacy. [26] Many commentators reported on the on-going revelations in the transformation of public power and institutions to private ones. Examples are prisons, schools, healthcare, transportation, old age benefits, guns, religion, and national parks. One billboard in my town reads, "The only wall that is needed is the one between church and state."

On the international scene *Time* wrote, "The world's only super power will sometimes partner with egotistical rogues to secure deals on favorable terms, but Trump's first days were outdoing all his predecessors with rogues in Russia, Egypt, Philippines, Turkey, France and China. Traditional allies and organizations such as England, Germany, The European Union, the United Nations and NATO were given short shrift.[27]

On January 30 the usually moderate *Time* magazine wrote about how Trump "reverses course on a century of U.S. leadership." One example was to replace a new universal healthcare system with a more expensive one to boost "the economy."[28] Trump's job ideas were confusing to many even though some had voted for him in the close states hopeful that he would use their coal mining for the steel that would build the wall, when, at this writing, no such event has

---

[25] "Parting Words," *The New Yorker*, Jan. 23, 2017, p. 17.

[26] "No to Both," J.V.P. Org. Ad, *The Nation*, Jan. 2/9, 2017.

[27] "Trump's New World Order Puts Nation over Globe," *Time*, Jan. 23, 2017, p. 24.

[28] "How to Make America White Again," *The Nation*, Jan. 30, 2017, p. 4.

occurred. With the call to resistance replacing the initial outrage, the Women's March and other groups are calling for a different replacement – that of Trump himself. In New York governmental leaders - Mayor De Blasio, Michael Bloomberg, and Governor Cuomo - were also out on the streets. As January came to an end, Trump opened with his well-known inauguration plan to make America White again.[29] The result of resistance in the streets and in the courts delaying his pet project to block immigration of Muslims from several Middle Eastern countries slammed the brakes on his campaign claims of first day Trump triumphs. Love your neighbor, not hate him/her was alive and well as Trump was reduced to pussyfooting along. And then there was February.

The First One Hundred Days

Another campaign promise was reinforced as the first hundred days began to add up in February. I will "get rid of and totally destroy" the Johnson Amendment,[30] which prohibits churches from participating in political campaigns and instructing their flocks to limit their voting issues and candidates to ones prescribed by their priests or ministers. The non-profit tax exemption status, if Trump is successful, should be removed and churches joining taxpayers in paying for that privilege. The same day, Trump appointed Jerry Falwell, Jr. to head a task force on higher education including both public and private providers. One commentator said the announcement was a shift from "the fundamentals of critical thinking and logic towards teaching

---

[29] "Trump's American Vision," *Time,* Jan. 30, 2017, p. 24
[30] Trump continues to say he will destroy the Johnson mendment by Executive Order.

a fundamentalism that is critical of thinking." [31] Such thinking includes Falwell's Liberty University, where Trump would become a graduation keynote speaker in May and where the creationist theory of the earth created five thousand years ago is taught as truth because biblical not scientific authority says it is. Three months later Trump issued an executive order to that effect, even though constitutional scholars are of the opinion that the Amendment cannot be vacated in this way.

When I was a legislator in the 1960s in Virginia, Jerry Falwell, Sr.'s church in Lynchburg, Virginia, only fifty miles away from Richmond where the Legislature met did not appear at hearings to liberalize the abortion statutes. Only two Catholic priests testified on that issue then. The issue did not become political until Ronald Reagan used it to entice Catholics to give up their Democratic Party affiliations for a republican one.

Trump signed one of many executive orders to come attacking the Affordable Care Act by directing federal agencies to prepare to unwind the law. Support for Obamacare had now risen to fifty-six percent and several town hall meetings became the voice for its preservation by both republicans and democrats. One of Trump's earliest orders was to shift federal funds to pay for the border wall. Then another killed the Trans Pacific Partnership and called for the renegotiation of NAFTA. By the same method he reinstated the public policy preventing foreign aid groups that receive U.S. assistance from promoting abortion. He announced his consideration to reactivate "black sites" where

---

[31] Trump spoke at Liberty University. One commentator engaged in the logic or lack of it in the speech.

persons could be tortured overseas and not subject to American law.[32]

The Nation followed with a John Nichols commentary noting that fifty-four percent of Americans who voted in the election backed someone other than Trump. He claimed that Trump prevailed only "because of an Electoral College that was established more than two centuries ago as a vehicle to thwart rather than confirm the will of the people."[33] Almost a month later, *The Nation* reported on a little publicized "act of the House of Representatives of January 3 reducing the salary of certain federal employees in order to get rid of individual (civil) servants who are not to their taste." Such attempts have been ruled unconstitutional in the past. Articles continued to flow on the Electoral College, gerrymandering, and restrictions on the Voting Rights Act.[34] Trump continued to talk about the wall, immigration, tax reform, the budget and Obamacare, but up to this point he had accomplished nothing substantive.

One of Trump's strong head-of-nation favorites, Israel's Netanyahu, seeking to legitimize Trump's presidency, put a hold on settlement expansion as a gift to the President and received big headlines. Two weeks later, without much fanfare, Netanyahu simply continued to do it again, further increasing Israel's attempt to outnumber indigenous Palestinians so that eventually the West Bank could be annexed without fear of a majority Arab vote. At the same time the Israeli Parliament retroactively legalized

---

[32] "How Trump is Trampling Precedent," *Time,* Feb. 6, 2017, pp. 9-10.
[33] "Trump Has No Mandate," *The Nation,* Feb. 6-13, 2017, p. 3."
[34] "You're Fired," *Id,* p. 10.

Jewish settlements, built on privately owned Palestinian land, that had been declared illegal by Israel's High Court.[35] The same *Guardian Weekly* carried a commentary on White supremacist Bannon's America first policy reinforced by isolationist Trump's declaration that NATO was obsolete.

Democrats began to find hope, even though republicans now controlled thirty-three governorships and sixty-seven of ninety-eight state legislatures. Americans were taking to the streets as never before in marches that were sponsored by women, scientists, and environmental activists. Even so, such liberal democratic senators as Elizabeth Warren and Sherrod Brown voted to confirm Ben Carson as Secretary of Housing and Urban Development. Ivanka and Jared were coming under fire for sharing their father's conflict of interest activities for which he is immune under the principle that "the king is above the law." The prince and princess are not, however. Nevertheless, at this writing, they have remained untouched. When I was in the state legislature, I authored a bill to hold all Virginia elected officials responsible for their conflicts of interest. By the time I was able to get the bill passed, it had been modified in such a way that it applied only to officials at the county level. Nevertheless, it was a first in 1968.

David Cole, Georgetown Law Center's eminent civil rights and constitutional law professor, and ACLU legal director, summed up Trump's violations of the Constitution in respect to the emoluments clause. Soon citizens would sue Trump over his conflict of interest in his Post Office building hotel venture and foreign dignitaries who feel it necessary to

---

[35] "Israeli Laws Retroactively Legalize Jewish settlements," *The Guardian Weekly,* Feb. 10-16, 2017, p. 13.

reward him by staying there so that they will receive proper attention on public issues.[36]

The month closed as Arizona republicans, inspired by Trump's far-right religious pronouncements, passed a law giving rapists the legal right to prevent women they impregnated from obtaining an abortion of "their child." A new Texas law made abortion a felony murder for both the woman and the provider.[37]

March activities would not be outdone even though a feeling was emerging that Trump's time table was, in fact, to be the first thing destroyed rather than Obamacare. The media began to poll people who voted for Trump. (I call them the "Ameri-can'ts") Many voted against Clinton, many voted not at all and a minority who voted for him were holding strong. The main reason given was that he was "tough, strong" etc. March saw the Russian investigation receiving renewed headlines. *The New Yorker* editors wrote a long piece about it claiming surveillance of the U.S. beginning in 1982 and including the meaning of the words "active measures." "Unlike classical espionage which involved the collection of foreign secrets, active measures aimed to influence events undermining a rival power."[38] That difference highlighted what was taking place. Trump had declared that Putin was "doing a great job" and that the Russian dictator was eligible to become "my best friend."

---

[36] Cole, David, "Trump Violates the Constitution," *New York Review of Books,* Feb. 23, 2017, pp. 4-5.

[37] "Hobby Lobby on Steroids," *The Nation,* Feb. 27, 2017, p. 7.

[38] "Active Measures," *The New Yorker,* March 6, 2017, pp. 40-41.

During the campaign he said that Putin was superior to Obama and his friends who were a "laughing stock."[39]

The March issue of *The New Yorker* contained non-stop articles on the "progress" of Trumpism, outlining the plusses of Obamacare, and the harm in proposed "Trumpcare" as drawn from Trump's several tweets. No legislation was yet forthcoming. It closed stating the purpose of the Russian intervention was to de-legitimize "the democratic process."[40] The media described Trump as "terrifying" and the "least popular or prepared presidential figure ... unfit for the job, ... bombastic, crude." Terrifying to a simple majority of Americans might be the case but not to a strong minority of the coalition we have been following – conservatives, Christians of a particular stamp, corporations, confederates, militarists who were now joined by democratic blue-collar workers, fired up by his strong man image. He remained what he had been – a billionaire investor and entertainer – who claimed he was smarter than others.[41] But cutting taxes for the wealthy, dropping rules and regulations, and ending public services in the name of the general welfare was at least a mixed message.

American scholars looked to a re-studying of the first liberal/conservative polarization in our history following Washington's presidency between the Hamilton/Adams conservative faction and the Madison/Jefferson liberal faction. The conservatives had great reservations about the value and stability of democracy. Hamilton was concerned

---

[39] *Ibid,* pp. 42-52.
[40] *Ibid.*
[41] "Terrifying Trump," *New York Review of Books,* March 19, 2017, p. 37.

about its economic restrictions and Adams about the prediction of Aristotle that all democracies commit suicide eventually and transfer temporarily into anarchy and finally end in autocracy. Madison was upset that government could subscribe to "the motive of private interest" and the theory of "free enterprise in place of public duty, converting its pecuniary dispensations into bounties to favorites or bribes to opponents, accommodating its measures to the avidity of a part of the nation instead the benefit of the whole."[42] Trump's ventures prior to his presidency, particularly one in Azerbaijan has been exposed as corrupt and linked to Iran's Revolutionary guard. Trump justified his action this way: "If American companies refused to give bribes, you'll do business nowhere."[43] Trump began to feel his omnipotence by asserting that the President had "unreviewable powers" beyond the founding fathers' wildest dreams.

A month before Trump's three military actions took place, his poll numbers, no higher than forty-four percent, had dropped to thirty-five percent. The *New York Review of Books* wrote "the lower his poll numbers the more outlandish his lies, the greater resistance from opponents within the bureaucracies, the thicker his scandals and chaos, the likelier he will be to seek to use a crisis, and all the opportunities it offers, to lever himself from a position of defensiveness to that of a dominating power."[44] About this time an insider conflict became public. Bannon's America first domestic

---

[42] "Alexander Hamilton's Trickle Down City," *The Nation*, March 13, 2017, p. 22.

[43] "Donald Trump's Worst Deal," *The New Yorker*, March 13, 2017, p. 48.

[44] "What He Could Do," *New York Review of Books*, March 23, 2017, p. 35.

policies would take second place to Kushner's international interventionist ones. As Trump tweeted his boldness on Syria, Afghanistan and North Korea, he would make the book reviewers' predictions come true by bombing the first two countries and threatening the third.

Worry about free speech First Amendment rights continued to surface. Such rights should be protected but in reality power not to do so resided in "a handful of wealthy tycoons and businesses in control of the most influential media outlets." Trump continued to say the media was his enemy.[45] His tweets were offered instead of hard evidence. "Fewer than half of all republican voters now believed that news organizations should be free to criticize political leaders." At the same time far-right churches should have the power to instruct their flocks on which political leaders to vote for.[46]

A shift back to the Russian hacking attack was highlighted by the revelation of General Flynn's relationship to the Russian influence for which he lost his job. The Logan Act was being considered, which declared: "Any citizen of the United States, who without authority of the United States, directly or indirectly commences or carries on any correspondence or intercourse with any foreign government ..., with intent to influence the measures or conduct of a foreign government or an officer or agent thereof ... in relation to any dispute or controversy with the United States or to defeat the measures of the United States, shall be fined under this title or imprisoned not more than three years or

---

[45] Cole, David, "Why Free Speech is Not Enough," *Id.*
[46] "Trump Isn't the Only Culprit in This Scandal," *The Guardian Weekly*, March 10, 2017, p. 16.

both."[47] Several of Trump's surrogates, it was said, may have violated these provisions as the FBI investigation continued.

To offset the publicity, Trump charged Obama with illegal surveillance of his campaign headquarters. Intelligence agencies of the government could not substantiate the claim. So he then went after Obama's National Security Advisor Susan Rice, claiming she broke rules in asking for more detailed information from the FBI and the same group found that she committed no wrongdoing as well. Meanwhile, two attempts to bar Muslims from entering the country were halted by temporary injunctions and the latest, claimed to be an improvement over the earlier one, was appealed, and set for hearing on the temporary injunction in late May.

Trump continued with his verbal commentary on Twitter too numerous to record all of them here. In March, he claimed, "America should never have given Canada its independence." Of course there was no United States of America in 1756 when the French ceded Canada to the British.[48] But in America today former slave colony North Carolina passed legislation banning transgender people (including gays) from rest rooms much like they had previously done with African Americans. A huge reaction nationally caused the former Confederate state to somewhat relax its rule.

The Atlantic magazine summed up what had been in the making for two months in "How to Build an Autocracy."

---

[47] *The Logan Act* Title 18, Chapter 45, Section 953, (1799).
[48] "Trolling the Press Corps," *The New Yorker,* March 20, 2017, pp. 52, 57.

It wrote: "Donald Trump can set the country down a path toward illiberalism, institutional subversion and endemic graft." It pointed out that "The U.S. may be a nation of laws, but the proper function of the law depends upon the compliance and integrity of those charged with executing it. A President, determined to thwart the law in order to protect himself and those in his circle, has many means to do so." The author had spoken, he said, with Trump supporters who favored a "troll army," modeled after Trump favorite dictators in Turkey and Russia, to control social media. A "piecemeal democratic erosion" is taking place."[49] A second article in the same magazine said the conclusion to be reached is that Trump is "an authoritarian threat to the survival of liberal democracy." It is backed by a decline in democracy worldwide over the least eleven years. A type of "army rule" seems to be in the offing.[50]

Moving into April, both fear of Trump and resistance to him increased. Some commentators felt the real focus for observers and activists has been the Republican Party's long time agenda. They simply found a voter-acceptable conduit for its implantation. One day they said that party must be held accountable for its complicity in supporting a person unfit for the job and unwilling to fulfill the duties of that office required by the Constitution. Moreover, Trump's associates, and primarily his Vice President, Pence, have been strong supporters as well of this attempt to destroy traditional American democracy. Speaker of the House Ryan is the one who must be most accountable for the actions of the Congress along with Senate Majority Leader McConnell.

---

[49] "How to Build an Autocracy," *Atlantic,* March 2017, pp. 44-59.
[50] "Containing Trump," *Id,* pp. 61-62.

Ryan's aim, he has publicly declared, has been "to dismantle the welfare state." He is seen as having made a bargain with the devil to do it, turning a blind eye to the inevitable consequences down the road, including a World War III nuclear war.[51]

The republican leadership violated a constitutional mandate requiring a hearing for presidential nominees to the Supreme Court. But no charge of obstruction of justice was forthcoming. Now the republicans got ready, with that success, to fill a vacancy they perpetuated for over a year, with an assured Senate majority to seat their own arch conservative nominee, which they changed the Senate rules in order to do so. Once again the great American pragmatic "ethics" of whatever works is ethical, worked. The republican nominee merrily succeeded to the Supreme Court, satisfying a minority of far right Christians hell bent on their theological views replacing constitutional ones. Their obsession with saving the emerging lives of embryos and fetuses is more important to them than the lives of human beings devastated in war, global warming, police violence, lack of health care and rape. Who are the greater killers? Those who espouse the right to live or those who vote only for the "right to life."

As for constitutional issues of judicial interpretation, nominee Gorsuch was hailed as an adequate successor to Justice Scalia's seat. He also claims to follow a so-called originalist interpretation, one that has not been followed by such republican jurists when it comes to the meaning of the Second Amendment. That absolute, fundamentalist position,

---

[51] "Trump: The Scramble," *New York Review of Books,* April 6, 2017, pp. 12-13.

which has its virtues as a *prima facie* starting point does injustice to the context of judicial issues. For example, slavery is an originalist concept, no longer tenable. To be set straight, we have only to consult the author of many parts of the Constitution and of the Bill of Rights, who as the original originalist never took such an absolute position. James Madison wrote in the *The Federalist No. 14:*

> Is it not the glory of the people of America, that, whilst they have paid a decent regard to the opinions of former times ... they have not suffered a blind veneration for antiquity, for custom, or for names, to overrule the suggestions of their own good sense, the knowledge of their own situation and the lessons of their own experience? ....Posterity will be indebted for the possession, and the world for the example, of the numerous innovations displayed .... Had no important step been taken by the leaders of the Revolution, for which a precedent could not be discovered, no government established of which an exact model did not present itself, the people of the United States might, at this moment, have been numbered among the melancholy victims of misguided councils, ... laboring under the weight of ... which have crushed the liberties of the rest of mankind. Happily, for America ... for the whole human race, they pursued a new and more noble course. ... which it is incumbent upon their successors to improve and perpetuate.

Let no one henceforth continue in the ignorance that James Madison had an absolute, fixed or irrevocable understanding of the Constitution and Bill of Rights that he authored.

With that understanding, as a constitutional lawyer, I have followed a logical and critical formula for applying the original meaning of the words and their adaption if necessary to modern needs commensurate with the intent of the Constitution. I call it a *prima facie* originalist interpretation, for that is my starting point. The first step is to see if the language consulted has a "plain" meaning to most who have the expertise to interpret it. If not, one should consult the legislative history and cultural context of the time it was composed. Finally, the needs of the current time in light of their constitutional relevance, round out a mature basis for moving in the direction that Madison foresaw. It is a living Constitution, which has as its primary objective, not its original words only, but the general welfare and a more perfect union. To hold the view with this in mind that expanding human knowledge and evolution should play no part is simply ludicrous. Nevertheless, another Scalia, perhaps a more rigid one, will be the deciding vote in the Supreme Court for many years to come in regard to the crucial issues of our times. It is expected that Gorsuch will side with the conservatives and corporation CEOs on *Citizens United* and with the religious theocrats who wish to take away the rights of the many for their particular doctrinal and dogmatic views in cases such as *Burwell v Hobby Lobby Stores, Inc.*[52] For my part, Trump's wall between Mexico and the U.S. should be left unfunded, which has temporarily been done by congressional action through September 17 and in its place the wall between church and state should remain in place for the benefit of both.

---

[52] "Case Studies," *The New Yorker*, April 3, 2017, pp. 33-34;

An anti-EPA advocate, Scott Pruitt, now heads the Environmental Protection Agency. Most Trump cabinet appointees are opposed to the very essence of the cabinet they now lead. The motivation, not hidden at all, is so these public service enterprises benefiting the common good should be de-regulated so that private enterprise will profit in every sense of that word. So it was natural that the EPA agency head announced on April 30 that its website would undergo changes to better represent the new direction the agency will take. Detailed scientific climate change data was deleted. Fact sheets on clean power and greenhouse emissions are among those removed as "out dated." Remember, its all a "hoax." And so "war is peace, etc., etc."[53] There are religious organizations that take a different position, not to mention that universally held by scientists. A Quaker magazine on earth care wrote: "A positive aspect of climate change is that it awakens us to how we are interconnected to every human being on this earth and beyond – and how fragile we are as an earth, as an island."[54] Nice words which must be followed up with active resistance.

Anxiety over health care destruction resurfaced as a bill satisfying moderate conservatives but not far right ones was withdrawn in April, only to come back to life in May and pass the House 217 to 214 when the far rights ones were enticed to vote for it once the needs of the poor, old and disabled were further compromised. The shortcomings of both bills were greatly publicized not only by democrats but

---

[53] "EPA Removes Several Climate-Related Websites," *Denver Post,* April 30, 2017, p. 62 .
[54] From a Quaker publication on the environment and earth care, *Befriending Creation,* March/April 2017.

also the American Medical Association and the American Association of Retired People, and only seventeen percent supported these bills of insurance companies attempting to practice medicine. One exception was the Kaiser Foundation that realized that allowing the states to determine whether Medicaid would keep its current expansion so that the republican ones could opt out would be harmful as part of any law that would later be passed by the Senate and House republicans together. Twenty republican votes that would not be needed anyway, saved republican congress people from a backlash of their voters in districts, which the democrats carried, by working out an arrangement so that they could vote against the bill as long as the number was limited so that the bill would pass.

The republicans claimed that protections for persons with pre-existing conditions remained in the bill, but because under the bill insurance companies, practicing medicine, were free to raise the cost of coverage for those persons, they would be unable to pay for health care. Older people were also inequitably discriminated against by being charged more than younger people as the party of the rich took from the poor, elderly and disabled and gave to their rich brethren, nothing new under the sun for the republican party of business. Many of these republicans praise their Christian religion, but dishonor Jesus as they love only their friends and act as if they hate the foreigner or any other group that stands in the way of worshipping money even though Jesus said it is the root of all evil. It was said that twenty-four million Americans would be deprived of healthcare under the first bill. The republicans decided not to get an estimate for the second bill. Trump now claimed three victories – his Supreme Court nominee, his international bombing interventions, and the passage of the House bill. The Senate thereafter announced it would write its own bill recognizing the extreme difficulties of the House measure. If not formally, the legislation is technically an amendment to the Obama law and not a repeal or replacement.[55]

Economic growth slowed towards the end of April. It had enjoyed a continuous upswing since Obama reversed the Great Recession in 2010 and significantly lowered unemployment. [56] Federal Communications Commission privacy rules were destroyed by Trump decree. Internets were deregulated, allowing servers to sell private users' information to the highest bidder. Private profit-makers celebrated the emergence of the corporate state. Government was taking the form of what was called corporatism, invented by Mussolini in the 1920s, where autocratic government and corporate capitalism partnered. You may remember that Mussolini wound up upside down at his end after twenty-five years of Italian autocratic rule.[57]

Even before the first one hundred days was completed, pundits began their summaries. Trump noted his accomplishments during these days and when others were not so complimentary he said that the first hundred days don't mean much. His concentration on himself coincided with a *Guardian Weekly* article entitled "Trump Puts America Second." His U-turn from America first domestic priority to interventionist world actions was noted as another

---

[55] "What Would it Mean for 24 Million Americans to Lose Health Insurance?" *The Nation,* April 10, 2017, pp. 21-24.
[56] "U.S. Growth and Consumer Spending is Low," *Denver Post,* April 29, 2017, p. 17A.
[57] "Transparent You," *The Nation,* April 24/May1, 2017, p. 3.

of his less than mature actions. Republican establishment "good old boys" in Congress applauded, hoping that this would stabilize Trump's presidency from here on out. Others responded "not so fast" since he has been known to include three different and contradictory policy directions in one policy statement.[58]

While the vote on the republican House healthcare bill took the major headlines, Trump's Ambassador to the U.N., Nikki Haley, called for renewed weapons tests and the demise of the nuclear test ban, while claiming "the U.S. is the moral conscience of the world." Later she added that her boss was its chief "CEO."[59]

The New Yorker published one of the first articles on a Trump demise, "What Would it Take to Cut Short Trump's Presidency?" And answered, impeachment or removal under the 25th Amendment by the Vice President with a majority of the cabinet, if he is judged to be "unable to discharge the powers and duties of his office."[60] Both seemed unlikely at that writing because the republicans control the Congress and Trump is able to discharge his duties but is simply doing so in a way that violates not his power but his legitimate duty and is leading to a demise of American democracy. The voters who elected him to office through the Electoral College were well aware of his personality and character and lack of political, military or religious experience or expertise.

---

[58] "Trump Puts America Second," *The Guardian Weekly,* April 21-27, 2017, pp. 1, 4.

[59] "United States says 'Yes' to Nuclear Weapons Tests, 'No' to a Treaty Ban," *Counterpunch,* May 5, 2017

[60] "End Game: What Would it Take to Cut Short Trump's Presidency?" *The New Yorker,* May 8, 2017, pp. 38-45.

Ninety-eight percent of Trump voters polled still enthusiastically supported everything he says and does.

In the first week in May Arkansas chose to execute four people within days of each other. The push to this "barbarism" is in sharp contrast "to prevailing thinking about capital punishment." Support for it in 1994 was at eighty percent. Today it is at its lowest since 1971, forty-nine percent with Trump joining that number.[61] The confederate coalition of republican southern states in the past forty years has led in this slaughter with 1,184 executions compared to only four in the north. Homicide figures in 2015 showed they were seventy-nine percent higher there proving again that the death penalty as a deterrent is a fallacy. The Bible belt opts for revenge, retribution, and retaliation rather than reconciliation and rehabilitation. Certainly, the forgiving seventy times seven of Jesus takes second place to an eye for an eye from Moses.

In March Trump had called drug prices "outrageous," speaking to his voting constituency. But when he met with drug company executives in May, he made no mention of anything outrageous, but told them "price fixing stifles innovation." It seems that what is stifled is the need of human beings for healthcare at the expense of the needs of business investors to maximize their profits.[62]

Trump moved to other economic roadblocks for such people when he promised to destroy the Dodd-Frank law, which attempted to control predator banks by re-establishing

---

[61] "Out of Time," *Id,* pp. 15-16.

[62] "The Issue: An Insider's Guide to Why Drug Prices Keep Rising Despite Widespread Complaining," *AARP Bulletin,* May 2017, pp. 17-24.

the Volcker rule that acts to separate regular banks from investment or predator banks. He threatened to break up the U.S. 9th Circuit Court of Appeals, angry with their ruling on immigration and to withdraw from international climate change obligations, reverse positions on NAFTA, renew oil drilling in the arctic and deregulate nutritional information and warnings required on labels of consumers products. Observers commented on the expense of his alternative White House weekend trips, paid by taxpayers in the millions. To top it all off, he decided to terminate White House interviews and to not attend the annual White House correspondents' dinner. Meanwhile, Jared Kushner's sister pushed China to invest in her business while Trump was meeting with the Chinese president on North Korean aggression.

The most complete one hundred days summary was compiled by *The New Yorker* editors who quoted Trump as saying "I am what I am." That reminded me of the Old Testament God who described himself as "I am who am." Writing for *The New Yorker*, David Remnick began: "He undermines the country he has been elected to serve and the stability he has pledged to ensure." And that he is "scarcely more reliable than any of the world's autocrats." One day NATO is obsolete, the next day it is "no longer obsolete." The Chinese are "grand champions of currency manipulation." Later, they are really good friends. At one time he loves Wikileaks and now he doesn't. His one consistency centers on his plutocratic propensities. His inherited real estate empire has been "distinguished by racist federal housing violations." It is recalled that he was a frequent visitor in the past to Studio 54. Always with a commentary, he was quoted as saying, "I would watch super models getting screwed ... on a bench in the middle of the room."[63] A true voyeur, one could say he now watches the ninety-nine percent getting screwed by his top one percent cabinet appointees. His cabinet appointees for the most part are either ignorant of their cabinet function or have already taken a stand contrary to its mission.

Trump has admitted that "the day I realized it can be smart to be shallow was for me a deep experience." His similarities to Huey Long and George Wallace and his Mussolini-like expressions that Alec Baldwin imitates so well would be funny if not so scary. On the Chinese president's first visit, his daughter Ivanka was present, while she was also selling her shoes and handbags in his country.

David Remnick concluded with "the Trump presidency represents a rebellion against liberalism itself – an angry assault on the advance of groups of people who have experienced profound, if fitful, empowerment over the past half century." He has not "welcomed these moral advances; his language, his tone, his personal behavior, and his policies all suggest and foster, a politics of resentment.... The task now is not merely to recognize the presidency for the emergency it is, and to resist its assault on the principles of reality and the values of liberal democracy, but to devise a fabric, to debate, to hear one another, to pursue and revive precious things."[64]

Summer Heat

The pace quickened after reaching the first one hundred days and conclusion of the month of May found the

---

[63] "One Hundred Days," *The New Yorker,* May 1, 2017, p. 24.
[64] *Ibid*

Presidency reeling in shock over new revelations. Trump's firing of the FBI Director on May 9 was the spark that set it off. Trump claimed that the "Trump-Russia" investigation was a "taxpayer funded charade," and James Comey was accused of "atrocities."[65]

While little legislation was forthcoming, a bi-partisan effort to defeat some oil and gas regulations was defeated in the Senate 49-51. Comparisons of Trump to Nixon and Watergate began to be the subject of discussion. Was there an obstruction of justice or a "clear and present danger of a cover up" as in Watergate? Commentators were reluctant to agree that this was the case yet.

Former Director of National Intelligence, James Clapper, lamented that American democracy was "under assault," both internally and externally. "America's founding fathers had created three co-equal branches of government with checks and balances, but with Trump as President that was now eroding."[66]

Virtually forgotten, recused Attorney General Sessions spoke up by issuing a sweeping new drug policy, instructing his federal prosecutors to charge defendants with the greatest crimes and penalties, destroying former Attorney General Holder's policy to consider the facts in each case where they might result in lesser charges and penalties.[67] As an aside, this would also help to rebuild private prisons, a Trump business aim, with increased prison population

---

[65] "100 Days in Office," *Guardian Weekly,* May 5, 2017, p. 16.
[66] "U.S. Government Under Assault, Clapper Says," *Denver Post,* May 2017.
[67] "Sessions Issues Sweeping New Drug Charging Policy," *Denver Post,* May 13, 2017, p. 16A

profits. Still under the belief that fraud was the reason for Clinton's winning three million votes, Trump, with yet another executive order created a commission to investigate what many considered non-existent.

By May 17, the world was given new facts on Trump's conversation with the Russian Foreign Minister and Ambassador to the U.S. in the Oval Office, where the American press was prohibited from attending. It was revealed that Trump disclosed classified information to the Russians, which came from Israel. On May 18 the stock market plunged in reaction. Trump's proposed budget to be released in forthcoming days had a provision that it would cut ten billion dollars from college programs and would channel part of that sum into private school choice enterprises. A day later it came out that Trump had asked Comey to put out the word that he was not under investigation. His chief of staff had also asked that Comey "push back" on the Russian investigation.

Senator Rich Bluementhal of Connecticut commented that "here we have the theft of democracy." Trump described it in another way: "No politician in history has been treated worse or more unfairly." The reports kept coming out as Comey's February notes indicated, according to a close friend, that Trump pressed him to drop the Flynn prob. News releases by cabinet members tried to get other issues in the headlines. Treasury Secretary Steven Mnuchin expressed his view that efforts to break up banks were a huge mistake as a deterrent to recession, and the Trump administration did not support the separation of regular banks and investment banks, in order to end a conflict of interest, because it hurt financial markets. The Trump administration continued on its raids of undocumented immigrants. It was reported that the ones Trump deported included an increase of one hundred and fifty percent of those without criminal records.

The last straw, which had always seemed to be until the next day, was the report that Trump, at the same time he revealed classified information had described Comey as a "crazy nut job" and that his removal eased "great pressure" on the investigation. Trump had already described Comey as a "grand stander and show boat." On the same day, May 19, it was reported that a senior Trump White House staff advisor was another subject of FBI investigation. The day before, Robert Mueller was appointed Special Independent Counsel with prosecutorial power to take over the investigation. McCain saw this as shades of Watergate and impeachment scenarios began.[68] Trump characteristically described the alarming events as a "witch hunt." But he admitted that he had disclosed to the Russians the comments reported by the press, but as President he was free to do so. He added, "I think it's totally ridiculous. Everyone thinks so."[69]

During the campaign Trump said he knew the answers to everything: "I know more about ISIS than the generals do." To confront terrorism you have to use methods that are "frankly unthinkable" and "a hell of a lot worse than waterboarding." Trump's methods, as President, were easily predicted from a description of the methods he used which

---

[68] "Special Counsel Appointed," *Denver Post,* May 18, 2017, pp. 1-6A

[69] "Trump Claims Witch Hunt," *Denver Post,* May 19, 2017, pp. 1-16A

he stated in one of his books: "Always get even. When you are in business you need to get even with people who screw you. You need to screw them back fifteen times harder ... go for the jugular, attack them in spades!" Trump was asked at a meeting with Evangelical voters Iowa whether he had ever had a reason to ask for God's forgiveness. He responded "why do I have to, you know, repent, why do I have to ask for forgiveness if I'm not making mistakes?"[70] Nevertheless, almost eighty-one percent of White Evangelical voters backed Donald Trump for President and fifty-seven percent believed "God had a direct hand in elevating Trump to the Presidency." In appreciation for such overwhelming Christian support the new President issued one of his first proclamations designating the date of his inauguration as a "national patriotic day of devotion." His latest executive order sought to empower Christian employers with the right to prohibit health coverage for contraceptives even though pediatrician and obstetrician organizations oppose his action.[71] He earlier said: "I want to take everything back from the world that we have given them." There goes the Sermon on the Mount on it's better to give than receive.

It was easy to figure out how Trump as President would end the civil service permanent employment, which was designed to protect government employees from political coercion. "The public employee unions will just come unglued." Next, he went after the media: "We have to repeal our libel laws" that protect reporters so that "we can

---

[70] "A Look at Trump and His Inside 'Alleged Christian Faith,'" *Colorado Springs Gazette,* Sept. 17, 2015
[71] "Masters of Schism," *The Nation,* June 5/12, 2017, p. 42; "Roll Back of Birth Control Mandate," *Denver Post,* May 31, 2017, pp. 1A, 11A

sue them and win lots of money." Earlier he had said about the Russians, but not to their face, "fuck you." Today the Russians are his buddies. A former White House official commented: "Honestly, the problem with Donald is he doesn't know what he doesn't know."[72] Ignoring that, Trump gave himself a one hundred day grade of A for achievement and his communications staff a C.[73]

Leading up to his trip abroad, still faced with the firing of Comey and the sharing of classified information with the Russians, a new leak came out that Comey had told his colleagues that he considered Trump to be "outside the realm of normal" and even "crazy."[74] But more was to come. Jared Kushner became "a person of interest" with revelations that he had talked several times with the Russians during the campaign, with General Flynn present, about setting up a private line of communications, using Russian systems, designed to shield comments from American intelligence intercepts.

With that the Trump entourage took off for trips to Muslim Saudi Arabia where a one hundred and ten billion dollar weapons deal with the Saudis was headlined. Thereafter he met with Israel's Netanyahu, Palestine's Abbas, the Vatican's Pope Francis and summit meetings in Belgium and Italy. The Saudis and Israelis praised him for his stand on using military and financial threats against Iran,

---

[72] "President Trump," *The New Yorker,* September 26, 2016, pp. 49-32.
[73] "May Days," *The New Yorker,* May 29, 2017, p. 16
[74] The Goldwater Rule, *The New Yorker,* May 22, 2017, pp. 18-23.

ending Obama's diplomatic alternatives. Some editorials lauded him for acting "presidential."[75]

There was a sigh of relief as Trump was scheduled to meet with two nations, which were at odds with Obama and would welcome the new President with honors and praise. Egypt, a nation charged with oppression against human rights, and Israel, a nation that had violated U.N. resolutions condemning it for its aggressive fifty-year military occupation of Palestine and for its illegal one hundred and twenty-six colonies there. A quick aside with the Palestinian President, Abbas, was followed with a public and private meeting with the Pope. During the campaign the Pope had said, "a person who sets about building walls and not building bridges is not a Christian." Trump tweeted that the Pope's comments were "disgraceful." It was reported that their meeting found them at odds on issues involving the poor, healthcare, immigration and climate control.

Moving to the Brussels conference with NATO, Trump's previous comments followed him there as well, since he described the place as "a hell hole." Several differences with NATO members resulted in Trump's refusal to support Article V defined as the Defense Doctrine of "one for all, all for one." He criticized NATO members for their financial obligation failures, but no one mentioned that the U.S. is billions of dollars behind in U.N. support. He could not refrain from criticizing Germany. Chancellor Merkel retorted that Germany can no longer rely on the U.S. and that it must take its fate into its own hands. Trump tweeted, "Germany is very bad for us." Moving to Sicily, Trump

---

[75] "Trump on Foreign Trip With Fresh Baggage," *Denver Post,* May 20, 2017, pp. 1A, 11A.

attended the G7 conference where he was in disagreement with the six other nations supporting climate control. He would not say whether he would attend the June conference on that topic or change U.S. policy supporting it, since he claims it is a Chinese hoax.[76]

Back at home; Trump's budget was released in its final form. Eight hundred billion dollars will be removed from Medicaid. But the Russian investigation continued to dominate the headlines. It now seems that Trump had not only contacted Comey but the Directors of National Security and National Intelligence as well, asking them to desist from their Russian investigation. Meanwhile, Michael Flynn said he would "take the fifth" instead of testifying. Trump preferred to reflect on his trip abroad, describing it as "a home run, historic and groundbreaking." A White House official claimed he had "united the entire Muslim world."[77]

Before him remained several major issues. 1) The immigration ban imposed by the federal courts would go to the Supreme Court. 2) Healthcare, said to deprive twenty-three million Americans of their coverage was before the Senate. 3) Comey would testify before the Senate Intelligence Committee on the Russian investigation the first week in June, and 4) the Paris Climate Change Conference awaited Trump's decision on whether it was all a hoax. Sixty-seven percent of Americans support the Paris Accords. After four months in the Presidency, Trump was indeed inventing a new Presidency.

---

[76] "Trump Claims Home Run," *Denver Post*, May 28, 2017, pp. 1A, 6A
[77] *Ibid*

David Cole, National Legal Director of the ACLU and a professor at Georgetown University Law Center, summed it all up in an article in *The Nation*.[78] He asked the question "whether there is any norm that Donald Trump will not defy?" He reviewed in a paragraph much of what has been written here. Trump refused "to release his tax returns, threatening to jail his opponent, demeaning veterans, and having bragged about grabbing women 'by the pussy.' As President he imposed a travel ban on people from predominately Muslim countries and explained on television that he intended to favor Christians. He has called the media 'enemy of the people' and the judge who enjoined his first travel ban a 'so-called judge.' He has shared highly classified intelligence with Russian officials and pressured Comey to drop the criminal investigation of Gen. Michael Flynn, his national-security advisor. And he's admitted that 'this Russia thing with Trump' was on his mind when he decided to let Comey go, just as the FBI investigation into Russia's interference in the presidential election – and the Trump campaign's possible collusion was heating up."

Cole continues, our democracy includes "notions that presidents should respect the other branches of government, that lying is unacceptable, and that the President, who technically oversees all federal law enforcement, should not interfere in criminal or counter intelligence investigations – especially those that concern the President himself or his close friends and advisors."

One of Trump's closest and most loyal allies is his Vice President, Mike Pence. He has agreed to Trump's agenda and actions, supported Trump's fake news, is

---

[78] "Making Trump Pay," *Denver Post,* June 5/12, 2017, pp. 3-4.

complicit in responsibility for them, and as a consequence he must be held equally liable for all that has been done to diminish American democracy.

With the arrival of June, subpoenas were issued to Kushner, Flynn, Manafort and others to testify before the Senate, House and Intelligence Committee. Comey was to testify on June 8. The month opened with the two contrasting and conflicting approaches to the current state of affairs. One pursued the Trump administration's efforts to pass negative and deregulating congressional legislation and presidential executive orders. The other continued the attempt to resist the impending movement of authoritative government by investigations, demonstrations and calls to remove the President or impeach him for collusion by him or his associates with Russia, a foreign power, or for obstruction of justice through him or his associates by interfering with the FBI investigation.

The month heated up physically with triple-digit temperatures throughout the southwest, preceded by Trump's withdrawal from the Climate Change Accords, joining only Syria, which rejected its intrusion and Nicaragua, which believed it didn't do enough. Former U.S. Secretary of State Kerry, who was instrumental in the Accords had this to say: "He promised to put America first but he has put America last. This is one of the most self-destructive moves and self-defeating actions any president has ever undertaken"[79]

Trump also made good on his promise to far-right Christians to allow organizations such as the Denver-based Little Sisters of the Poor to exclude contraceptives from their

---

[79] From his June press release and interview on MSNBC.

health care insurance coverage for their employees who didn't share their personal, theocratic views. Currently, the U.S. rate of pregnancy fatalities is the highest in the world. Apparently, contraceptives are bad but oil and gas development in Arctic wildlife regions is good or so says another Trump executive order.

Fake news and lies continued from the President's mouth. I am reminded of Jill Lepore's inclusion in one of her articles, of Hitler's writings in *Mein Kampf* that most people "are more easily victimized by a large than by a small lie, since they sometimes tell petty lies themselves, but would be ashamed to tell big ones." Archibald McLeish wrote: "Democracy is never a thing done. Democracy is always something a nation must be doing."[80] The President and many in this nation are not now doing it.

Comey testified on June 8, stating publically under oath that Trump asked him to back off on the Russian election investigation. He refused to do so, he said. Comey testified in open session and later behind closed doors with classified information. In an attempt to gain the headlines, the Republican House majority passed a bill to repeal Dodd-Frank and the Volcker rule, which restored banks to their pre-recession unregulated, destructive power. Nevertheless, between June 8 and June 12, Comey's testimony and its import was center stage. Discussion continued as the White House reiterated that the President is not responsible to laws, which are applied to other governmental representatives and therefore is above the law, like the kings of old. Trump began to privatize air traffic control next in order to

---

[80] "The Strategy of Truth," *The New Yorker,* 5/12, 2017, pp. 57-58.

disassemble the union, which protects such employees. Returning to comments on global warming and oil and gas increases, he tweeted: "The U.S. is the most clean and environmentally friendly country."

Comey's testimony was released in legal form the day before he testified. On the same day two FBI directors, NSA Director Rogers and DNI Director Coates testified with much of what they knew, but only in closed session by their own choice. Both stated that it was "inappropriate" to speak of the President in public and consequentially citizens and voters could not hear whether they would testify in closed session that Trump attempted to influence them to halt the Russian investigation. Comey had no such reservations in open session. He stated: "It is my judgment that I was fired because of the Russian investigation. …The Russians interfered …" with the election. Trump said afterward that Comey was the liar and Republicans picked up on Comey's allowing a professor friend of his to release his version of meeting with the President where other members of his cabinet were asked to leave and Trump then asked him for his loyalty. He also read from his notes that he was invited to a dinner with the impression that there would be other people present, but it turned out to be only he and Trump in private conversation.

The Russian investigation got ever deeper as it was revealed that they had infiltrated voting systems in the election. As Trump's popularity dropped to thirty-six percent in mid-June, his actions on the Climate Change Accords was disapproved by sixty percent of those polled. Attorney General Sessions, who would testify on June 16, was heard by intercepts to have had more than two conversations with the Russians, although under oath at his nomination hearing, he stated he had none. Meanwhile Trump announced his intention to hand back two diplomatic compounds to Russia, which Obama had taken away earlier.

The Middle East got hotter, the Sunni nations, taking on Qatar for aiding the Shiites. Trump was with the "Faith and Freedom" evangelists, one thousand of them, giving their renewed support to him at a breakfast where he was the main speaker. The AARP pleaded again against Obama health care repeal and the Senate narrowly overturned federal guidelines for states establishing retirement plans to benefit employees who found themselves working in the private sector but were not offered one by their employer.[81]

Trump's final comment on Comey was that he would be willing to testify "one hundred percent" to show Comey was the liar and had intimated, without proof, that he had taped Comey in their conversations.

Elizabeth Drew wrote a stellar article for the *New York Review of Books* on the issue of collusion. She cited persons "close to the President" who were under surveillance by the FBI, including Manafort, Stone, Page, Kushner and now Sessions. Special Counsel Mueller would initiate investigation into criminal acts, while the Senate and House would continue their investigations into non-criminal acts, which could lead to impeachment or removal. She quoted 19th century British parliamentarian, Edmund Burke who said: "Statesmen, who abuse their power ... upon the enlarged and solid principles of state morality."[82] The

---

[81] AARP.org/Bulletin, June 2017.
[82] Drew, Elizabeth, "Trump: The Presidency in Peril," *New York Review of Books,* June 22, 2017, p. 59.

specific issue that now would constitute an abuse of our democratic principles of state morality is not whether Trump or his associates influenced the FBI or other agencies to deter their investigation, but whether they attempted to do so. That would be obstruction of justice. The issue of collusion turns on whether somewhere in the numerous conversations many Trumpites had with Russians before Trump was elected constituted a violation of the Logan Act, making it criminal for non-governmental persons to attempt to interfere with American foreign policy and practices.

One Hundred and Sixty Days and Counting

As we approached our 241st Independence Day, Trump's first six months in office will come shortly thereafter. We waited six weeks for Trump to tell us whether he taped Comey. He didn't. The words of the Senate health care bill were next to be revealed as the continuing Russian investigation revelations were still before us as were the further testimonies of Attorney General Sessions, General Flynn, Coates and Rogers.

Comey's testimony necessitated Sessions' appearance before congress on June 16. He was grilled on denying he ever had contact with Russians on matters concerning the campaign or administration. It turned out that he did, not twice but three times. Trump was not happy with his Attorney General nor was he with Special Counsel Mueller's investigation, which he described as "the greatest witch hunt in American political history" and threatened to fire him, ala Nixon.

Terrorist attacks continued abroad and here at home where statistics showed that there is at least one shooting each day in America where more than one in four people die or are wounded. At the same time stricter gun laws are dead as well.[83]

Trump's taxes remained a secret but his financial records were revealed with several discrepancies between what he claimed and what the actual figures were. Conflicts of interest and suspicious business partnerships were scrutinized.

To please his base, Trump announced his tougher attitudes towards Cuba, presumably with the intent to replace leftist President Castro with a new Batista-type conservative who will reinstate privileged land development opportunities, casinos and prostitutes, all of which Trump has had dealings with in the past. (If not prostitutes, he claimed "pussies.")

On June 19 it was announced that closed-door secret drafts of a new Trumpcare bill was in progress, which would not be released for anyone other than thirteen republicans to see before June 22 and would be voted on by June 27 without hearings or amendments before congress adjourned for the summer. Senator Bluementhal referred to the process as "a very toxic recipe for democracy." Toxicity is also in the air as a new scientific study reported, "the killer heat is getting worse. ...The United States is going to be an oven if the government fails to act" on this "lethal heat condition."[84] Triple digit temperatures were back in half the nation.

The same day another report on lethal power came out of the U.S. Supreme Court, which decided to hear a case

---

[83] Coll, Steve, "A Politics of Anger," *The New Yorker,* June 26, 2017, p. 17.

[84] "Too Hot to Handle," *Denver Post,* June 20, 2017, p. 1A,4A.

this fall on gerrymandering and redistricting. A lower court in Wisconsin had struck down redistricting there. However, the Court decided to keep it in place until they reached a final vote in the fall. Newly appointed Justice Gorsuch was the deciding vote on continuing the undemocratic process so that it could effect the next election in favor of the republicans regardless of how the Supreme Court finally decides.[85] Meanwhile, a new study indicated that a type of redistricting and gerrymandering that the Supreme Court prohibited in the past because it resulted in a definite advantage for one party, did so in the states of Michigan, Pennsylvania, Wisconsin, Virginia, Florida and North Carolina. Trump won in close races in all these states except Virginia.[86] Another poll showed that one- party rules now in forty-two percent of state races, mostly republican.[87] The one-party state was a favorite of Stalin, Mussolini, Hitler, Mao and Castro.

More undemocratic events followed. The Trump administration decided to limit news briefings on the basis that meetings with the media "had ceased to pay dividends." A former Reagan communications team member, Eric Dezenhall said, "Its terrifying from a democracy standpoint." Later Trump would end the use of cameras in reduced briefings. Interestingly, John Toland, in his book *Adolph Hitler,* reminded us that one of the first things Hitler did when he gained power was to limit the media and then

---

[85] "Power Shift Could Come," *Denver Post,* June 20, 2017, p. 1A, 4A

[86] "Re-examining Redistricting," *Denver Post,* June 25, 2017, P. 6A

[87] "More Running Unopposed," *Denver Post,* June 24, 2017

control it.[88] Democratically elected authoritarian Trump puts new meaning in the word "brief" in news briefings.

While all of this was taking place and to get away from it, I was reading a biography of Albert Einstein, which at the same time was on TV in a mini series entitled "Genius." I was struck by Einstein's attitude and comments, such as "Blind respect for authority is the greatest enemy of truth," and "we are dealing with a threat to the basic existence of humanity," referring to the threatened use of atom weaponry.[89] Einstein's portrayal also reminded me of the House Un-American Activities Committee and McCarthy investigations of Americans in the 50s, including Einstein, where scientists among others were suspected of being Communists, disloyal to the government. Hitler also required that scientists take a pledge of loyalty to Hitler and the new "Aryan science."[90]

New revelations on the further extent of Russian infiltration into the American 2016 election contained the report that twenty-one states were under attack through hacking and were under Putin's direction. Voter records were obtained and databases, as reported by the *New York Times*, but again the disclaimer was included that these activities had no affect on the election's outcome.[91] More Trump promises went by the board because Trump claimed he would not touch Medicaid, but the new Senate Trumpcare

---

[88] Toland, John, *Adolph Hitler,* Ware, England (Wordsworth: 1997) p. 295.

[89] Isaacson, Walter, *Einstein, His Life and Universe,* New York, (Simon and Schuster: 2007) p. 68.

[90] *Id* "Red Scare," pp. 524-534.

[91] CNN TV news report, June 23, 2017.

bill deeply affected such coverage. Doctors, AARP, Nurses, and many other medical professionals, including drug companies, came out against it again. Disabled people committed civil disobedience in front of republican Majority Leader Mitch McConnell's office.

The period between June 22 and 27 featured an intense consideration of the senate healthcare bill and its subsequent re-writing when several republicans on both the left and right said they could not support the bill unless there were changes made to accommodate their concerns. As far as this author is concerned, among the several reasons why the bill is not acceptable, the most important one doesn't seem to be addressed by anyone. It was not addressed in Obamacare and is the main reason why its costs increased, and not because the republicans believed it was Obama's fault. The fault lies in the fact that unless those who are raising the costs – insurance companies and pharmaceuticals, have a cap on their costs and opt-outs, it will kill any bill.[92]

During the last week of June, Trump's popularity held steady between thirty-six to forty percent but only twenty percent of Americans approved of the senate bill when it came out of committee. One reason for its disapproval was the thirty-one states that have enacted Medicaid extensions in the past, would take on the extra burden of paying for them. They are mostly democratic states. The republican national government, however, would relieve itself of the burden of Medicaid expansion in order to free up monies to aid the needy rich. Eighteen mostly southern and western republican states would not seriously

---

[92] "Putting Profits Ahead of Patients," *The New York Review of Books,* July 13, 2017, p. 47. Single payer would not do so.

be affected since they did not take on extended Medicaid in the first place.[93] "Trumpcare" is looking more and more like "no care."

Another Trump promise not kept was to stop jobs from going out of the country. But after six months they continue to do so. Support for democratic control of the government rose to forty-three percent and republican support fell to twenty-six percent. That left thirty-one percent who didn't seem to be convinced that the conditions of the day were of any import, after all that has been said.

The Vice-President kept his promise to be "an unwavering ally" of the President. Speaking in Colorado Springs to the Focus on the Family Christian/military supporters with offices next to the Air Force Academy, he declared, "Under this President's leadership, life is winning in America."[94] Good choice of words since living doesn't seem to be winning. As if it will never end, further limitations on the rights of federal employees were announced with a new law that makes it easier for the President to fire any employee who doesn't agree with him.[95]

Back to the Paris Agreement on Climate Change and Trump's animosity toward it, at least eighty mayors have come out in support of the Agreement in spite of Trump.[96] They plan to initiate their own applications of the Agreement's requirements in their cities and towns. Not to

---

[93] *Ibid.* June 24, 2017

[94] "Pence Speaks," *Denver Post,* June 24, 2017

[95] "New Law Makes it Easier to Fire Agency Employees," *Denver Post,* June 27, 2017, p. 16A

[96] "U.S. Mayors Focusing on Climate," *Denver Post,* June 25, 2017.

be outdone, Trump announced the removal from his proposed budget support for earthquake alerts.

Democrats began to question themselves, as commentators wrote and spoke about what's wrong with the Democratic Party. Seemingly everything, but most often cited is that the party "has no message." Something is wrong when polls show that forty-two percent of Americans believe the democrats are the party of the rich, twice the number who consider that true of Trump's agenda.[97] Peter Emerson of Huffpost claimed that "anti-Trump is played out," and "our values are under attack" is not message. He spoke on MSNBC with that notion on June 24, but had no suggestions on what to do about it. Since this book, from beginning to end is an alert to resist the powers and principalities because "our values are under attack," if he is right this book is obsolete before it is ever published. But I believe otherwise.

Naomi Klein, in the July issue of *The Nation*,[98] wrote that the limited establishment options, which are being used worldwide to fight the right wing corporate coup insurgents, need to be replaced by a greater resurgence. She recognizes that the resistance movement has reached "levels beyond which organizers say they have never seen before." The new option she suggests combines with that to form a positive and not only negative emphasis called "progressive transformational change." It names many of the human, civil and constitutional programs and legislation that have been put forth in this book to replace the negative surge of right

---

[97] See also Foer, Franklin, "What's Wrong With the Democrats?" *The Atlantic,* July/August 2017, p, 48-58.
[98] Klein, Naomi, "Daring to Dream in the Age od Trump," *The Nation,* July 3/10, 2017, pp. 14-16.

wing conservatism. Resistance stops the negative progressive movements; restarts the positives.

At this point in the continuing saga many Americans ask themselves what is the limit to the republican administration's disparagement of democratic process by its president? Is there any? Donald Trump boasted, "I could stand in the middle of 5th Avenue and shoot somebody and I would not lose any voters." He is almost right. Polls indicate he has lost only about two percent of his hard core. John Nichols writes, as calls heighten for impeachment that "the separation of powers protections outlined in the Constitution have taken a beating on the long march from George Washington's prudent administration to the imperial presidency that Trump inherited." Patriots have always feared "a king for four years." Forty-eight percent, at Nichols' writing, now support impeachment with forty-one percent opposed. Impeachment appears to be the only tool for errant presidents.[99]

The period between the last week in June and the 4th of July holidays marking Trump's first 160 in office arrived with the republican attempt in the U.S. Senate to vote through a health care repeal and replacement bill. The text proved unsatisfactory to at least four moderate and four conservative republicans for different reasons. Two days before the final vote scheduled for June 29, it was postponed until after the holidays. One of the crucial blows to it, of several, was the Congressional Budget Office report that twenty-two million would not be covered by 2026 and fifteen million already in 2018. The bill cost three hundred

---

[99] Nichols, John, "For Impeachment," *The Nation,* June 19/26, 2017, p. 4.

million dollars less over a period of ten years as a result of less coverage. Premiums would be cut out, but out-of-pocket expenses would increase. Cuts in Medicaid would also add to the savings of money, the republicans chose to obtain, rather than the savings of life and limb of human beings. A poll, out on June 28 by Marist/PBS, found only seventeen percent approval of the Senate bill, even with attempts at further revision and with fifty-five percent disapproval. Statistics released earlier in the week indicated that presently Medicaid covers twenty percent of all Americans, thirty-nine percent children, forty-nine percent of births and sixty-four percent of nursing homes. Not only the public, but also the professionals were still opposed and were joined by a republican minority.[100] For these reasons, the democrats held fast against it.

Our final take on the undemocratic attempt to repeal and replace the Affordable Care Act with the so-called Better Care Reconciliation Act comes from Amy Davidson's commentary in the July 3 issue of *The New Yorker.*[101] "Before Obamacare, when people who had insurance developed a serious health condition, they often discovered that it wasn't covered by their policy." Co-payments, deductibles, caps – "their coverage amounted to little more than a discount coupon on something that remained unaffordable." – hospitalization, pediatrics and chronic disease care. The Obama bill defined these services as "essential health benefits" which required private insurance plans to cover. The House and Senate bills allow states to

---

[100] "Health Bill Puts Focus on GOP Goal," *Denver Post* reprint of *Washington Post* article, June 25, 2017, p. 21A; TV news reports June 26-27, 2017.
[101] "Feeling Worse," July 3, 2017, p. 17-19.

waive coverage of "essential benefits." This is all the more reason for a single payer option to be an essential part of any improved health plan.

The republican disappointment had been preceded by a slight lift when the U.S. Supreme Court agreed to hear the merits of the Trump travel ban in the fall in spite of almost unanimous lower court support of the ban. All nine Justices agreed to do so and to lift the ban preventing foreign nationals from the six Middle Eastern nations affected who have contacts or ties with U.S. relatives or other connections established, but to continue the ban until the fall for any who have no such contacts or ties. In any case, the ban was to run for ninety days beginning several months ago, but that amount of time will again be consumed before the Court hears the case, which by that time may be moot.[102]

While bills and bans were the decisions of the day, the White House decided to create one of its own. First it limited the number of White House briefings, then banned media personnel from sitting in on health care discussions, and finally decided to disallow photo coverage of White House briefings whenever it cared to.

To detract from the on-going Russian investigation Trump switched the blame to Obama, accusing the former President of collusion and obstruction by not acting at all to counter the Russian hacking during the campaign. The facts proved otherwise, as Obama added sanctions, removed Russian officials from their mansions in the U.S. and sent them home, and spoke to Putin personally. No matter.

---

[102] "Officials Finalizing Details of Trump's Revised Restrictions," *Denver Post,* June 29, 2017, p. 13A.

What's true is what's Trump. Another attempt was to focus the news on Trump allegations that the Syrians were preparing for another chemical attack. Whether to believe Trump took another blow when the *New York Times* published a document consisting of all the lies that Trump, in the first one hundred and fifty-four days, averaging, they said, about one a day.

More bad news came out on June 28 when it turned out that former Trump campaign manager, Paul Manafort, finally registered retroactively as a foreign lobbyist, having made millions from his clients, some of which during the time when he was managing the campaign. Meanwhile, Ivanka Trump's way offshore Chinese factory, which could hardly employ American workers, was charged with low pay and abuse of its employees.[103]

One of the most serious pending issues, a hoax to Trump, but a horror to most others, is global warming and climate change. Secretary of Energy, Perry, who at one time wanted to terminate the department, admitted that "climate change is happening" and "it will have a tremendous impact on the economy." Sadly missing was its impact on us humans. Bill Nye, well known scientist, speaking on the Velshi and Ruhle MSNBC news commentary on June 28, noted that Perry doesn't "buy that the science is settled" and added that it is with ninety-seven percent of all scientists. He sees it as the "most serious problem facing humankind."

---

[103] "Low Pay, Abuses Described at an Ivanka Trump Plant," *Denver Post*, June 28, 2017.

Conclusion

As we draw to a close, fundamental issues remain to be resolved that specifically impact our understanding of democracy and our efforts to resist its demise. Among these are health care, global warming, immigration, budget and tax reform, allies and enemies, and the ever increasing of inequality in our citizenship. These issues and all the others discussed in the first and second editions of this book, must be continually and actively addressed in the coming months. For Trump will continue his attempts to establish a more permanent authoritarian, one-party system. Its aim is to disassemble parts of American government and transfer their power to the organizations of the coalition of conservatives that we have spoken of earlier as they become the locus of that transferred power.

Imbedded in this effort is the underlying threat not only to the right to life but also the right to live, an issue examined extensively in the first edition. If we are concerned about the right to life but also the right to live, beyond the existence of the zygote, embryo and fetus stages of human development, we must recognize that the threat to our human existence is frighteningly apparent as the efforts of the rogue Trump and Tea Party republicans foster the collapse of American civilization as we know it. Particular threats when joined together can have the consequence of just that. In summary, these are, but not limited to, the erosion of adequate health care, the abuse of the poor by the rich, the idolatry of gun violence, the intention to overheat the planet, the desecration of human beings on the basis of their color, all of which are threats to the lives of the living. The process of one political party, bent on ending the rule of law, the pursuit of justice and the yearning for a more perfect union, must be stopped now in a nonviolent resistance movement coupled with the remaining democratic structures and the good consciences of more than half of our American governmental representatives. Such alternative powers must surely prevail in the end if we are guided by the love of neighbor and the eternal light that marks our way.

Although I am sure many more items of "breaking news" will be released, many more individual comments generated, and an equal number of tweets forthcoming from Trump, the Twitterer, after this writing, there is enough information and evidence accumulated so far to ensure our awareness that our American democracy is definitely in demise, if the present conditions are allowed to continue and prevail.

How will the story end? Will the newcomers to the resistance movement be able to respect and cooperate with the old time resisters, who have been at it these last forty years? Will the resistance forge ahead on two fronts – on the streets by conscientious objectors and civil disobedients, and in the courts and legislative bodies sworn to uphold the Constitution? Will democracy prevail over the Mussolinian aspects of authoritarian state corporatism and Hitlerian characteristics of political autocracy? Everything has an end and this precarious threat to the continuation of the long evolutionary trek towards the perfection of participatory social democracy must ultimately be resolved one way or another. Nonviolent resistance and conflict resolution remain the best process.

If this book and its Preface and Afterword were a legal brief holding President Trump responsible for intending to complete the demise of democracy begun by Ronald Reagan and continued by Republican representatives, I believe I would have made my case. What remains is to continue the memorialization, which I began with the 800th anniversary of *Magna Carta*, and the 75th anniversary of Roosevelt's Four Freedoms. May 29, 2017 was the 100th anniversary of the birth of President, John Fitzgerald Kennedy. The year 2017 is also the 230th anniversary of the oldest living constitution in world history. Will it survive?

Gordon Wood eminent historian wrote recently about the "inventor of the presidency." He quoted Washington saying to Madison that precedent had to be "fixed on true principles." And later speaking at a Jewish Synagogue in Newport Massachusetts, he said that America had established "an enlarged and liberal policy worthy of invention. …All possess alike liberties of conscience and immunities of citizenship." In comparison it was said of Trump that "an illiberal man who respects no limits on his lust for power" is attacking the "great virtues" of the U.S. Constitution, which is impotent to withstand him because "a written constitution cannot protect the country from a determined assault on its democracy."[104]

Washington, Madison and Jefferson, rejecting the conservative path of the British monarchy, founded America on a liberal foundation. As the remaining days of the Trump conservative republican presidency unfold it is my hope that there will be a return to those liberal foundations. They characterize the origin of this country and its evolution of democracy. Americans must reject the autocratic,

---

[104] Wood, Gordon, "The Inventor of the Presidency," *New York Review of Books,* May 25, 2017, p. 34.

unconstitutional and undemocratic regime that holds on to power through its control of the republican presidency and Congress.

President Trump's first six months in office have been described as a modern dystopia. Dystopia is defined as "an imagined place or state in which everything is unpleasant or bad, typically a totalitarian or environmentally degraded one." It is the opposite of a utopia. The argument for dystopianism is that "perfection comes at the cost of freedom." "Perfection" in the security of the autocratic state is at the expense of the citizens it represents. Many novels have been written imagining such a time and place. The more recent ones are *Brave New World, The Lord of the Flies, 1984,* and *Atlas Shrugged.* Today there exists a polarization of a small majority opposing the authoritarian Trump regime and a large minority who feel empowered by the demise of democracy.[105] And now the news that Trump, Jr. allegedly conspired with Russia to influence the election.

Eric Fromm writes "George Orwell's *1984* is an expression of a mood, and it is a warning. The mood it expresses is that of near despair about the future of man, and the warning is that unless the course of history changes, men all over the world will lose their most human quality, will become soulless automatons and will not ever be aware of it."[106] House Representative Elijah Cummings, ranking member of its Oversight Committee, has repeatedly warned us, "this is the fight for the soul of our democracy. The U.S. recently ranked 21st among democracies.

---

[105] "No We Cannot: The New Pessimism Comes of Age," *The New Yorker*, June 5/12, 2017, pp. 102-106

[106] Orwell, George, *1984,* London, (Signet Classics: 1980) p. 313.

The fight for the soul of our democracy will be by those who, with their resistance and resilience, will restore American democracy to a time before Trump and generate a resurgence of the American experiment to, yet again, a new birth of freedom.

One example of such efforts going on for some time is close to home for my wife, Genie and me where sanctuary movement is alive and well again. We joined the new movement when cities and churches declared themselves sanctuaries for undocumented U.S. residents, many of whom have no criminal records and yet they are being deported daily across the country, in many cases rending families apart. Our own fight to protect such refugees and residents began in 1980 and continued for almost a decade. Frightened people were fleeing from their own countries where their lives were threatened and the U.S. had laws designed to protect them. But in the Reagan years those laws were not honored and people were held in concentration-like camps in the southwest. Our house church and community in Colorado Springs was recognized as one of the first publicly declared sanctuaries. Much of our work was part of an over-ground "railroad" helping those that were refused hospitality so that they could be safe here or in Canada. We cooperated with members of the Mountain View Friends Meeting (Quakers) in Denver and southwest border organizations to do so.

So it was inevitable that when we moved from Colorado Springs to the Denver area, during Trump's first week in power, we joined the Mountain View Meeting, which is working as part of the Denver Sanctuary Coalition. Trump's executive order and legislation prohibiting sanctuary cities, passed by the House minutes before they departed on their July 4 holiday, does not deter us. When we joined, around the first of February, Mountain View already had a young woman and her baby living in sanctuary in the meetinghouse. She was eventually given a stay of her deportation order and was able to move out of sanctuary to be with the rest of her family. It is unclear what will eventually happen to her but part of the Coalition's work is to accompany such people whenever they must appear at an ICE hearing or check-in to provide visible support as a witness to ICE.

After Ingrid was able to leave sanctuary, another young woman was to accept our hospitality. However, when she appeared at her ICE check-in before moving into the meetinghouse, ICE agents detained her and refused to hear her attorney or supporters speak on her behalf although she has lived in the U.S. since she was four years old, does not remember Mexico at all and has three small children born in the U.S. Within a week she was bused to the Mexican border and deported, depriving her citizen children of their mother and placing her, alone, in extreme danger in the middle of the night. We will continue to invite undocumented people to share our hospitality in spite of such setbacks and are heartened that similar things are happening in other churches in Denver and around the world.

After the congress adjourned on June 29, several more unusual events occurred besides Trump's daily twitter insults. There were accusations of bribes by him, refusals by the states over his call to investigate what has been determined to be no fraud in elections. It appeared to be just a cover for the White House to gain valuable voter documents that otherwise would not qualify for access to.

Trump declared his support for repealing Obamacare and replacing it later, moved to end heating aid for the poor,[107] while North Korea launched yet another missile.

It appears, after all the events recorded here, that American democracy may not be replaced either. When historians look back on the attempts to disempower American democracy from 1980 through the present day, they might well determine that the turning point beginning American democratic restoration and resurgence was the day after Trump was inaugurated. Now, almost six months later, there is an indication that in the words of Sherlock Holmes, "the game's afoot." Let us hope that by Election Day 2018 we'll see that it has proved successful. After Congress returned in mid-July, my effort, through this book, to unveil the threat and resist it intellectually ended. But my wife and I will continue our physical resistance and witness. I am inspired by Senator Ted Kennedy's words: "The work goes on, the cause endures, the hope still lives, and the dream shall never die."[108]

As I bring this Afterword to its conclusion, I am reminded that May 30, 1867, a day to decorate the graves of fallen Confederate and Union soldiers and civilians in the American Civil War, was set aside as "Decoration Day." We now call it Memorial Day instead. It originated as a day of reconciliation not memorialization. Reconciliation is the last step in a new birth of freedom, reconciling modern conservatives and liberals to the work of re-inventing the American presidency and experiment in line with Washington's words of "an enlarged and liberal policy

---

[107] See *Denver Post* July 3, 2017, pp. 12A, 13A
[108] Words from his eulogy for his brother, Bobby.

worthy of invention." The "American Experiment" that Madison envisioned, paraphrasing the words of Charles Dickens, has seen the best of times and the worst of times. At my advanced age, I may not be fortunate enough to experience and write about the final resolution of this most serious attempt to cause democracy's demise.

Today there burns an Eternal Flame at the gravesites of the Kennedy brothers permanently placed there fifty years ago. That flame will outlast the resolution of the pending issues that threaten our democracy, will outlast Donald Trump's presidency, and outlast my life as well. And "the glow from that fire can truly light the world."[109] So it stands, for me, as a symbol of the light that paves the way through this darkness. It lights the cover of this book and is a symbol of hope for the future that the final demise of American democracy shall not occur.[110] As has been repeatedly said,

---

[109] The quotation is from President Kennedy's Inaugural Address.

[110] The Kennedy era played a huge part in my early adult life. I wrote to Senator Kennedy after he announced his candidacy for President in January 1960. I received a prompt reply from him saying that he appreciated my "confidence and support" and hoped I would "stay in touch." After his death I was a visitor to the home of the Robert Kennedys, having met the Senator in 1964 and his wife and family in 1967. After his death, my kick-off gathering in 1972 as a peace candidate for Congress was held at their home. Earlier, in 1965, I was elected to the Virginia Legislature inspired by the Kennedy "Camelot" years. As I write this Afterword, his example as President compared to the current one, has caused me to ponder whether my sixty years of public service and activism has all been in vain. But remembering the symbol of the eternal Flame has helped to renew my "confidence" and "support" of the American experiment and to believe, once again, in its ultimate perfection.

the past is prologue and the future is forever uncertain. But faith, hope and love endure and empowered by those values we must be confident that American democracy will permanently persevere.

One thing is certain, every book, like life itself, must come to its end but this struggle shall not. May justice obstruct democracy's demise and may all obstructions of justice in democracy's path ultimately suffer their own demise, so that the movement to a more perfect union may reach its ultimate goal, and the spirit that first moved its founders will move us forward once again.

APPENDIX

20 Similarities of Hitler and Trump

1. Both supported by business corporate executives.
2. Both rejected "old" generals and organized their own.
3. Both claimed to support workers and poor, but did not.
4. Both said they were true Christians and supported churches.
5. Both ridiculed minorities, limiting voting rights.
6. Both chastised democratic judges.
7. Both campaigned to close borders to foreigners.
8. Both religiously racist, one of Jews, the other of Muslims.
9. Both anti-feminist, White-supremacist and nationalist.
10. Both would unleash weapons of mass destruction.
11. Both utilized propaganda policy of the "Big Lie".
12. Both sought after conservative politicians.
13. Both rejected democratic diversity of governmental power.
14. Both recognized marriage only between heterosexuals.
15. Both vowed to end international law and organizations.
16. Both were candidates not initially supported by major parties.
17. Both criticized and broke away from other countries and alliances but admired dictators.
18. Both received tremendous media coverage, but rejected free media.
19. Both supported private possession of military style weapons.
20. Both campaigned on negative attacks and won by a minority of votes due to several candidates dividing the votes.

BIBIOGRAPHY

Arendt, Hannah, *The Human Condition*, Chicago (University of Chicago Press: 1958)

Bosworth, David, *The Demise of Virtue in Virtual America*, New York (Front Porch Press: 2015)

Durland, William, *Immoral Wars and Illegal Laws*, Colorado Springs, CO (Createspace: 2011)

_____, "History as Prologue" published by Center on Law and Human Rights, 2010, revised, 2016

_____, "Resistance, Resilience and Restoration," presented to Colorado Regional Meeting of Friends, April 2017, reprinted in *Western Friend,* July/August 2017, pp. 26-28

_____, *The Price of Folly: A Layperson's Guide to American Plutocracy*, Colorado Springs CO (Createspace: 2013)

_____, *William Penn, James Madison and the Historical Crisis in American Federalism,* Lewiston, NY (The Edwin Mellen Press: 2000)

Hacker, Jacob and Pierson, Paul, *American Amnesia,* New York (Simon and Shuster: 2016)

Hamilton, Alexander, John Jay, James Madison, *The Federalist*, Norwalk, CT (The Easton Press: 1979)

Hutchinson, William and Rachel, William, eds. *The Papers of James Madison*, Chicago (University of Chicago Press: 1969)

Kruse Kevin, *One Nation Under God: How Corporate America Invented Christian America,* New York

(Basic Books: 2015: *Writings*, New York   (Libraryof
    America: 1948)

Orwell, George, *1984,* New York (Signet Classics: 1980)

Roth, Philip, *The Plot Against America,* New York (Vintage:
    2004)

Madison, James, *Notes of Debates in the Federal Convention
    of 1787,* New York (W.W. Norton & Co: 1987)

Runciman, David, *The Confidence Trap: A History of
    Democracy in Crisis from World War I,* Princeton,
    NJ (Princeton University Press: 2015)

Seger, Linda, *Jesus Rode a Donkey*, Rev. 2nd ed. N.
    Hollywood, CA (Havenbooks: 2014)

Smith, James, ed. *The Republic of Letters*, New York
    (William Norton & Co.: 1995)

Thomas, Gordon, *Gideon's Spies: the Secret History of the
    Mossad,* New York (Thomas Dunn Books: 1998)

Toland, John, *Adolph Hitler,* Ware, England (Wordsworth:
    1997)

Williams, Richard, *The Cooperative Movement*, Hampshire,
    England (Ashgate Publishers, Ltd: 2007)

Wirbel, Loring, *Star Wars: U.S. Tools of Space Supremacy*,
    London (Pluto Press: 2004)

I quoted from *The Guardian Weekly* of London, *The New
Yorker*, *The Nation*, *The New York Review of Books*, *The
New York Times, Washington Post* and *Denver Post*
newspapers. I am grateful for the depth of journalism and the
breadth of opinion expressed in their pages.

INDEX

Made in the USA
Lexington, KY
13 April 2018